ACTA UNIVERSITATIS UPSALIENSIS
Historia litterarum
26

The Prose of the World
Flaubert and the Art of Making Things Visible

SARA DANIUS

UPPSALA UNIVERSITET

For Stefan

© Sara Danius 2006

ISSN: 0440-9078
ISBN: 91-554-6599-4

Typesetting: Uppsala University, Electronic Publishing Centre
Printed in Sweden by 08 Tryck, Bromma 2006
Distributor: Uppsala University Library, Box 510,
SE-751 20 Uppsala, Sweden
www.uu.se, acta@ub.uu.se

Contents

Preface 7

Introduction 9

Chapter 1: Realism and the Advent of the Visible 19
Realism and the Rejection of Allegory / From Rhetoric to Style / The Metropolis and the Gaze / Balzac and the Loss of the Real

Chapter 2: The Image in Action: On *Madame Bovary* 59
The Look of Commodities / The Moving Sidewalk / Emma As Image / As She Lies Dying / Two Scenes of Writing / The Indestructible Scribbler / The Utopia of the Image

Chapter 3: The Aesthetics of the Colon: On *L'éducation sentimentale* 127
Like A Vision / Where the Action Is / Narrate or Describe / The Universal Eye / Realism and Derealization

Epilogue: The Scandal of Realism 177

Bibliography 189

Index 201

Preface

This book is part of a larger enterprise, and a remark is in order here about format. For while *The Prose of the World* is a free-standing study of Flaubert, it is also part of a projected trilogy on realism. In this larger work, I take a closer new look at the realist novel from Stendhal to Balzac and Flaubert, and I do so by inquiring into a little understood and undertheorized subject: the art of making things visible. My central claim is that the interest in the visible aspects of the world takes a radically new turn with the rise of realism. It is not only a quantitative change, it is also, and above all, a qualitative one. In this history, moreover, Flaubert represents a turning-point. What follows, then, is not merely a study of Flaubert. It is an episode from a history of *la visibilité romanesque*.

This project was conceived during a year's fellowship in 2001–2002 at the Wissenschaftskolleg in Berlin. It was an invaluable time of retreat, but even more important is that the Wissenschaftskolleg offered daily encounters with forty fellows from all over the world, representing all modes of scientific inquiry. It was in this environment, as stimulating as it was challenging, that I decided to pursue the questions that are at the heart of this book. I wish to thank the Rector, Wolf Lepenies, for the invitation. I am most grateful to Gesine Bottomley, the head librarian at the Wissenschaftskolleg, and her excellent staff for their assistance.

The book was finished during a fellowship year at the Swedish Collegium for Advanced Study in the Social Sciences in Uppsala (SCASSS). I owe a special debt of gratitude to its principal, Björn Wittrock, who helped launch the Torgny Segerstedt Pro Futura Fellowship, a four-year postdoctoral research program aimed at scholars in the humanities and the social sciences. I have been fortunate enough to hold a Pro Futura Fellowship, and I am grateful to professor Wittrock for his generous support and unfailing kindness. I also wish to thank Barbro Klein, vice director of SCASSS. The Bank of Sweden Tercentenary Foundation, under the tutelage of Dan Brändström, has provided generous funding. The Tercentenary Foundation has also assisted with the publication of this book. The Swedish Foundation for International Cooperation in Research and Higher Education (STINT) supported my year in Berlin.

Many conversations have found their way into the pages of this book. I am especially grateful to the late Reinhard Baumgart, whose insightful comments meant a great deal in the early stages of writing. I also owe thanks to Gottfried Boehm, Françoise Bottero, Gerd Carling, Giuliana Carugati, Heinrich Detering, Christoph Harbsmeier, Sheila Jasanoff, Hans Joas, Caroline Jones, David MacDougall, Reinhart Meyer-Kalkus, Ann E. Kaplan, Ernst Osterkamp, Ioana Parvulescu, Marie Peterson, and Hanns Zischler. Finally, I am grateful to my colleagues and students in the Department of Literature at Uppsala University, in particular, Bengt Landgren and Håkan Möller.

My work has benefited greatly from questions, comments, and criticism I received at various invited lectures and conference talks. I am especially grateful to John Guillory, who responded to a lecture I gave at New York University.

Morten Nøjgaard and Brynja Svane, romance studies scholars in Odense and Uppsala respectively, invited me to participate in conferences and workshops on French realism. I thank them both. These occasions were great learning experiences. I am also grateful to Pierre-Marc de Biasi and Philippe Dufour for valuable advice and to Martine Mesureur-Ceyrat at the Equipe Flaubert at the ITEM/CNRS in Paris for her gracious assistance.

I owe a special debt of gratitude to Aris Fioretos, Sepp Gumbrecht, Toril Moi, and Anders Olsson, who read my manuscript in its entirety. I have learned much from their comments. My copy editor, Herman Rapaport, guided the manuscript through its final stages with swiftness, precision, and good humor.

To study Flaubert is also to study a great critical tradition, stretching from Albert Thibaudet to Gérard Genette, from Marcel Proust to Nathalie Sarraute. I have tried to acknowledge what I owe to previous writers on Flaubert in the footnotes. Finally, I also wish to acknowledge my debt to Fredric Jameson, with whom I studied at Duke University— it's already long ago. His commitment to apprehending how matters of style intersect with history remains an inspiration. I am grateful for his example.

Stefan Jonsson, my husband, has followed this book project with unflagging enthusiasm from beginning to end. It gives me great pleasure to thank him: he made the work worthwhile. This book is for him.

Ann Arbor, Michigan, February 2006

Introduction

> There is a widespread assumption that if one is interested in the visual, one's interest must be limited to a technique of somehow *treating* the visual. Thus the visual is divided into categories of special interest: painting, photography, real appearances, dreams and so on. And what is forgotten—like all essential questions in a positivist culture—is the meaning and enigma of visibility itself.
>
> *John Berger*

> The only thing that is different from one time to another is what is seen and what is seen depends upon how everybody is doing everything. This makes the thing we are looking at very different and this makes what those who describe it make of it, it makes a composition, it confuses, it shows, it is, it looks, it likes it as it is, and this makes what is seen as it is seen. Nothing changes from generation to generation except the thing seen and that makes a composition.
>
> *Gertrude Stein*

One day—it's already long ago—I happened upon a newspaper piece by Italo Calvino. The article originally appeared in *La Repubblica* in 1980 on the occasion of the one hundredth anniversary of Gustave Flaubert's death. It is a tribute to the French writer and, in particular, to his last work of fiction, *Trois contes,* or *Three Tales,* from 1877. At first glance, it is an unremarkable piece, but Calvino makes a brilliant observation.

Calvino does not say a word about how the omniscient narrator disappears with Flaubert, nor does he mention Flaubert's obsession with finding *le mot juste*. Calvino also does not talk about Flaubert's time-consuming pursuit of authentic details, or the scandal that surrounded the publication of *Madame Bovary* (1857). Nor does he touch on Flaubert's biography. Instead, Calvino concentrates on a single feature of Flaubert's writings, and a purely formal one, namely, their fundamentally visual quality. Foregrounding Flaubert's extraordinary ability to make the reader see, he describes how that acute power of imagination makes itself felt in *Trois contes*.

Half way through his characterization, Calvino changes pace, and it is now that he drops his brilliant observation. He opens an invisible parenthesis, inserting a digression that throws open a new perspective. The reader may not even notice it, because the digression is so well integrated into the discussion of Flaubert, but what Calvino does here, in four dense lines, is to offer a miniature history of the French novel. The literary history that he has in mind is organized around a particular theme, that of the visible:

> C'è una storia della visività romanzesca—del romanzo come arte di *far vedere* persone e cose—, che coincide con alcuni momenti della storia del romanzo, ma non con tutti. Da Madame de Lafayette a Constant il romanzo esplora l'animo umano con un'acutezza prodigiosa, ma le pagine sono come persiane chiuse che non lasciano vedere niente. La visività romanzesca comincia con Stendhal e Balzac, e tocca con Flaubert il rapporto perfetto tra parola e immagine (il massimo d'economia col massimo rendimento). La crisi della visività romanzesca comincerà mezzo secolo dopo, contemporaneamente all'avvento del cinema.[1]

> There is a history of visibility in the novel—of the novel as the art of making persons and things *visible*—which coincides with some of the phases of the history of the novel itself, though not with all of them. From Madame de Lafayette to Benjamin Constant the novel explores the human mind with prodigious accuracy, but these pages are like closed shutters which prevent anything else from being seen. Visibility in the novel begins with Stendhal and Balzac, and reaches in Flaubert the ideal rapport between word and image (supreme economy with maximum effect). The crisis of visibility in the novel will begin about half a century later, coinciding with the advent of the cinema.[2]

That's all. Having used four lines to say something that others would say in two hundred pages, Calvino closes the invisible parenthesis. He then continues his gloss on the visual aspect of Flaubert's style.

When I came across Calvino's article, I had just finished a book on modernism—on sight and hearing in the modernist period, and on how habits of perception are affected by modern technologies of perception. I had decided to work my way back to the nineteenth century and to

---

[1] Italo Calvino, "L'occhio del gufo," *La Repubblica,* May 8, 1980; reprinted as "Gustave Flaubert, *Trois contes*," in *Perché leggere i classici* (Milan: Mondadori, 1995), 168.
[2] Calvino, "Gustave Flaubert, *Trois contes*," in *Why Read the Classics?* trans. Martin McLaughlin (New York: Pantheon, 1999), 151–2.

shift the focus of attention from the modernist novel to the realist novel. I wanted to write a prehistory of modernism.

In reading Calvino's lines, I was immediately intrigued. I decided to pursue a history of how the novel conquers the visible. Such an enterprise would not only entail a new perspective on nineteenth-century realism. It could also usefully be thought of as a prehistory of modernism.

What makes Calvino's digression so thought-provoking? At least three things. First and foremost: the very idea that there is a history of visibility in the novel, a *visività romanzesca*.[3] Calvino is not concerned with the general question of how a piece of verbal representation may render the world visible. Rather, his claim is that a mode of literary visibility exists that is peculiar to the literary genre known as the novel. What is more, he suggests that it would be possible to trace the evolution of the art of making things visible through the history of the novel.

Second, Calvino maintains that this history is a very recent one, indeed, a modern one. He speaks about a mere hundred years, a period stretching from Stendhal and Balzac to, say, Proust. It is as though that period were a distinct phase within the history of the novel. This history, furthermore, knows shifts and breaks. Calvino even states, as though it were a known fact, that the early twentieth century sees a crisis of visibility, a crisis that he connects to an extra-literary phenomenon—the advent of cinematography. Style, then, is a historically mediated practice and may usefully be approached as such.

Third, because he emphasizes that novelistic visibility begins in earnest with Stendhal and Balzac, Calvino intimates that the advent of realism coincides with the advent of visibility. It is true that he never says as much—the word "realism" never once occurs in the article—but he clearly implies that the realist novel is intimately connected with the art of making things visible.

---

[3] The central term in Calvino's passage is *visività*, not *visibilità*. It is clear that he made some kind of distinction between these two terms, but whether it is a sharp one is hard to say. Readers familiar with Calvino's work will recall that he devotes an entire chapter to "visibilità" in *Lezioni americane*, translated as *Six Memos for the Next Millennium*. "Visibilità" is thus one of the six literary values that Calvino upholds in this last book of his. In reflecting on "visibility," Calvino dwells primary on the nature and power of imagination, that is, the visual part of literary imagination. He begins with the role of the imagination in Dante's *Commedia* and ends with the fantastic in Balzac's *Le chef-d'oeuvre inconnu*. See Calvino, "Visibilità," in *Lezioni americane. Sei proposte per il prossimo millennio* (Milano: Mondadori, 1993), 89–110; "Visibility," in *Six Memos for the Next Millennium,* trans. Patrick Creagh (Cambridge, Mass.: Harvard University Press, 1988), 81–99. I thank Giuliana Carugati for discussing Calvino's texts with me.

Of course, the entire history of literature as we know it, from Homer and Greek tragedy onwards, can be approached as a history of the art of making persons and things visible. We can see Odysseus's scar in front of us, just as we can see Don Quijote and Sancho Panza fighting those invisible knights that turn out to be wind mills; or to take more recent examples, think of Leopold Bloom burning that breakfast kidney in James Joyce's *Ulysses* (1922), or Mrs. Ramsay knitting that brown stocking in Virginia Woolf's *To the Lighthouse* (1922).

What Calvino is suggesting, however, and what makes his train of thought so interesting, is that the art of making persons and things visible takes a radically new turn with the advent of realism. He even goes so far as to maintain that the history of novelistic visibility proper begins with Stendhal and Balzac. For although Calvino speaks of *la visività romanzesca*, he is not arguing that the art of the making things visible is intrinsic to the novel *per se*. The tradition begins only in the early nineteenth century. Calvino's intuition thus opens a historicizing perspective.

What, then, came before the realist novel? If, as Calvino suggests, pre-realist novels do not make things and persons visible, what do they do? How best to describe the early novel and its accomplishments from the point of view of *la visività romanzesca*?

Calvino mobilizes an image. It is an image that stands out like a sore thumb in a passage otherwise characterized by simplicity, clarity, and transparency. In seeking to make the early novel visible, he resorts to a metaphor, a wonderfully mind-boggling metaphor: "Da Madame de Lafayette a Constant il romanzo esplora l'animo umano con un'acutezza prodigiosa, *ma le pagine sono come persiane chiuse che non lasciano vedere niente*." Literally speaking: "From Madame de Lafayette to Constant the novel explores the human mind with prodigious accuracy, *but these pages are like closed shutters that do not let us see anything*."

This is the missing part of Calvino's miniature history of the French novel. It stretches from 1678, the year when Madame de Lafayette published *La Princesse de Clèves,* often considered as the first French modern novel, to the early nineteenth century and the writings of Benjamin Constant. This tradition, in all its variety and richness, is summed up in Calvino's image of the closed shutters.

Closed shutters? This is a metaphor that encourages us to think of the pre-realist novel in unexpectedly material terms. Its "pages" are no longer to be grasped as a mere figure of speech. Thanks to the image of the shutters, we can see before us those book pages in all their stubborn concrete reality: as rectangular sheets of paper typically appearing in pairs, each endowed with uniform lines of black letters that run horizontally across the flat surface. The analogy is a striking one, and it operates on a visual level. Indeed, just as the sheet margins correspond to the frame of the shutter, so the sequence of signs marching across the page corresponds to the space between the wooden slats.[4]

But if the analogy is perfectly symmetrical on the visual plane, it is asymmetrical on the conceptual one. And this is precisely what animates Calvino's metaphor and makes it so thought-provoking. We open a book, and we open shutters, but we cannot open shutters the way in which we open a book. All this can be put differently. What happens as a result of Calvino's metaphor is that the common notion that the book represents a world—indeed, *is* a world—falls apart. For the underlying idea in Calvino's passage is that the early novel represents some kind of world, and that it does so in the most rigorous, penetrating, and exact way possible, but that the reader is not made to see it. Carefully set off from the outer world, the world of the pre-realist novel is an emphatically interior space.

The paradox is that the early novel offers a world while at the same time being closed off from the world. In fact, not only is it closed off from the exterior, it also prevents the reader from seeing it. The world offered is so precisely rendered that it does not even occur to the reader that there is a world out there. The open book shuts the world out. The point is not that the pre-realist novel considers the art of making things visible less important, or less honorable, or less urgent. Visibility, quite simply, is not yet an issue. It is only in the early nineteenth century that Calvino's closed shutters will be thrust open. And it is only then that one may perceive the relative paucity of visual description in the early history of the novel.

Why, then, do so many writers in the nineteenth century exhibit such a passionate interest in representing how things, persons, and settings look? In short, what is the historical meaning of realist visibility?

I resolved to explore Calvino's suggestion, and to treat it as a thesis. My project would have as its working hypothesis that the early nineteenth

---

[4] My gloss on the *persiane* in Calvino is partly inspired by an essay on Roman shutters by the classicist Jesper Svenbro. Svenbro, like Calvino, establishes a parallel between the physical appearance of the written page and that of the shutter. See Svenbro, "Om fönsterluckor," in *Ljuset och rummet. Rom 1949 fotograferat av Lennart af Petersens* (Stockholm: Wahlström & Widstrand, 2004), 29–40. Kafka, too, used the image of the shutters as a metaphor, but in a different context: as a metaphor of the cinematographic projection on the screen. According to Gustav Janouch, Kafka once said that, "Filme sind eiserne Fensterläden." See Janouch, *Gespräche mit Kafka,* enl. ed. (Frankfurt am Main: Fischer, 1968), 216. Hanns Zischler brought Kafka's shutters to my attention.

century sees a radically new interest in the visible aspects of the phenomenal world.[5] What, specifically, does the realist novel make visible, and how? And what is not made visible? Guided by Calvino's digression, I would seek to bring into relief the features and effects of this new preoccupation with the visible world.

As I considered these issues, I came to ask the question of why there could not be a history of visibility—as distinct from a history of visuality. In discussing literary means of evocation, scholars and critics typically speak of "word" and "image," and of "verbalization" and "visualization." In the field of textual analysis, these are reassuringly familiar terms, but it seemed to me that the thrust of Calvino's historical anecdote pointed in a somewhat different direction. Calvino's concern is not so much with visualization *per se* as with the art of making things and persons visible. The emphasis, I think, is less on the mental activity of imagination and more on the craft of making things visible.

In other words, there is a distinction to be made between visuality and visibility. To be sure, the meaning of these two terms often overlaps, as do the ways in which they are used. What is more, the words "visual" and "visible" ultimately derive from the same etymological root, the Latin word *videre,* to see. Just how close the Italian word for "seeing" is to its Latin origin becomes evident in Calvino's phrase, "C'è una storia della visività romanzesca—del romanzo come arte di *far vedere* persone e cose…"

Yet it is clear that the "visible" and the "visual" tend to refer to two distinct conceptual realms.[6] Let me offer a few preliminary remarks. In

---

[5] For a similar perspective on realism, see Peter Brooks's excellent new study, *Realist Vision* (New Haven: Yale University Press, 2005). Brooks's book appeared just as I had finished my manuscript, and I therefore cannot discuss his approach to realism and the visible in detail. But it is clear that *Realist Vision* is a contribution to the revisionist study of nineteenth-century realism as well as an insightful inquiry into how realist works of art go about the task of conjuring up the real. Brooks deals with both French and British realism, and also engages with painting from Courbet through Lucian Freud. The book contains a chapter on *Madame Bovary,* in which Brooks specifically discusses perspective. He focuses on the representation of Emma, arguing that there "seems to be a problem of vision or perspective in this intensely visual novel, in that the central object of vision, Emma as a physical presence, never quite seems to cohere into a whole" (55). For Brooks, such fragmentation is primarily linked to fetishism.

[6] Yet another important term here is "vision." Vision typically refers to "sight" in a narrowly empirical sense, but also to visionary experience. Yet the distinction between "vision" and "visuality," as Hal Foster has underscored, is not as clear cut as one may think. "Although vision suggests sight as a physical operation, and visuality as a social fact, the two are not opposed as nature to culture: vision is social and historical too, and visuality involves the body and the psyche" (preface to *Vision and Visuality,* ed. Hal Foster [Seattle: Bay Press, 1988], ix). For a wide-ranging, historicizing, and culturally specific approach to the issue of vision and visuality, see the essays collected in *Visuality Before*

literary studies, the visual is intimately related to the notion of a subject or an instance that visualizes—the author, the narrator, the reader, a character, or an omniscient eye. Visuality, especially in contemporary scholarly discussions, is also tightly bound up with notions of a "system."

The domain of the visible, on the other hand, is predominantly associated with the exterior world and its immediate *thereness*. I take the visible to be more directly connected with the sensuous, concrete, empirical world. A pilot, for example, speaks of *visibility*. To raise questions of visibility in the realm of the novel is immediately to invite issues such as range of vision and level of precision—classic realist themes.

I evolved the following hypothesis. If visuality is chiefly concerned with *seeing*, visibility is primarily concerned with the *seen*: both the thing-made-visible and the making-visible-of-the-thing-made-visible. Visibility, then, is not so much concerned with the observing subject as with the art of making something visible. Why, indeed, could there not be a literary history of the seen?

I imagined a history of the realist novel that would place not so much the *subject* but rather the *object* at the center of the inquiry. My project would not be a history of realist imagery, or a history of the gaze, or a history of visual regimes.[7] It would also not entail an attempt at reconstructing a "period eye."[8] It would, rather, be a history of narrative figuration in the realist period as seen from the point of view of the visible.

To be sure, these distinctions are far from airtight ones. To foreground the visible rather than the visual is, to some extent, a mere shift of emphasis. The category of the "seen" necessarily implies an instance of "seeing," a vantage point of observation. In the following pages, moreover, there will be plenty of talk about looks and looking, gazes and gazing, images and imagery, and other typically "visual" phenomena. This only proves that there are unavoidable contiguities between the visible and the visual.

---

and Beyond the Renaissance: Seeing as Others Saw, ed. Robert S. Nelson (Cambridge: Cambridge University Press, 2000).

[7] See, for example, Jonathan Crary, *Techniques of the Observer: On Vision and Modernity in the Nineteenth Century* (Cambridge, Mass.: MIT Press, 1990); Martin Jay, *Downcast Eyes: The Denigration of Vision in Twentieth-Century Thought* (Berkeley and Los Angeles: University of California Press, 1993); David Michael Levin, ed., *Modernity and the Hegemony of Vision* (Berkeley and Los Angeles: University of California Press, 1993); Laura Mulvey, "Visual Pleasure and Narrative Cinema," in *Visual and Other Pleasures* (London: Macmillan, 1989), 14–26.

[8] Michael Baxandall's term. See his classic study, *Painting and Experience in Fifteenth Century Italy: A Primer in the Social History of Pictorial Style,* 2nd ed. (New York: Oxford University Press, 1972), esp. 29–108.

But there is a deeper motivation behind my foregrounding of the category of the visible. It is also theoretically motivated. The distinction between visibility and visuality that I propose here usefully opens a new conceptual space that allows for a reconsideration of the realist novel. For to follow the path of the visible rather than that of the visual allows us to trace a cultural-historical shift that realism itself helped to bring about. I shall explain what I mean.

If we approach realism by way of the category of the "visual," the perspective is readily refracted through the question of the "image." But the domain of the visible ranges far wider than that of the image. What is more, at the heart of the realist enterprise is an essentially anti-allegorical impulse—allegory here conceived in the widest possible sense. To insist on the visible rather than the visual is to strike a note that resonates deeply within realism itself. The realist novel wants to make the reader see and to call forth the world, but it rejects the time-honored tradition of pictorial representation.[9] Renouncing the transcendental in favor of the immanent, realism places a taboo on allegory. As Emile Zola once underscored, realist writing should aim at "the exact reproduction of life, without any novelistic element."[10] The distinction between the visual and the visible thus opens a perspective that has the further advantage of allowing us to rediscover the novelty of the realist enterprise: its strangeness, its shocking nature, its scandalous ambitions.

This book, then, is an inquiry into nineteenth-century realism and the art of making things visible, with Flaubert at the center. It offers a glimpse of what happens when Calvino's shutters have been thrown open. Beginning with Stendhal and culminating with Balzac, a whole new interest in the visual appearance of the real makes itself felt in the early nineteenth century. I trace this transformation in chapter 1, and there I also develop the conceptual tools needed to understand it. The change is not only a quantitative one; it is also a qualitative one. And this becomes apparent as the nineteenth century wears on, and nowhere more so than in the writings of Flaubert. For what I shall be proposing in this book is that Flaubert represents a new chapter in the history of literary visibility.

My discussion of Flaubert and the visible will center on his most important novels, *Madame Bovary* (1857) and *L'éducation sentimentale* (1869). Beginning with *Madame Bovary*, Flaubert effects a thorough-

---

[9] Philippe Hamon develops a similar argument in *Imageries. Littérature et image au XIXe siècle* (Paris: José Corti, 2001). I shall have more to say about Hamon's study in chapter 1.

[10] Emile Zola, *Les romanciers naturalistes* (Paris: Charpentier, 1890), 126.

going change that will reverberate far into the twentieth century, and that can be traced in writers such as Joseph Conrad, Franz Kafka, Marcel Proust, James Joyce, Vladimir Nabokov, and Gertrude Stein. I devote a chapter to each novel, subjecting both to close textual analysis. I pay detailed attention to questions of syntax, for as Proust once suggested in a brilliant essay on Flaubert's style, this is where the action is. Flaubert breaks new ground in the history of the novel by manipulating rules of syntax. My readings of *Madame Bovary* and *L'éducation sentimentale* are to be found in chapters 2 and 3, respectively; and while they can be read as free-standing studies, they are part of a larger trajectory, the story of how the realist writers discover the visible.

It has often been observed that Flaubert's writings tend heavily toward the descriptive mode and that description, in Flaubert, frequently assumes the form of an image, a still life, or even a tableau. In this view, Flaubert's novels, from *Madame Bovary* on, can be seen as a string of tableaux interspersed with narrative interludes. Consider the image of Rouen hovering like a painterly mirage on the horizon, a tableau studded with carefully selected details such as those tall masts appearing like a forest of needles. Or consider the portrait of Madame Arnoux, complete with a pair of dazzling eyes and a deliciously blue background.

Numerous critics have also noted the proto-cinematic character of many of Flaubert's descriptions, as in the agricultural show episode in *Madame Bovary* where the narrator engages in something like crosscutting, or in the opening scenario of *L'éducation sentimentale*, where the banks of the river Seine slide past us as though we, too, were present on that vessel and watching that panoramic scenery.

Description, tableau, image, panorama, cinema: I want to go further than this. To push things as far as possible, I want to suggest that Flaubert invents a wholly new representational space. Flaubert produces a historically new type of literary image. Indeed, the Flaubertian image is a new object in the history of the novel.

And because the Flaubertian image is a new object in the history of the novel, it calls for a literary-critical vocabulary that does not quite exist and that would be capable of articulating both the newness and peculiarity of that new representational space. Ekphrasis, as we shall see, is an utterly inadequate term. In fact, description, too, is an inadequate term. This book thus seeks to map the architecture of the new space of representation that emerges on a grand scale in the pages of Flaubert's ground-breaking novels.

Chapter 1
Realism and the Advent of the Visible

What does the advent of visibility mean when we are discussing the history of the novel? It means that for the first time in the history of Western literature, a writer will tell the reader that the soap in a particular bedroom is blue.

Blue soap? It might be objected that there is nothing remarkable about that. In order to bring out the extraordinary nature of this blueness, let me discuss briefly a novella by an early nineteenth-century writer, Heinrich von Kleist. This is how Kleist opens one of his most famous stories, "Die Marquise von O…" from 1808:

> In M…, einer bedeutenden Stadt im oberen Italien, ließ die verwitwete Marquise von O…, eine Dame von vortrefflichem Ruf, und Mutter von mehreren wohlerzogenen Kindern, durch die Zeitungen bekannt machen: daß sie, ohne ihr Wissen, in andre Umstände gekommen sei, daß der Vater zu dem Kinde, das sie gebären würde, sich melden solle; und daß sie, aus Familienrücksichten, entschlossen wäre, ihn zu heiraten. Die Dame, die einen so sonderbaren, den Spott der Welt reizenden Schritt beim Drang unabänderlicher Umstände, mit solcher Sicherheit tat, war die Tochter des Herrn von G…, Kommandanten der Zitadelle bei M… Sie hatte, vor ungefähr drei Jahren, ihren Gemahl, den Marquis von O…, dem sie auf das innigste und zärtlichste zugetan war, auf einer Reise verloren, die er, in Geschäften der Familie, nach Paris gemacht hatte.[1]

> In M…, an important town in northern Italy, the widowed Marquise of O…, a lady of unblemished reputation and the mother of several well-brought-up children, inserted the following announcement in the newspapers: that she had, without knowledge of the cause, come to find herself in a certain situation; that she would like the father of the child she was expecting to disclose his identity to her; and that she was resolved, out of consideration for her family, to marry him. The lady who, under the constraint of unalterable circumstances, had with such boldness taken so strange a step and thus exposed herself to the derision of society, was the

---

[1] Heinrich von Kleist, "Die Marquise von O…," in *Erzählungen* (Frankfurt am Main: Insel, 1997), 117.

daughter of Colonel G..., the Commandant of the citadel at M... About three years earlier her husband, the Marquis of O..., to whom she was most deeply and tenderly attached, had lost his life in the course of a journey to Paris on family business.[2]

Kleist's opening is dramatic. It begins with the Marquise's public announcement and then recounts the background of her remarkable mode of action. What has happened? That is the question at the heart of Kleist's story.

After her husband's premature death, the Marquise and her children decided to withdraw to her parental home. There they lead a secluded life, quiet and predictable, and several years pass by. One day Russian troops arrive and take the fortress by storm. As the Marquise and her children try to escape the burning building, a group of riflemen seizes the panic-stricken woman with the intention to rape her. A Russian officer discovers what is about to happen and drives the men away with his sword. The Marquise, utterly relieved and grateful, has a fainting fit. Shortly thereafter, she is shocked to realize that she is pregnant. She does not know how it may have happened, nor when, nor by whom.

Within a mere two pages, the narrative has acquired considerable speed, and the reader has moved deep into the plot. But where do the characters live? Where do they come from? When does the action take place? Kleist does not say. The novella is poor in images, atmosphere, concrete circumstances. Kleist also dwells precious little on how the Marquise, or her children, or her parents, look, dress, move, behave, and speak.

To be sure, Kleist wants us to believe that the places and the individuals he tells us about do exist. He even asserts that the narrative is "based on a true incident, the setting of which has been transposed from the north to the south," thus seeking to convince us that this is a story about real events. But visual appearance is in the end unimportant. Kleist spends all of his genius on the plot and its moral significance. No blue soap.

It may be objected that "Die Marquise von O..." is a novella; that the genre itself presents Kleist with natural constraints; that he cannot afford to describe in detail where things take place, how his characters look, and the like. This is true. But it is also true that a mid-nineteenth-century writer like Flaubert wrote short stories that were packed with visual facts, so much so that they caused Roland Barthes to reflect on

---

[2] Kleist, "The Marquise of O—," in *The Marquise of O— and Other Stories,* trans. David Luke and Nigel Reeves (London: Penguin, 1978), 68.

the actual function of all this seemingly meaningless information. We usually think of such information as "detail."

In one of these stories, "Un coeur simple" from 1877, Flaubert describes the middle-class household in the provinces where his protagonist, Félicité, is employed as a serving-woman. This is one of the tales that Calvino discusses in the article I mentioned in the introduction. In describing the household, Flaubert's narrator moves through the various rooms of the little house. He makes a stop in the drawing-room, mentioning the yellow tiled oven, the temple-shaped clock, and the eight mahogany chairs lining the wall. In the middle of the description, he inserts: "Un vieux piano supportait, sous un baromètre, un tas pyramidal de boîtes et de cartons [A barometer hung on the wall above an old piano, piled high with a pyramid-shaped assortment of packets and cardboard boxes]."[3]

Why does Flaubert tell us that there is a barometer on the wall? Barthes makes a provocative suggestion. Such objects may seem insignificant, superfluous, non-functional, but they carry out an important job. To be sure, they lack narratological justification, and they denote little, but they are anything but semiotically meaningless. They do signify, and what they signify is the category of the real itself. They simply say: "*we are the real.*"[4] They serve to authenticate the illusion of the real—as naked fact, as indisputable truth—to which nineteenth-century realist modes of representation so emphatically aspire. The barometer, Barthes argues, is there to put an end to meaning. The barometer says: *I am pure immanence, I am absolute particularity.*

Now remove the barometer, and the yellow color from the tiled oven, and Flaubert's story will be a little less true to life. But—and this is a crucial question—will the story become less intelligible?

All this brings me to an important point. If we felt that Flaubert's visual facts added something to our understanding of, say, the poor serving woman's psychological profile, or the larger world in which Flaubert's characters move, then we would be unlikely to even think of these details in terms of visibility. To discover that there is something like a history of visibility in the novel, visibility must have become visible. There must be too much of it. Visibility must have become a "problem,"

---

[3] Gustave Flaubert, "Un coeur simple," in *Oeuvres,* ed. Albert Thibaudet and René Dumesnil (Paris: Gallimard, 1952), 2:591; "A Simple Heart," in *Three Tales,* trans. Roger Whitehouse (London: Penguin, 2005), 3.
[4] Roland Barthes, "L'effet de réel" [1968], in *Oeuvres complètes,* ed. Eric Marty (Paris: Seuil, 1994), 2:479–84, quotation, 484; "The Reality Effect," in *French Literary Theory Today: A Reader,* ed. Tzvetan Todorov, trans. R. Carter (Cambridge: Cambridge University Press, 1982), 17.

or else we would not pay attention to it.[5] Of course, there are visual descriptions in early nineteenth-century writers such as Austen, Goethe, and Kleist, but they tend to be brief and are easily absorbed by the narrative structure. To make the reader see may be relevant, perhaps even desirable, but it is not a primary goal.

With the emergence of realist writing, all this changes. Little by little, a new notion enters the critical vocabulary: "the exact reproduction of life, without any novelistic element." This is how Zola characterized the literary method associated with the realist writers, especially the naturalists.[6] To be "exact" was as important as to "reproduce." And this is where visibility enters the picture. But it enters the picture as excess. In realism, the real world is not just visible; it is, and has to be, excessively visible.

Realism and the Rejection of Allegory

One of the most radical but also least understood changes that took place with the advent of realism is that it set out to show things the way they really were, not how they should be. Idealism, whose most famous proponent was George Sand, became a thing of the past.[7] This is the context in which we should understand Stendhal's famous lines on the vocation of the novel in *Le rouge et le noir* from 1830. One of the characters,

---

[5] What does Aristotle's *Poetics*, one of the oldest treatises on the nature of art and of representation, have to say about the art of making things visible? Aristotle remains silent on the issue. The category of the visible appears nowhere in Poetics, in all likelihood because the philosopher is centrally concerned with the category of action. For Aristotle, mimesis is always the mimesis of action, and he therefore privileges questions of narration, not those of description. This, of course, is linked to the fact that Aristotle's inquiry is centered on drama, especially tragedy. See Aristotle, *Poetics*, trans. Stephen Halliwell (Cambridge, Mass.: Harvard University Press, 1995), 27–141. Plato's conception of mimesis, on the other hand, builds on a visual and pictorial, and therefore also more static, model. For a substantial and thoroughly argued inquiry into how Plato and Aristotle conceived of mimesis, see Stephen Halliwell, *The Aesthetics of Mimesis: Ancient Texts and Modern Problems* (Princeton: Princeton University Press, 2002), 37–72 (Plato), 151–76 (Aristotle). See also Antoine Compagnon, who observes that things in themselves are of no interest to Aristotle: *Le démon de la théorie. Littérature et sens commun* (Paris: Seuil, 1998), 119; *Literature, Theory, and Common Sense,* trans. Carol Cosman (Princeton: Princeton University Press, 2004), 74. Compagnon, like Paul Ricoeur before him, even goes so far as to argue that Aristotle's poetics is a narratology. See also Umberto Eco, "The Poetics and Us," in On *Literature,* trans. Martin McLaughlin (London: Secker & Warburg, 2005), esp. 244.

[6] Emile Zola, *Les romanciers naturalistes* (Paris: Charpentier, 1890), 126.

[7] See Naomi Schor, *George Sand and Idealism* (New York: Columbia University Press, 1993).

a young aristocratic woman, has behaved in a manner one might find unsuitable. The episode relates her mode of action, but refrains from condemning it. Instead, Stendhal's narrator emerges from the wings to explain why he treats the young woman the way he does. At the same time, he offers us his literary program in a nutshell:

> Eh, monsieur, un roman est un miroir qui se promène sur une grande route. Tantôt il reflète à vos yeux l'azur des cieux, tantôt la fange des bourbiers de la route. Et l'homme qui porte le miroir dans sa hotte sera par vous accusé d'être immoral! Son miroir montre la fange, et vous accusez le miroir! Accusez bien plutôt le grand chemin où est le bourbier, et plus encore l'inspecteur des routes qui laisse l'eau croupir et le bourbier se former.[8]

> Why, my good sir, a novel is a mirror journeying down the high road. Sometimes it reflects to your view the azure blue of heaven, sometimes the mire in the puddles on the road below. And the man who carries the mirror in his pack will be accused by you of being immoral! His mirror reflects the mire, and you blame the mirror! Blame rather the high road on which the puddle lies, and still more the inspector of roads and highways who lets the water stand there and the puddle form.[9]

Between the sublime beauty of the blue skies and the raw facts of the muddy road, a new literary paradigm of modern serious realism is about to emerge.[10] Life is both beautiful and appalling, sublime and disgusting. The task of the writer, who journeys through a changing reality, is to reproduce the world as it is. The writer should not intervene, nor mediate; he should simply reproduce.

And yet life is more than what can be seen with the naked eye. Think of moral behavior, for example, the very issue that motivated the digression. It is therefore all the more interesting that Stendhal uses the optical device of the mirror as his central image. Tools such as pen and paper would have suggested that the writer invents, selects, and composes. Instead, Stendhal settled for the metaphor of the mirror, as though the literary product were a mere receptacle. The beginnings of realism are intimately connected to the importance of that which can be seen.

To be able to depict things the way they really were, not how they should be, realism had to make a rigorous, hardheaded, muscular at-

---

[8] Stendhal, *Le rouge et le noir,* ed. Michel Crouzet (Paris: Livre de Poche, 1997), 362.
[9] Stendhal, *Scarlet and Black: A Chronicle of the Nineteenth Century,* trans. Margaret R. B. Shaw (Harmondsworth: Penguin, 1953), 365–6.
[10] Auerbach's term; see Auerbach, *Mimesis* (Tübingen: Francke, 1946), 422–59; *Mimesis,* trans. Willard R. Trask (Princeton: Princeton University Press, 1953), 454–92.

tempt at remaining true to life and to nature. This meant, among other things, that realism had to closely observe outward appearances and to find stylistic means of reproducing them. It also meant that realism had to renounce allegory.

And this anti-allegorical impulse helps explain the shock of the new. It equally helps explain the appeal of blue soap. Indeed, as Hayden White underscores, nineteenth-century realism resolutely turned away from traditional modes of figuration by which to generate an allegorical or secondary meaning. "The advent of realism meant, among other things, the rejection of allegory, the search for a perfect literality of expression, and the achievement of a style from which every element of rhetorical artifice had been expunged."[11]

What, more specifically, does this mean? Consider a famous painting by Botticelli, *The Birth of Venus,* executed in Florence in the 1480s. In looking at Botticelli's nude, we understand immediately that she is not of our world. If she is rising out of the sea, that water is mythic water. It would be ridiculous to look for blue soap, so much so that I hesitate to underscore it.

Botticelli's woman is an idealized creature. She will not die, not become ill, not suffer pain, for she exists outside human temporality. She might bear children, that is true, but in that case her offspring would also be mythic. And yet, for all her stubborn transcendence, her body is all-important, though not as an empirical phenomenon but rather as a signifier. And this signifier is meant to mediate transcendental meanings: beauty, youth, fertility, love, desire, origin, femininity, and so on. In a word, Botticelli's woman is an allegory.

Now consider a modern painting of a nude executed by Pierre Bonnard in 1936, *Nu dans le bain* (Nude in the bath). Unlike Botticelli's Venus, Bonnard's woman is inhabited by time. She will definitely die. In fact, her flattened body and the bold yellow-pink-greenish color spectrum make her look rather sickly, as though she were taking a bath in order to cure herself of some ailment. We would not be surprised to find blue soap in the picture, perhaps in a small bowl on a stool next to the bath tub.

If Botticelli's Venus is an entity that mediates other meanings, Bonnard's nude is immediate. She is immanent to herself. She is a particular woman in a particular bathtub on a particular day, and she happens to be Bonnard's wife. She might well be typical of other women in other

---

[11] Hayden White, "The Problem of Style in Realistic Representation: Marx and Flaubert," in *The Concept of Style,* ed. Berel Lang (Philadelphia, PA.: University of Pennsylvania Press, 1979), 213.

bathtubs, but she is not meant to generate secondary meanings in the way Botticelli's goddess does. She is there, and the painter is there, and Bonnard wants to convey something of that being-there-ness, in particular, the ways in which her skin absorbs and reflects the soft, vibrant, tremulous light that flows through the window somewhere outside the frame. Her skin, one might say, is a canvas within the canvas.

If we step back a little from the image, we realize that Bonnard's painting also seeks to remain faithful to the optical experience of the woman resting in the tub and how the image presents itself to the painter's eyes. Not only the nude is particular; the visual impression, too, is particular.

Because realism celebrated the immediate and the given, it had to reject allegory. Literal meaning was, and should be, everything. Meaning was on the surface. If the world had been seen, then it had in some sense also been understood. We can now begin to appreciate the historically new importance of visibility.

From Rhetoric to Style

Literary realism has typically been connected with the rise of the middle classes; the industrial revolution; secularization; economic individualism; the emergence of a large female readership and of a specifically modern kind of historical consciousness for which historical change becomes part of individual self-understanding.[12] The novel, Georg Lukács once suggested, is the epic of a godforsaken world.[13]

From a more properly literary point of view—and here I follow Erich Auerbach—realism has typically been seen as what happens when those rules of style promulgated by classical aesthetics lose legitimacy. According to these rules, tragedy should deal with humans drawn from the upper classes, whereas comedy should concern itself with the people. It was unthinkable that a tragedy should have as its hero a shoe maker, or a butcher, or a midwife. Moreover, tragedy should deal with the ideal

---

[12] See Ian Watt, *The Rise of the Novel: Studies in Defoe, Richardson, and Fielding* (Harmondsworth: Penguin, [1957] 1983). See also Auerbach, *Mimesis*, 422–59. For a critical survey of theories of realism, see Torsten Pettersson, "Den gemensamma världen. Realismen som litteraturform," in *Dolda principer. Kultur- och litteraturteoretiska studier* (Lund: Studentlitteratur, 2002), 149–71.
[13] Georg Lukács, *Die Theorie des Romans. Ein geschichtsphilosophischer Versuch über die Formen der grossen Epik* [1920] (Munich: dtv, 1994), 77; *The Theory of the Novel: A Historico-Philosophical Essay in the Forms of Great Epic Literature,* trans. Anna Bostock (London: Merlin, 1971), 88.

spheres of human existence, with the universal, the eternal, the transcendental. Comedy, on the other hand, should deal with human existence in its emphatically material, physical, and social aspects. To put the difference in Northrop Frye's terms, the comedy represents the low mimetic mode, and the hero is one of us; the tragedy represents the high mimetic mode, and the hero is above us.[14]

With the emergence of modern serious realism, high and low were mixed together. The son of a simple carpenter could now become the tragic hero of a novel of epic proportions. The protagonist I have in mind, Julien Sorel in Stendhal's *Le rouge et le noir* (1830), is in effect something much more vulgar than a mere carpenter's son: he is an upstart. Determined to rise above his station, he eventually makes his way to the highest levels of society—only to be executed at the end of the novel.

Decades before the word "realism" entered literary discussions, Stendhal wrote a pamphlet called *Racine et Shakespeare* (1823). In it, Stendhal plays out classicism against romanticism, or purity against heterogeneity. The hour of classicism has struck, he claims. Classical poetics has run its course: it merely fetters genius. What purpose does the alexandrine serve? It only conceals stupidity. Stendhal even goes so far as to suggest that tragedy should be in prose. What is more, all literature should be oriented toward present-day needs.

In this way, Stendhal spells out his own proto-realistic ideals. He maintains that writers should explore the style of contemporary modes of expression rather than relying on the ancient tradition of rhetoric. Indeed, although it may be less poetical, the style of current conversation is far more natural and therefore true to experience.

Three decades later, with the publication of *Madame Bovary,* Flaubert was to make a clean sweep of rhetoric in the novel once and for all. And this, as numerous critics have stressed, is the true literary-historical significance of Flaubert's 1857 novel.

Besides this mixture of "tragic" and "comic" properties, and the equally important discovery of everyday middle-class life as a serious topic, realism also meant that a strong emphasis was placed on originality, novelty, and invention. The idea that a writer should imitate old masters and adhere to certain aesthetic rules definitely lost its hold.

What is more, the emergence of realist discourse meant that description began to pervade the art of narration.[15] Paul Valéry, incidentally, saw

---

[14] Northrop Frye, *Anatomy of Criticism* (Princeton: Princeton University Press, 1957), 33–67.

[15] See, for example, Lukács, "Erzählen oder Beschreiben? Zur Diskussion über Natura-

a close connection between the advent of photography and the growing importance of description in nineteenth-century literature. "The moment that photography appeared, the descriptive genre began to invade Letters," he wrote. "In verse as in prose, the décor and the exterior aspects of life took an almost excessive place."[16]

Realism, indeed, was accompanied by a historically new emphasis on things: on inert matter, everyday objects, household goods, commodities, kitsch, curiosities, *bibélots*.[17] And because realism wanted to incorporate the thingness of the world into its descriptive discourse, it developed a penchant for the detail—say, blue soap.[18] The French critic Francis Wey, who also happened to be Courbet's patron, even went so far as to speak of a "cult of details." This was as early as in 1845, well before Flaubert and Zola. Wey remarked that "the taste for and close attention to details characterizes young and strong literatures; the abuse, the profusion of an excess of details signals decadent literature."[19]

Visibility in the realist novel is directly connected with both description and the detail. It may usefully be understood in relation to both. But this is also true: not all realist description is visually oriented; conversely, visually oriented accounts are not always descriptions. By the same token, the detail does not always derive from the order of the visible. All this is to say that visibility in the novel—*la visibilité romanesque*—is a critical and literary category in its own right, and that it deserves to be approached as such. This also implies that novelistic visibility has its own relatively autonomous history. From a literary-historical point of view, the modern art of making things visible can be traced as far

---

lismus und Formalismus," in *Probleme des Realismus* (Berlin: Aufbau, 1955), 103–45; Philippe Hamon, *Du descriptif* (Paris: Hachette, 1993). See also the essays collected in *Beschreibungs-kunst – Kunstbeschreibung: Ekphrasis von der Antike bis zur Gegenwart,* ed. Gottfried Boehm and Helmut Pfotenhauer (Munich: Fink, 1995).

[16] Quoted in Linda Nochlin, *Realism* (London: Penguin, [1971] 1990), 45.

[17] On the status of the thing in French realism, see Juliette Frølich, *Des hommes, des femmes et des choses. Langages de l'objet dans le roman de Balzac à Proust* (Saint-Denis: Presses Universitaires de Vincennes, 1997). On things in British realism, see Harry E. Shaw, *Narrating Reality: Austen, Scott, Eliot* (Ithaca, N.Y.: Cornell University Press, 1999), 38–89. On things in American realism, see Bill Brown, *A Sense of Things: The Object Matter of American Literature* (Chicago: University of Chicago Press, 2003); see also the special issue on "Things," ed. Bill Brown, *Critical Inquiry* 16, no. 1 (Fall 2001). On the *bibélot* in French realism, see Janell Watson, *Literature and Material Culture from Balzac to Proust: The Collection and Consumption of Curiosities* (Cambridge: Cambridge University Press, 1999).

[18] For a superior analysis of the realist detail, and of the ways in which the category of the detail has been framed in critical discussions and aesthetic debates, see Naomi Schor, *Reading in Detail: Aesthetics and the Feminine* (New York: Routledge, 1987).

[19] Francis Wey, *Remarques sur la langue française au dix-neuvième siècle* (Paris: Firmin Dodot, 1845), 2:374; quoted in Schor, *Reading in Detail,* 43.

back as to the role of ekphrasis in classical rhetoric. By ekphrasis, a minor genre of ancient rhetoric, is typically meant a speech or text that contains a description of a visual artifact, in particular, a work of visual art. The locus classicus is the shield of Achilles, the celebrated episode in the *Iliad* where Homer slows down the narrative speed in order to render in detail the shield of the Greek warrior hero.[20] But ekphrasis is also often understood in a more general sense, as any kind of substantial description that serves to represent—that is, to make the reader see—visual artifacts as well as persons, objects, settings, views, and the like. In contemporary critical discourse, ekphrasis has become subject to widespread and theoretically sustained reflection, and it is frequently approached as "the verbal representation of visual representation."[21]

Ekphrasis as the verbal representation of visual representation: this is a reformulation that throws into relief an issue that has always been part of the ekphrastic—the ontological difference between verbal and visual modes of representation and the utter impossibility for the text or spoken word to be capable of doing what the image can do: to show, to actualize, to bring forth.

For Sigurd Burckhardt, all poetic images aim at transcending the very verbal means with which the image is created and ultimately seek to achieve the kind of plasticity and physical thereness that one typically finds in the visual arts, especially painting and sculpture.

> The painter's tree *is* an image; but if the poet writes "tree," he does not create an image. He *uses* one; the poetic "image" is one only in a metaphorical sense. Actually it is something that evokes an image, a sign pointing to a certain pre-established configuration in our visual memory [...]. The so-called poetic image achieves its effects only by denying its essence; it *is* a word, but it functions by making us aware of something other than it is. If many key terms of literary analysis—"color," "texture" and "image," for example—are in fact metaphors borrowed from the other arts, this is the reason: poetry has no material cause. Words already have what the artist first wants to give them—body.[22]

---

[20] See, for example, Murray Krieger's influential essay, "The Ekphrastic Principle and the Still Moment of Poetry; or *Laokoön* revisited," in *The Play and Place of Criticism* (Baltimore: Johns Hopkins University Press, 1967), 105–28. For a survey of contemporary discussions of the nature of ekphrasis, with a useful bibliography, see W. J. T. Mitchell, "Ekphrasis and the Other," in *Picture Theory* (Chicago: University of Chicago Press, 1994), 151–81. See also Gotthold Ephraim Lessing, *Laokoon, oder über die Grenzen der Malerei und Poesie* (Stuttgart: Reklam, 1964), esp. 114–21.

[21] This is how James Heffernan, for example, defines his object of study; see Heffernan, *Museum of Words: The Poetics of Ekphrasis from Homer to Ashbery* (Chicago: University of Chicago Press, 1993), 3.

[22] Sigurd Burckhardt, "The Poet as Fool and Priest," *ELH* 23 (1956), 280; quoted in Krieger, "The Ekphrastic Principle," 108.

The ekphrastic lineage is an instructive one because more or less all the aesthetic and philosophical problems that the realist visible turns around, implicitly or explicitly, are reviewed in the literature on this poetic mode. Yet although the realist art of making things visible can be interestingly related to the Western tradition of ekphrasis, the history of visibility in the novel is a more wide-ranging and also more complicated affair.[23]

First, and as I shall be arguing throughout this book, the pursuit of the visible is by and large an eminently modern phenomenon. Second, the mode of making things visible in the nineteenth-century novel represents a break with what went before it. Third, realist visibility is not limited to the verbal representation of visual representation; it also includes natural objects and artifacts, such as a buttonhole, a crease, a bar of soap, a sunset, a view, a rooftop, a human face, a fingernail.

In fact, it is in the nature of realist visiblity to be non-ekphrastic, even anti-ekphrastic. Just as nineteenth-century realism may be seen as a conscious attempt at stripping literary discourse of all "novelistic" elements, as Zola once put it, so it also tends to evade the grand tradition of the visual arts. Realism has a marked affinity with the brute facts of everyday life. And if paintings are to be dealt with, they had better be unknown masterpieces, as in Balzac's novella.

---

[23] Apart from ekphrasis, classical rhetoric provides a rich supply of terms that help us to conceptualize the art of making things visible, that is, the attempt to evoke something visually before the reader or the audience—think of terms such as *evidentia, enargeia, illustratio, phantasia, hypotyposis.* Greek and Roman rhetoricians possessed a tremendously well-developed critical and analytical apparatus, and much of what goes on in nineteenth-century realism may usefully be approached in rhetorical terms. Yet it is clear that *la visibilité romanesque* represents something new in the history of literature, not just in terms of scope but also in terms of function. Historically speaking, moreover, realism is a post-rhetorical phenomenon. To put things as simply as possible: the sheer existence of that blue soap should alert us to the possibility that the visible ultimately means something very different in nineteenth-century realism than in, say, a poetic verse by Homer or an elevated speech by Quintilian. For an instructive discussion of hypotyposis, see Eco, "Les Sémaphores sous la Pluie," in *On Literature,* 180–211. Eco reminds us that hypotyposis represents the opposite of ekphrasis; the former invites the reader to construct a visual representation, the latter attempts to represent a visual construction, that is, an image. This is why Eco argues that hypotyposis, strictly speaking, is not a trope. "Hypotyposis is [...] a semantic-pragmatic phenomenon (besides, inasmuch as it is a figure of thought, like irony and similar figures, it requires complex textual strategies and can never be exemplified through brief quotations or formulas) and is a prime example of interpretative cooperation. It is not so much a representation as a technique for eliciting an effort to compose a visual representation (on the reader's part)" (199). This is a distinction that may usefully be applied to nineteenth-century realism; the visible in the realist novel builds less on tropes than on specific techniques for provoking the reader to imagine things that can be seen.

Philippe Hamon develops a similar argument in his wonderfully capacious book *Imageries. Littérature et image au XIXe siècle* (2001). He even goes so far as to claim that the nineteenth century saw the emergence of a new kind of imagery. To be sure, the period certainly did not invent the image, Hamon emphasizes; nor did it invent literature, nor the relation between image and text, nor the presence of images and of figurative objects in literature. But a major change took place all the same, for the nineteenth century witnessed a transformation of the relationship between the image and the literary text.

> [Le XIXe siècle] a modifié profondément et radicalement cette relation en inventant, ou en mettant au point, ou en industrialisant, ou faisant circuler, ou en généralisant dans des proportions radicalement nouvelles une nouvelle *imagerie*, – le terme se généralise au XIXe siècle – faite de nouveaux objets et de nouvelles pratiques. [...] Cette modification prend place entre les lanternes magiques et les panoramas de la fin du XVIIIe siècle et le cinéma à l'extrême fin du XIXe siècle.[24]

What, more specifically, was new about nineteenth-century literature? In Hamon's view, two things in particular. First, the literary image had now become an utterly heterogeneous affair. It was diverse and mobile, and it no longer originated in the literary realm alone. Up until the nineteenth century, the treatment of the textual image had been governed by practices inherent in the great literary-historical tradition. One imitated handed-down images, or one reacted against the tradition, Hamon writes, but one always moved within the boundaries of the literary-historical domain. From now on, however, the art of fiction began to turn to extra-literary realms and to their corresponding, newly emerged image worlds.

> [L]e dix-neuvième siècle semble rompre avec une longue tradition de l'évolution littéraire qui " progressait " par imitations (on imite les anciens) ou réactions (on fait tout le contraire des anciens), imitations et réactions qui restaient en quelque sorte endogènes, qu'elles fussent internes (on imite les classiques du XVIIe siècle) ou externes (on imite Shakespeare, ou Ossian, ou W. Scott), mais toujours intérieures au champ des belles-lettres.[25]

This is the sense in which the nineteenth-century image bears witness to a rupture with the literary-historical tradition. Rhetoric loses its hold;

---

[24] Philippe Hamon, *Imageries. Littérature et image au XIXe siècle* (Paris: José Corti, 2001), 11.
[25] Ibid., 31–2.

painting no longer reigns supreme as model; and the ekphrastic lineage undergoes a mutation. According to Hamon, therefore, the nineteenth-century iconosphere is of a fundamentally different kind: the grandeur of painting, and the nobility of its historical, biblical, or mythological motifs, are replaced by emphatically trivial images. By the same token, three-dimensionality gives way to flatness. The literary image is now readily two-dimensional, level, and plane; it is also angular, cropped, and framed.

But this is not quite all. The nineteenth century breaks with the past in yet another way. In the spirit of Roman Jakobson's theory of figuration, Hamon suggests that in the nineteenth century, metonymy is substituted for metaphor.[26] Metaphor, according to Jakobson, operates by way of similarity (likeness, superposition, identification, the paradigmatic); metonymy, by contrast, is based on the principle of contiguity (combination, context, differentiation, the syntagmatic). The opposition is not only a classificatory tool; it also provides a periodizing device. Jakobson thus suggests that if the metaphoric procedure prevails in romanticism, the metonymic procedure comes to predominate in realist discourse.[27]

---

[26] See Roman Jakobson, "Two Aspects of Language and Two Types of Aphasic Disturbances," in Jakobson and Morris Halle, *Fundamentals of Language,* 2d, rev. ed. (The Hague: Mouton, 1971), 69–96. For Jakobson, the metaphoric and the metonymic modes are present in all language; there is continuous oscillation between the two poles in any sign system, even non-verbal ones. Jakobson argues, however, that just as the metaphoric mode prevails in romanticism, so the metonymic one prevails in realism. And while the metaphoric process has generated much discussion, the metonymic still awaits its critics and theorists: "The primacy of the metaphoric process in the literary schools of romanticism and symbolism has been repeatedly acknowledged, but it is still insufficiently realized that it is the predominance of metonymy which underlies and actually predetermines the so-called 'realistic' trend, which belongs to an intermediary stage between the decline of romanticism and the rise of symbolism and is opposed to both. Following the path of contiguous relationships, the realist author metonymically digresses from the plot to the atmosphere and from the characters to the setting in space and time. He is fond of synecdochic details. In the scene of Anna Karenina's suicide Tolstoj's artistic attention is focused on the heroine's handbag; and in *War and Peace* the synecdoches 'hair on the upper lip' and 'bare shoulders' are used by the same writer to stand for the female characters to whom these features belong" (91–2). It is also interesting to note that Jakobson's distinction between metaphor and metonymy works to explain the difference between poetry and prose, so that the former is governed by the principle of similarity, whereas prose is "forwarded essentially by contiguity" (96). But if it is true that all prose is essentially metonymic, what—if anything—then sets realistic prose apart?

[27] Jakobson connects his theory of the metaphoric and metonymic processes to Freud's theory of dream language in *Traumdeutung.* The metonymic mode thus corresponds to Freud's notion of "displacement"; the synecdochic mode (in Jakobson, the synecdoche is closely related to metonymy) finds its counterpart in "condensation"; and the metaphoric, finally, is linked to "identification and symbolism" (95).

In Hamon's scheme of things, the metonymic mode is part and parcel of the transformation of the relation between text and image in the nineteenth century, especially when it comes to the function, appearance, and pragmatics of the literary image. Consider a metonymic instance in *Madame Bovary*. In describing Rouen, Flaubert's narrator compares the islands in the river to "de grands poissons noirs arrêtés."[28] As Hamon suggests, this is a peculiar image in that it locates the second term (fish at a standstill) in the vicinity of the first (islands in a river), thus insisting on spatial as well as referential contiguity.[29] Any comparison, to be effective, has to build on difference, distance, or tension, and this is why Flaubert's image achieves virtually nothing. The narrative flow comes to a halt. Why? The second term, because it is so close to the first, hampers the transfer of meaning that we expect from a comparison. The word is forced to turn back on itself; and the reader's hermeneutic activity is short-circuited. To realize that those Flaubertian islands are likened to immobile fish is to move into a world without secrets, without significance, without meaning.

If nineteenth-century realism celebrated the literal, and if it therefore also rejected allegory, it is easy to see why metonymy came to be the privileged mode of figuration. For the metonymic is rigorously non-transcendental and anti-hierarchical: it always refers us back to the material substance of the world, to the brute facticity of the real, in a never-ending movement of continuous displacement.

The second feature that in Hamon's view characterizes nineteenth-century literature is that the image tends to be situated in a precise topography. Indeed, for all its diversity and mobility, the image is always placed in a carefully articulated and highly individualized site. Every icon comes with its own "iconothèque." A certain logic may be discerned, Hamon suggests: the image is readily located in sites that are related either to "production" or to "storage." Together these sites help organize a system, constituting a veritable "iconotope" specific to the nineteenth century.[30]

Hamon's book is a pioneering study. For although critics and scholars have always agreed that the visible is overwhelmingly important to nineteenth-century writers, very little has been written on the subject. The modern art of making things visible has not been subjected to sustained

---

[28] Philippe Neefs, in his notes to *Madame Bovary,* underscores that the passage has become a veritable model of Flaubertian description, especially in the genetic study of Flaubert's manuscripts. See *Madame Bovary,* ed. Philippe Neefs (Paris: Livre de Poche, 1999), 394.
[29] Hamon, *Imageries,* 302–5.
[30] Ibid., 31.

critical attention. Hamon's study is an exception, as is Isabelle Daunais's recent work on the French novel. In *Frontière du roman* (2002), Daunais traces a development that stretches from Balzac to Maupassant and Proust.[31] Like Hamon, she is concerned with the emergence of the modern notion of *style,* a process whose first stirrings can be observed during the second half of the eighteenth century. Style now begins to be understood in the singular. Style is no longer thought of as a set of discursive registers available to the writer, but rather as something that is irreducibly individual. Indeed, style is now the author's personal signature, his or her unique fingerprints. To put things a little differently: style is substituted for rhetoric. In this process, the author of *Madame Bovary* is a key figure, for with Flaubert we witness the fullblown emergence of style.[32]

In Daunais's view, the shift from rhetoric to style in French nineteenth-century literature is accompanied by a shift from orality to visuality.[33] If rhetoric in the novel reflected the existence of a literary public, and a relatively homogeneous one at that, then the advent of style in the modern sense reflects the growing distance between the writer and his or her audience. And if, furthermore, rhetoric in the novel reflected a mode of crafting narratives that was based in an essentially oral conversation culture, then style marks the emergence of an autonomous language. Indeed, in the course of the nineteenth century, "print culture becomes the site of an autonomous language."[34]

It is at this point that the question of the visible enters the picture. As style is substituted for rhetoric, the art of making things visible gains a new urgency. Visual description becomes imperative, especially in Balzac. As we shall see in a moment, Balzac excels in the visual exposition of the world, all the way down to the parameters that govern the social order. But if, in Balzac, the oral component still makes itself strongly felt, then after Balzac a new development begins to take shape. Daunais argues that the spoken period gives way to a new literary unit—*la phrase*. It may be a sentence, or a passage, or a paragraph, but it is never just a *phrase*: it is a thing, an object, an artifact. And nowhere do these

---

[31] See Isabelle Daunais, "Le spectacle du roman," in *Frontière du roman. Le personnage réaliste et ses fictions* (Montréal: Presses de l'Université de Montréal, 2002), 49–111.

[32] Marcel Proust develops this argument with great force in "Sainte-Beuve et Balzac", in *Contre Sainte-Beuve précédé de Pastiches et mélanges et suivi de Essais et articles,* ed. Pierre Clarac and Yves Sandre (Paris: Gallimard, 1971), 263–94.

[33] Daunais's point of departure is Marc Fumaroli's work on French conversation culture; see Fumaroli, *Trois institutions littéraires* (Paris: Gallimard, 1992).

[34] Daunais, "Spectacle du roman," 59–60.

historical changes become so palpable as in the case of Flaubert.[35] For with Flaubert, this new textual space—the sentence—very often coincides with a visual description, an image, or a tableau:

> Comme souvent, Flaubert marque ici un tournant: à partir de *Madame Bovary* (de son deuxième chapitre, pour être exact), le roman ne se donne plus à lire dans le relais d'une parole conteuse. La visibilité de la phrase s'allie à la visibilité du monde (les objets, les détails de la matière) pour créer une conception de la représentation et de l'écriture qui conduit doublement à une oeuvre "visible."[36]

The novel of the latter half of the nineteenth century establishes a distance to its reader, Daunais underscores. For the textual unit known as *la phrase* is aimed at a reader, not at a listener. It presupposes that the narrative is processed by the eye, not by the ear. With Flaubert onward, the organizing unit of the narrative text is no longer *le récit* but rather *la phrase*. Daunais even goes so far as to suggest that in *Madame Bovary*, *le récit* is effaced in the presence of things; and these things, in their turn, are reduced to their visible features.

The Metropolis and the Gaze

Why does the birth of realism coincide with the advent of novelistic visibility? The question requires careful consideration of nineteenth-century visual culture at large. First and foremost one has to consider painting—Courbet, of course, and artists such as Manet, Monet, and Degas—but also the advent of photography, the emergence of illustrated newspapers, and the spread of commercial images in public spaces.[37] The rise of visibility in the history of the novel is an overdetermined phenomenon.

In the early nineteenth century, an extraordinary multitude of new image objects and visual practices began to emerge.[38] In addition, new

---

[35] Roland Barthes beautifully makes this point in "Flaubert et la phrase" [1967], in *Oeuvres complètes,* 2:1382; "Flaubert and the Sentence," in *Barthes: Selected Writings,* ed. Susan Sontag (London: Fontana/Collins, 1983), 303.

[36] Daunais, "Spectacle du roman," 58.

[37] On the relations of photography and nineteenth-century literature, see Nancy Armstrong, *Fiction in the Age of Photography: The Legacy of British Realism* (Cambridge, Mass.: Harvard University Press, 1999); Bernd Stiegler, *Philologie des Auges. Die photographische Entdeckung der Welt im 19. Jahrhundert* (Munich: Fink, 2001); and Philippe Ortel, *La litterature à l'ère de la photographie. Enquête sur une révolution invisible* (Nîmes: Jacqueline Chambon, 2002).

[38] For a survey of "ocularcentric" tendencies in French culture, from the late eighteenth

forms of interference, mediation, and circulation came into being. The realist novel, especially in France, is an excellent record of these historical changes. It not only records such events but also thematizes them.

Yet another factor is the rise of the metropolis as a site of visual excess. As the nineteenth century progressed, private and public spaces alike were invaded by images, visual messages, and figurative objects of all kinds. Apartments, public monuments, commercial buildings, railway cars, horse-driven cars, billboards, sandwich men, department stores, shop windows, arcades, walls, streets, boulevards: all helped produce a single yet heterogeneous space in which spectacular artifacts and messages moved, circulated, and communicated. Among them were photographs, drawings, reproductions, industrially produced kitsch objects, political advertisements, posters, images of actors and actresses, post cards, illustrated magazines.[39]

The nineteenth-century city did more than just constitute a vast spectacle. It also worked the other way around by motivating a continuous realization of the visible. Generally speaking, the evolution of nineteenth-century urban space—its tremendous growth; its ever-changing realities; its flows of traffic, humans, goods, and information; its shaping and reshaping of social relations—necessarily excited the sense of sight. Now startled and dulled, now intoxicated and bored, the urban eye and its habits were shaped by a peculiar dialectic that the modern city itself helped to enforce. This, of course, is a major theme in Walter Benjamin's work on Paris in the Second Empire.

But what I have in mind is something much more fundamental, even banal: urban space literally made one see. Like never before, the nineteenth-century metropolitan city encouraged the discovery of the visible as such. And it did so by triangulating the relation between the observer and the observed, between the perceiving subject and the visible world.[40] For a gloss on the dynamics of this process, I can think of no richer source than Balzac.

---

century through the mid nineteenth century, see Martin Jay, *Downcast Eyes: The Denigration of Vision in Twentieth-Century French Thought* (Berkeley and Los Angeles: University of California Press, 1993), 83–148.

[39] On Paris as consumerist spectacle, especially during the Second Empire, see, for example, Walter Benjamin, *Das Passagen-Werk* (Frankfurt am Main: Suhrkamp, 1982); T. J. Clark, *The Painting of Modern Life: Paris in the Art of Manet and His Followers* (Princeton: Princeton University Press, 1984), 3–22; David Harvey, *Paris, Capital of Modernity* (New York: Routledge, 2003), 209–24.

[40] On the "triangulation of desire," especially in the French nineteenth-century novel, see René Girard, *Mensonge romantique et verité romanesque* (Paris: Grasset, 1961); *Deceit, Desire, and the Novel: Self and Other in Literary Structure,* trans. Yvonne Freccero (Baltimore: Johns Hopkins University Press, 1965).

Balzac's realism testifies to the discovery of modern metropolitan space, or to be more accurate, Paris. In Balzac, Paris is a world unto itself, and it knows no alternatives. Paris is not a place-name. It is also not the capital of France. Paris is a sign system, a mythology, a galaxy, a living essence, a giant organism. It is always in motion, and what makes it tick is the money form. Whoever you are, and whatever you want to become, Paris always precedes you, marks you, conditions you. In Balzac, the city is a character in its own right.[41]

Paris as protagonist: this is especially true of *Illusions perdues* (1837–43). Balzac's story offers an exemplary entry into the nineteenth-century novel and its discovery of metropolitan space—and, hence, of the visible as such. Lucien de Rubempré, an aspiring poet and handsome young man of low station, has decided to leave the provinces to go to Paris. He is in love with Madame de Bargeton, a witty, cultivated, and wealthy woman who represents the summit of society in the little place where he has grown up. For him, she is Beauty, Intelligence, Spirit incarnate. Madame de Bargeton, for her part, has fallen for the poet's charms and, much to the surprise of her friends, established him in her salon. They meet regularly and often in private. Eventually, they make a secret plan to leave Angoulême for Paris.

During his first days in the French capital, Lucien visits a series of public spaces, places to see and to be seen. Thrilled and confused, he wanders along the boulevards, strolls through parks, passes by cafés and shops. In the evening, he pays a visit to the theater to watch a vaudeville performance in the company of Madame de Bargeton and her friend, a certain Baron du Châtelet. Although nothing has happened, Madame de Bargeton undergoes a transformation in Lucien's eyes. That good taste of hers melts into air; that famed elegance appears as a chimera. A hitherto unseen being emerges into view, mercilessly framed as she now is by the other women at the theater.

---

[41] That Paris serves as a character in its own right in Balzac's oeuvre has been observed by numerous critics and scholars. See, for example, Italo Calvino, "The City as Novel in Balzac," in *Why Read the Classics?,* trans. Martin McLaughlin (New York: Pantheon, 1999), 139–43. Henry James, too, noted that, "Paris became [Balzac's] world, his universe." A truly perceptive reader, James went on to remark that "Wherever in his novels Paris is not directly presented she is even more vividly implied; the great negative to his brilliant positive, that *vie de province* of which he produced such elaborate pictures, is always observed from the standpoint of the Boulevard. [...] He never perceived with any especial directness that the civilized world was made up of something else than Paris and the provinces" ("Honoré de Balzac," in *European Writers & The Prefaces* [New York: Library of America, 1984], 35).

> Le cercle s'élargissait, la société prenait d'autres proportions. Le voisinage de plusieurs jolies Parisiennes si élégamment, si fraîchement mises, lui fit remarquer la vieillerie de la toilette de Mme de Bargeton, quoiqu'elle fût passablement ambitieuse: ni les étoffes, ni les façons, ni les couleurs n'étaient de mode. La coiffure qui le séduisait tant à Angoulême lui parut d'un goût affreux comparée aux délicates inventions par lesquelles se recommandait chaque femme.[42]

> His little world was broadening out and society was assuming vaster proportions. The proximity of several beautiful Parisian women, so elegantly and so daintily attired, made him aware that Madame de Bargeton's *toilette*, though passably ambitious, was behind the times: neither the material, nor the way it was cut, nor the colours were in fashion. The hair-style he had found so seductive at Angoulême struck him as being in deplorable taste compared with the delicate inventiveness which lent distinction to the other women present.[43]

Lucien rediscovers Madame de Bargeton: he comes to look at her with the eyes of others. What has happened? Balzac's answer is Paris. Indeed, Paris is represented as the great mediator, here and elsewhere in *Illusions perdues*. For what has taken place is that the relationship between Lucien and Madame de Bargeton is no longer a dual one; it is a triple relationship. Indeed, the gaze of desire that once seemed so spontaneous and immediate has been subjected to a cruel logic of triangulation.

In this process, Paris is the third term. And what is more, Julien's desire can barely survive the advent of a third term. From now on, there may be gazing, but precious little desire—at least in so far as Julien's feelings for Madame de Bargeton are concerned. Balzac explains: "En province il n'y a ni choix ni comparaison à faire: l'habitude de voir les physionomies leur donne une beauté conventionnelle [In the provinces no occasion arises for choice or comparison: one sees the same physiognomies day by day and confers a conventional beauty on them]" (193/161).

But there is more to the episode, for the revelation is perfectly symmetrical. When Madame de Bargeton casts an eye on her young admirer, he too emerges in a new and less flattering light, mercilessly framed as he now is by the other men at the theater.

> De son côté, Mme de Bargeton se permettait d'étranges réflexions sur son amant. Malgré son étrange beauté, le pauvre poète n'avait point de tour-

---
[42] Honoré de Balzac, *Illusions perdues,* ed. Philippe Berthier (Paris: Flammarion, 1990), 192–3. Further page references are given in the main text.
[43] Balzac, *Lost Illusions,* trans. Herbert J. Hunt (Harmondsworth: Penguin, 1971), 161. Further page references are given in the main text.

> nure. Sa redingote dont les manches étaient trop courtes, ses méchants gants de province, son gilet étriqué, le rendaient prodigieusement ridicule auprès des jeunes gens du balcon: Mme de Bargeton lui trouvait un air piteux. (193)

> Madame de Bargeton too was indulging in strange reflections about her admirer. The poor poet was singularly handsome, but he cut a sorry figure. His frock-coat, too short in the sleeves, his cheap provincial gloves and his skimpy waistcoat gave him a prodigiously ridiculous appearance in comparison with the young men in the dress-circle: Madame de Bargeton found him pitiable to look at. (161)

Balzac hastens to stress, once more, what has happened between the two lovers, and why it had to happen the way it did.

> Il se préparait chez Mme de Bargeton et chez Lucien un désenchantement sur eux-mêmes dont la cause était Paris. La vie s'y agrandissait aux yeux du poète, comme la société prenait une face nouvelle aux yeux de Louise. À l'un et à l'autre, il ne fallait plus qu'un accident pour trancher les liens qui les unissaient. (193)

> In the case both of Madame de Bargeton and Lucien, mutual disenchantment was setting in, and Paris was the cause of it. The poet was seeing life on a larger scale and society was taking on a new aspect in Louise's eyes. With both of them, only a chance event was needed to sever the bonds between them. (162)

The logic of the triangulated gaze does not stop here. Its symmetry extends further, all the way into Lucien's self-understanding. He is quick to internalize the gaze of the Parisian other, and he does it successfully—so successfully, in fact, that he even comes to look at himself with radically different eyes.

The day after the visit to the theater, Lucien learns that he is invited to go the opera in the company of Madame de Bargeton and her distinguished cousin, the Marquise d'Espard. Overjoyed at the prospect, Lucien decides to spend the morning taking a walk in the Tuileries Gardens. He leaves his hotel and begins to stroll, as happy as can be. Soon enough, his sense of joy is replaced by the most agonizing kind of dissatisfaction. He now discovers what his exterior signifies in the eyes of others. Paris has made him see, and he does not like what he sees:

> Lucien passa deux cruelles heures dans les Tuileries: il y fit un violent retour sur lui-même et se jugea. D'abord il ne vit pas un seul habit à ces jeunes élégants. S'il apercevait un homme en habit, c'était un vieillard hors la loi, quelque pauvre diable, un rentier venu du Marais, ou quelque

garçon de bureau. Après avoir reconnu qu'il y avait une mise du matin et une mise du soir, le poète aux émotions vives, au regard pénétrant, reconnut la laideur de sa défroque, les défectuosités qui frappaient de ridicule son habit dont la coupe était passée de mode, dont le bleu était faux, dont le collet était outrageusement disgracieux, dont les basques de devant, trop longtemps portées, penchaient l'une vers l'autre; les boutons avaient rougi, les plis dessinaient de fatales lignes blanches. Puis son gilet était trop court et la façon si grotesquement provinciale que, pour le cacher, il boutonna brusquement son habit. Enfin il ne voyait de pantalon de nankin qu'aux gens communs. Les gens comme il faut portaient de délicieuses étoffes de fantaisie ou le blanc toujours irréprochable! D'ailleurs tous les pantalons étaient à sous-pieds, et le sien se mariait très mal avec les talons de ses bottes, pour lesquels les bords de l'étoffe recroquevillée manifestaient une violente antipathie. Il avait une cravate blanche à bouts brodés par sa soeur […]. Non seulement personne, excepté les gens graves, quelques vieux financiers, quelques sévères administrateurs, ne portait de cravate blanche le matin; mais encore le pauvre Lucien vit passer de l'autre côté de la grille, sur le trottoir de la rue de Rivoli; un garçon épicier tenant un panier sur sa tête, et sur qui l'homme d'Angoulême surprit deux bouts de cravate brodés par la main de quelque grisette adorée. À cet aspect, Lucien reçut un coup à la poitrine […]. (195–6)

Lucien spent two hours of torment in the Tuileries: he angrily took stock of his own appearance and condemned it. In the first place, not one of these elegant young men was wearing a cut-away coat: if he saw one at all it was worn by some disreputable old man, or some poor down-at-heel, or a *rentier* from the Marais quartier, or a commissionaire. Having realized the difference between morning and evening wear, this highly sensitive and keen-sighted poet recognized the ugliness of his own apparel, which was fit only for the rag-bag, the out-of-date cut of his coat, its dubious blue, its outrageously ungainly collar and its tails nearly meeting in front through too long usage; the buttons were rusty and there were tell-tale white lines along the creases. Also his waistcoat was too short and so grotesquely provincial in style that he hastily buttoned up his coat in order to hide it. Lastly, only common people were wearing nankeen trousers. Fashionable people were wearing attractively patterned or immaculately white material! Moreover everyone wore gaitered trousers; the bottoms of his fell in ugly crinkles on the heels of his boots. He wore a white cravat with embroidered ends […]. Only grave personages, a few aged financiers and austere public officials wore white cravats; worse still, the unhappy native of Angoulême saw a grocer's errand-boy with a basket on his head passing along the other side of the railings on the pavement of the rue de Rivoli, and he was wearing a cravat with its two ends embroidered by some adoring shop-girl. For Lucien this was like a blow in the chest […]. (164–5)

This passage is a mere fragment of the episode that renders how Lucien comes to see himself with the eyes of others. Yet the comedy of these pages should be clear, and the formidable skill with which Balzac's narrator approaches the descriptive task he has set himself. For what Balzac achieves here is something quite remarkable. The passage appears at first glance to offer an elaborate characterization of Lucien's appearance and little more. But Balzac in effect accomplishes two things at once. The scene also manages to expose—to make visible—the very parameters that govern the fashion system in relation to which Lucien's exterior takes on meaning.

And it does so in brutal detail. A collar is never just a collar, a crease is never just a crease, a button never just a button. During his random stroll through the Tuileries, it quickly dawns on Lucien that he is the unwitting carrier of so many signs that have already assigned him a place within a visually determined signifying system, that is, a hermeneutics of class. And when Lucien discovers what kind of place he occupies within this very signifying system, the gap between his self-image and what he represents in the eyes of others begins to yawn terrifyingly.

> "J'ai l'air du fils d'un apothicaire, d'un vrai cortaud de boutique!" se dit-il à lui-même avec rage en voyant passer les gracieux, les coquets, les élégants jeunes gens des familles du faubourg Saint-Germain, qui tous avaient une manière à eux qui les rendait tous semblables par la finesse des contours, par la noblesse de la tenue, par l'air du visage; et tous différents par le cadre que chacun s'était choisi pour se faire valoir. Tous faisaient ressortir leurs avantages par une espèce de mise en scène que les jeunes gens entendent à Paris aussi bien que les femmes. (196–7)

> "I look just like an apothecary's son, a mere shop-assistant!" he told himself, as he watched the passers-by, graceful, smart, elegant young men of the Faubourg Saint-Germain: all of them having a certain *cachet*, all alike in their trimness of line, their dignity of bearing and their self-confident air; yet all different thanks to the setting each had chosen in order to show himself to advantage. The best points in all of them were brought out by a kind of *mise en scène* at which the young men of Paris are as skilful as the women. (165)

It is as though Lucien, in casting a critical eye on his own appearance, has stepped out of himself. He has been pulled into a strange dialectic: he is both the subject of perception and its object. Lucien, after all, is indeed the son of an apothecary, but what he now discovers—what Paris makes him see—is that he is a *mere* apothecary's son. As he looks at the others, he also looks at himself—and then turns into an other in his own eyes.

Balzac here performs an exercise in comparative criticism. What is more, he crafts a passage that, in its accumulation of tell-tale detail, recreates on the stylistic level the very distinction about which it speaks. A whole series of particulars, all pregnant with unexpected social significance, parade before our eyes: the look of a button, the shape of a collar, the texture of a cravat, the cut of a waistcoat, the length of a trouser pant.

For Lucien there is a simple lesson to be drawn. On learning how he appears in the eyes of others, Lucien decides to refashion himself, especially now that he is to appear at the opera in distinguished company. Spending a sum of money that is the equivalent of some four month's existence in Angoulême, he buys himself a new outfit, including expensive boots. He even has his hair waved by a professional hairdresser.

At the opera, he takes a seat in the Marquise's box right at the back of the auditorium. Balzac motivates the scene that will follow by underscoring that in this box "on y est vu comme on y voit de tous côtés [in it one can see everyone and be seen by everyone]" (199/169). Balzac has set the stage, and the spectacle can begin.

In the intermission after the first act, Madame de Bargeton looks at Lucien with approval and compliments him on his successful transformation. As he gazes at her in return, Lucien can only conclude that she has failed to change. She remains the same; and her boring, deplorable, inexcusable sameness is brought out by that difference called Paris. All it takes is a quick glance for Lucien to realize that his seemingly ageless goddess, the beautiful and eloquent Madame de Bargeton, is a frumpy old woman from the provinces.

> Le voisinage d'une femme à la mode, de la marquise d'Espard, cette Mme de Bargeton de Paris, lui nuisait tant, la brillante Parisienne faisait si bien ressortir les imperfections de la femme de province, que Lucien, doublement éclairé par le beau monde de cette pompeuse salle et par cette femme éminente, vit enfin dans la pauvre Anaïs de Nègrepelisse la femme réelle, la femme que les gens de Paris voyaient: une femme grande, sèche, couperosée, fanée, plus que rousse, anguleuse, guindée, précieuse, prétentieuse, provinciale dans son parler, mal arrangée surtout! En effet, les plis d'une vieille robe de Paris attestent encore du goût, on se l'explique, on devine ce qu'elle fut, mais une vieille robe de province est inexplicable, elle est risible. La robe et la femme étaient sans grâce ni fraîcheur, le velours était miroité comme le teint. Lucien, honteux d'avoir aimé cet os de seiche, se promit de profiter du premier accès de vertu de sa Louise pour la quitter. (200)

> Proximity with a woman of fashion, the Marquise d'Espard, a Parisian Madame de Bargeton, was so prejudicial to her, her Parisian brilliance set in such strong relief the imperfections of her country cousin that Lucien, drawing two-fold enlightenment from the *beau monde* in this pompous assembly and the eminent Marquise, at last saw Anaïs de Nègrepelisse for what she was and as she was seen by the people of Paris: a tall, desiccated woman with freckled skin, faded complexion and strikingly red hair; angular, affected, pretentious, provincial of speech and above all badly dressed! In fact the very pleats of an outmoded Parisian dress can still reveal taste: one can make allowances and visualize it as it once was; but no allowances can be made for a superannuated up-country garment—it invites derision. Both the dress and the woman in it lacked grace and bloom: the mottled velvet went with a mottled complexion. Lucien was ashamed at having loved this cuttle-bone and promised himself to take advantage of Louise's next access of virtue by dropping her. (169–70)

In this passage, the same sort of clash is rehearsed as in the theater episode: a clash between error and truth, illusion and realism. But what appeared as a mere impression at the vaudeville theater emerges as an unshakeable fact at the opera. The verdict is unalterable. And the truth is there for all to see, including the young poet.

Balzac makes abundantly clear that Madame de Bargeton's magic is cruelly transmuted. In fact, she suffers more than one loss. As Lucien's gaze is triangulated by way of the visually determined system of signification known as Paris, she loses not only her aura of distinction; she also loses her individuality. Reduced to a mere example, she is now any old woman, any ridiculous provincial.

In Balzac, Paris is a relentless conveyor of truth, the great mediator, the third term that unexpectedly intervenes into any relation and bursts it open to the most unsettling kind of difference. Not only does Lucien perceive how the others perceive Madame de Bargeton, he also comes to see what they in fact see—a woman from the provinces, utterly lacking in distinction. In making the gaze of the others into his own, Lucien is thus able to perceive the naked truth with his own eyes. For to see "la femme réelle," as Balzac's narrator underscores, is to see "la femme que les gens de Paris voyaient" (200). In other words, the real woman is the woman as seen by the people of Paris (169).

And what do the people of Paris actually see? Balzac's narrator pedantically lists the visible evidence that amounts to Madame de Bargeton's truth, so that we—the readers—can see it before our eyes too: "une femme grande, sèche, couperosée, fanée, plus que rousse, anguleuse, guindée, précieuse, prétentieuse, provinciale dans son parler, mal arrangée surtout! [a tall, desiccated woman with freckled skin, faded complexion and strikingly red hair; angular, affected, pretentious, provincial of speech and above all badly dressed!" (200/169). Comparison leads to relativization, and relativization leads to dethronement. Such is Madame de Bargeton's Parisian fate. But the exclamation mark puts an end to relativization: the truth revealed is anything but a relative one.

This, then, is how Madame de Bargeton is apprehended by the people of Paris. Balzac means this quite literally, for the Parisian eye he has in mind is by no means only a metaphorical one. The episode reaches its climax when the image of Madame de Bargeton is juxtaposed with another image, as striking as the first: of how the people at the opera, equipped with viewing instruments, turn their eyes toward the Marquise's box and pass judgment on the sorry female figure from Angoulême.

Balzac motivates the description of the scene by appealing to Lucien's excellent eye-sight.

> Son excellente vue lui permettait de voir les lorgnettes braquées sur la loge aristocratique par excellence. Les femmes les plus élégantes examinaient certainement Mme de Bargeton, car elles souriaient toutes en se parlant. (200)
>
> His excellent eye-sight enabled him to see how many opera-glasses were levelled at their pre-eminently aristocratic box. The most elegant women were obviously scrutinizing Madame de Bargeton, for they were smiling as they chatted to one another. (169–70)

One piece of visible evidence is thus matched by another. Balzac offers us a paradigmatic scene in which the object of vision (the undistinguished Madame de Bargeton) is coordinated with the subjects of vision (the distinguished Parisians at the opera), in a vision that exerts a powerful influence on the young man. This, indeed, is Lucien before the Law. No wonder that he decides to drop Madame de Bargeton at his first convenience. He begins, instead, to develop an interest in her Parisian cousin, the distinguished Madame d'Espard.

But the logic of the triangulated gaze has one more twist. In the meantime, Madame d'Espard is shocked to realize that Lucien's real name is Chardon, not Rubempré, and that he is indeed the son of a simple shopkeeper in the provinces. Madame d'Espard tells her cousin to drop Lucien immediately, and Madame de Bargeton heeds her advice. The two ladies had originally decided to throw a dinner party to which they would invite the young poet and a few influential literary people, but they now decide to cancel it under the pretext that both of them are ill. In learning the news, Lucien is perplexed. Not only is Madame de Bargeton indisposed, she also refuses to receive him.

As he ponders the remarkable coldness of Madame de Bargeton's note, he walks down the Champs-Elysées. Thousands of elegant carriages pass by. All of a sudden the traffic comes to a halt, and Lucien catches sight of the two ladies in an extravagant vehicle. It appears to him that Madame de Bargeton has undergone a metamorphosis: she is wearing a whole new outfit, in exquisite materials that truly become her, and her comportment exudes the most natural kind of beauty, grace, and distinction. Her entire being is different. In fact, he finds it hard to recognize her.

As Lucien approaches the barouche to greet the ladies, he is thoroughly ignored. Madame de Bargeton pretends not to see the young man who bows before them; Madame d'Espard, for her part, is content merely to look at him through her lorgnette. And as if such disdain were not enough, a third person, a certain de Marsay, stares at Lucien through his monocle and then, with carefully calculated symbolism, lets it drop—to Lucien, it seems like the fall of a "guillotine blade."

The barouche is set in motion and moves away. The young man is seized by violent rage. Indeed, as befits a Balzacian protagonist endowed with truly Balzacian ambitions, Lucien is overcome by desire for social revenge: he wants to strangle Madame de Bargeton, send Madame d'Espard to the scaffold, and subject de Marsay to the most delicious kind of torture. The rage is powerful enough to carry him through six hundred pages, and the result is *Illusions perdues*.

I have dwelt at length on these episodes as I take Balzac's novel to be an ideal entry into the realist novel and the rise of the city as a narrative space. What Balzac does here is craft an archetypal tale of how a provincial arrives in the metropolis, discovering a social force field that is as vast and complex as it is opaque. And this discovery necessarily subjects the protagonist's previous experiences, convictions, and beliefs to painful relativization. Such relativization is another word for "lost illusions," and this, of course, is what *Illusions perdues* is all about. From now on, life will be a sequence of battles, and Balzac's handsome hero rises to the challenge. This is a paradigmatic story, one that both Stendhal and Flaubert rehearse, each in his own way. But what sets Balzac's version of the story apart from those of Stendhal and Flaubert, respectively, is his stubborn insistence on the visual aspects of this social comedy.

For Balzac's detailed descriptions of Lucien's first Parisian experiences also amount to an allegorical representation of how the protagonist comes to discover the visible. In the province, the gaze of the other was a known one, as the other could almost always be identified. The other may have been an other, but he or she was not a stranger, not an anonymous person. In much the same way, all visually determined signifying systems in Angoulême tended to be organic, transparent, and easy to decode.

In Paris, things are very different. And so it is that Lucien's introduction to Paris is staged as an essentially visual battle, first and foremost as a battle of the gazes. Because he so desperately wants to conquer Paris, he is immediately pulled into a socially significant field of vision. And Balzac is fast on the heels of his hero, explicating at length the hermeneutic parameters of the system and providing ample examples of how it works. Balzac wants his readers to really see this world in all its palpable visual reality, and above all he seeks to make it transparent, down to the most insignificant waist-coat button.

Yet I want to argue that these paradigmatic passages in *Illusions perdues* have an even larger and more wide-ranging significance. They do more than tell an emblematic tale about how the provincial comes to discover the visible. They also amount to an allegorical representation of how the realist novel itself discovers the visible.

This, of course, is an extravagant proposal. But there is good reason to entertain the idea that Balzac's story is an allegorization of how the realist novel discovers the visible, even if we limit the analysis to *Illusions perdues*. We have seen that Balzac's novel narrates the historical and social circumstances in which the visible as such becomes visible. Add to this that Lucien de Rubempré is more than a mere poet. He is also a figuration, a vehicle, a paradigm. He is a narrative device that permits new epic worlds to come into being. And so we should not be surprised when, a few hundred pages later, Balzac's protagonist is likened to "a serial novel": "Ce n'est pas un poète, ce garçon-là, c'est un roman continuel [He's not a poet, that young man: he's a serial novel!"], one of the characters exclaim (609/665).

Indeed, just as Lucien discovers the monstrous organism that is Paris, so the nineteenth-century realist novel falls into the visible.

Balzac and the Loss of the Real

Theodor W. Adorno once wrote an essay on Balzac called "Balzac-Lektüre," or "Reading Balzac." It dates from 1953, but it was not published until eight years later in the second volume of *Noten zur Literatur* (1961). On the face of it, the essay is a straightforward piece of literary criticism as typically practiced by Adorno. He focuses on Balzac's style and seeks to account for its historical specificity. But the title of the essay—"Balzac-Lektüre"—should also be grasped as literally as possible: as a report on the actual experience of reading Balzac.[44]

Adorno never really says as much, but anyone who reads the piece closely will discover what made him write about Balzac. Adorno was invaded by a sense of linguistic bewilderment, if not to say downright frustration. He found it exceedingly difficult to read Balzac. As a conscientious scholar, Adorno set out to read the great novelist in the original. And as a conscientious intellectual, he wanted to understand every single word. After all, what is Adorno if not the philosopher of the particular?

Now Adorno found that he had to consult his French dictionaries more or less all the time. So there he was, shuttling between his reading chair and his book case, looking up word after word, becoming ever more exasperated:

> Welcher deutsche Leser Balzacs, der gewissenhaft zum französischen Original greift, wäre nicht schon in Verzweiflung geraten über die unzähligen ihm unbekannten Vokabeln für spezifische Differenzen von Gegenständen, die er im Wörterbuch suchen muß, wenn nicht die Lektüre schwimmen soll; bis er dann resigniert und beschämt den Übersetzungen sich anvertraut. Die handwerkliche Genauigkeit des Französischen selber, der Respekt für Nuancen des Materials wie der Bearbeitung, in dem so viel von Kultur sich niederschlägt, mag dafür verantwortlich sein. Aber Balzac outriert das. (147)

> What German reader of Balzac, conscientiously turning to the French original, would not despair over the countless unfamiliar terms for specific differences between objects, terms he has to look up in the dictionary if his reading is not to flounder; until finally, resigned and humiliated, he entrusts himself to the translations. The craftsmanlike precision of the French language itself, the respect for nuances of material and workmanship in which so much of culture is sedimented, may be responsible for this. But Balzac takes it to extremes. (127–8)

What in the world did all these odd words in Balzac mean? And why did the French writer indulge in such specialized terminology?

Let us look at a random passage from *Illusions perdues*. Balzac's narrator is describing a certain monsieur Séchard, an aged printer who also happens to be the father of one of the major characters in the novel. The passage describes the pride *père* Séchard takes in his business; but it does more than that—it also serves to educate the reader in the art of

---

[44] Theodor W. Adorno, "Balzac-Lektüre," in *Noten zur Literatur* (Frankfurt am Main: Suhrkamp, 1981), 139–57; "Reading Balzac," in *Notes to Literature,* trans. Shierry Weber Nicholsen (New York: Columbia University Press, 1991), 121–36. Further page references are given in the main text.

printing. In fact, the second part of the passage reads like a veritable user's manual:

> Le père dégringola l'escalier raboteux, usé, tremblant, sans y chavirer; il ouvrit la porte de l'allée qui donnait dans l'atelier, se précipita sur la première de ses presses sournoisement huilées et nettoyées, il montra les fortes jumelles en bois de chêne frotté par son apprenti.
> "Est-ce là un amour de presse?" dit-il.
> Il s'y trouvait le *billet de faire-part* d'un mariage. Le vieil Ours abaissa la frisquette sur le tympan, le tympan sur le marbre qu'il fit rouler sous la presse; il tira le barreau, déroula la corde pour ramener le marbre, releva tympan et frisquette avec l'agilité qu'aurait mise un jeune Ours. La presse ainsi manoeuvrée jeta un si joli cri qui vous eussiez dit d'un oiseau qui serait venu heurter à une vitre et se serait enfui. (68)

> The old man clattered down the rugged, worn, rickety staircase without tumbling over himself, opened the alley door leading to the workshop, rushed to the first of the presses which he had been crafty enough to have oiled and cleaned, and pointed to the strong oaken side-pieces which his apprentices had polished.
> "Isn't that a jewel of a press?" he asked. There was a wedding-invitation on it. The old "bear" lowered the frisket on to the tympan and the tympan on to the carriage and rolled it under the press; he pulled the bar, unrolled the cord to draw back the carriage, and raised tympan and frisket with all the agility a young "bear" might have shown. Thus handled, the press gave a pretty little squeak like that of a bird fluttering away after striking against a window-pane. (11)

Why, Adorno asked himself, why does Balzac display such a consuming interest in concreteness, here and elsewhere? Why such obsessive precision? Why such advanced technical vocabulary?

It surely would have pleased Adorno that the most recent edition of *Illusions perdues*, edited by Philippe Berthier, has been provided with no fewer than 643 explanatory footnotes, so as to explain to the contemporary reader the nature and function of things such as a *jumelle*, a *tympan*, a *frisquette*... The contemporary *French* reader!

Balzac knew the printing industry by heart—he once ran a printing business, and his first-hand experience of that world everywhere makes itself felt in the novel. Adorno accordingly stresses that the major technical changes that enabled the rise of mass-produced literature are brilliantly—indeed, expertly—described in *Illusions perdues*. But the point is that Balzac's penchant for precision, concreteness, and specialized terminology is not limited to those spheres he knew well. It is a general tendency in Balzac. What is more, he takes it to extremes. Why?

After so much lexical research, and after a great deal of pondering, it obviously occurred to Adorno that his shuttling between his reading chair and his dictionaries had a reason. He had happened on a stylistic feature that marks Balzac's writings in particular and the nineteenth-century realist novel in general, a feature that could be interestingly related to social processes. In other words, Adorno decided to treat his sense of linguistic humiliation as a literary-historical problem in its own right.[45]

Hence the essay "Balzac-Lektüre." And hence the thought-provoking idea that the realist pursuit of concreteness and precision springs *not* from a familiarity with the phenomenal world but rather from a generalized loss of reality, a *Realitätsverlust*:

> Die Absonderlichkeit Balzacs wirft Licht auf einen Zug der Prosa des neunzehnten Jahrhunderts insgesamt seit Goethe. Der Realismus, dem auch idealisch Gesonnene nachhängen, ist nicht primär, sondern abgeleitet: Realismus aus Realitätsverlust. Epik, die des Gegenständlichen, das sie zu bergen trachtet, nicht mehr mächtig ist, muß es durch ihren Habitus übertreiben, die Welt mit exaggerierter Genauigkeit beschreiben, eben weil sie fremd geworden ist, nicht mehr in Leibnähe sich halten läßt. (148)

> Balzac's oddness sheds light on something that characterizes nineteenth century as a whole after Goethe. The realism with which even those who are idealistically inclined are preoccupied is not primary but derived: realism on the basis of a loss of reality. The epic that is no longer in command of the material concreteness it attempts to protect has to exaggerate it in its demeanor, has to describe the world with exaggerated precision precisely because it has become alien, can no longer be kept in physical proximity. (128)

Balzac, Adorno argues, is not so much attempting to *reproduce* a world, as he is attempting to *evoke* one. Contrary to what is commonly believed, the realist writer is not at home in the world, but fundamentally alienated from it, and this is why Balzac and other nineteenth-century writers tend to excel in concreteness. In realism, concreteness is not a

---

[45] Adorno had other reasons to shuttle between his reading chair and his book case. In addition to his French dictionaries, Adorno also consulted the *Dictionnaire biographique des personnages fictifs de la Comédie humaine*—in order to make sense of Balzac's ever-expanding, proto-paranoid universe and to track the complicated movements of the characters, their comings and goings, appearances and reappearances. Obviously these trips, too, occasioned philosophical reflection. The fact that Balzac's literary world is virtually impossible to survey, and that one even needs a guide to find one's way through it—this fact, for Adorno, was an interesting problem in its own right, deserving of critical reflection. So it is that parts of the essay dwell on the question of totality in Balzac.

transparent medium. It is anything but a sure path to literality. It is not a means of expressing some preexisting non-verbal reality. To the extent that literary concreteness expresses anything at all, it should be seen as a restitutional gesture and as a compensatory phenomenon. Concreteness in the realist novel, Adorno suggests, is motivated by a reality that is increasingly subjected to processes of abstraction.

To be sure, concreteness may seem to be an essential part of a literary strategy that permits us to see more clearly the world to which the representation refers. And very often, especially in realist discourse, this same world is also the historical context that occasioned the representation in the first place. But Adorno's point is that there is a significant difference between the act of looking *at* the world [*anschauen*] and that of seeing *through* it [*durchschauen*]. To be able to see through the world, one cannot merely look at it. Or to be more precise: when we reach the realist period, it is no longer enough merely to look at the world, nor is it enough simply to show what the world looks like. A world made visible is not necessarily a transparent one.[46] By the same token, concreteness does not automatically warrant understanding.

> Präzision fingiert äußerste Nähe zu den Sachgehalten und damit leibhaftige Gegenwart. Balzac übt die Suggestion des Konkreten aus. Sie ist aber so übermertig, daß man ihr nicht arglos nachgeben, sie nicht der ominösen Fülle epischer Anschauung gutschreiben soll. Viel eher ist jene Konkretheit, worauf ihr Eifer verweist: Beschwörung. Um durchschaut zu werden, kann die Welt nicht mehr angeschaut werden. (147)

> Precision simulates extreme closeness to the matter at hand and hence physical presence. Balzac uses the suggestion of concreteness. But it is so excessive that one cannot yield to it naively, cannot credit it to the ominous richness of epic vision. Rather, that concreteness is what its ardor suggests: an evocation. If the world is to be seen *through*, it can no longer be looked *at*. (128)

The visual aspect of Balzac's style is everywhere implicated in Adorno's essay, and he also notes the "penchant for the visual" in Balzac's writings, though it is not an explicit concern. It is therefore all the more interesting that Adorno associates questions of concreteness and exac-

---

[46] Hayden White makes a similar point in "The Problem of Style in Realistic Representation" wherein he suggests that in the realist novel understanding is readily conflated with perception. For in the realist period, "it was no longer the manner or form of utterance that constituted style, but rather the matter or content of the discourse […]. This meant that style had to do with cognitive perspicuity, the insight which the writer had into 'the nature of things.' To *see* clearly was to *understand* aright, and understanding was nothing other than the clear perception of the 'way things are'" ("Problem of Style," 214).

titude with the issue of seeing, as though they were inextricably linked. This is inherent in his play on the verb "schauen," as in *anschauen* and *durchschauen*. Concreteness and exactitude, for Adorno, point to the cognitive dimension of nineteenth-century realism or, to be more precise, its cognitive ambitions. In mobilizing the vocabulary of vision, Adorno turns "seeing" into an epistemological metaphor, to be sure, but it also confirms the utter importance of the visible in Balzac.

To make the world concrete is to make it visible, but to make it visible is not necessarily to make it intelligible. Rather, the concreteness of the visible, and the visibility of the concrete, is a compensatory strategy on the part of the realist writer, for whom the meaning of the world constantly escapes. The question then becomes: is it at all possible to see through nineteenth-century society and the historical factors that help shape it? Adorno says no.

> Eben weil in der bürgerlichen Welt vom Entscheidenden nicht sich erzählen läßt, geht das Erzählen zugrunde. Die immanenten Mängel des Balzacschen Realismus sind potentiell bereits das Verdikt über den realistischen Roman. (153–4)

> It is precisely because in the bourgeois world one can no longer tell stories about the things that are decisive that storytelling is dying out. The deficiencies inherent in Balzacian realism already represent, in latent form, the verdict on the realistic novel. (133)

Buried within this passage is an entire history of philosophy, one that also includes a theory of how art relates to history. For what Adorno suggests here is that a complex yet intimate relation exists between the practice of storytelling and the social formation. If the nineteenth century sees the decay of storytelling, it is ultimately because the mode of production is entering a new phase, the beginnings of full-blown capitalism, sometimes also called the period of classic or monopoly capitalism.

As a result, social life as a whole, and particularly the socioeconomic factors that help shape the early industrial world, are becoming increasingly more abstract and hence more difficult to grasp. Adorno invokes Max Weber's terminology, especially when he speaks of "disenchantment." He clearly suggests that the vast social universe unfolding in Balzac's writings must be understood against the background of that newly emergent worldly asceticism that, according to Weber, was vital to the rise of the protestant work ethic and industrial capitalism. Balzac offers an exemplary entry into a world that bears witness to that destructive process known as disenchantment, a general elimination of magic that sweeps through all spheres of social life and that goes hand in hand with the logic of rationalization:

> So bunt ist der Einbruch des Graus, so bezaubernd die Entzauberung der Welt, so viel läßt von dem Prozeß sich erzählen, dessen Prosa dafür sorgt, daß es bald nichts mehr zu erzählen gibt. (146)
>
> So colorful is the emergence of gray and so enchanting the disenchantment of the world; there is so much to be told about the process whose prose makes sure that soon there will be nothing left to tell. (127)

In Balzac's works one may trace such processes, Adorno suggests, not only on the level of content but also, and above all, on that of form. Concreteness, a preeminently formal feature, is a case in point: it is the surest key to the historical moment that Balzac seeks to chronicle—provided that it is grasped as a dialectical response. Balzac's passion for the concrete and, by implication, the visible should therefore not be seen as part of an attempt to produce a copy of true reality but rather as a formal trace, a textual figuration of a certain historical content. Concreteness, in Adorno's view, is an inverted—and distorted—mirror-image of processes of abstraction. It is the negative imprint of the disenchanted world.

But Balzac also opens a window onto another historical scenario. Like few other realist writers, Adorno suggests, Balzac exposes how the early industrial world is subjected to a formidable re-enchantment. The nineteenth century sees the return of mythic powers, but these no longer emanate from a god but rather from the spread of the commodity form. Little by little, a whole new social imaginary emerges, namely the dream world of modernity. To excavate that brilliant, enchanting, sumptuous dream world: this was Walter Benjamin's great objective in *Das Passagen-Werk*. And just as Adorno invokes the Weberian framework, so he also alludes to Benjamin's notion of re-enchantment and the theory of cultural modernity of which it was a crucial part.[47]

---

[47] For an incisive discussion of how Benjamin approached the "re-enchantment" of the modern world, see Susan Buck-Morss, *The Dialectics of Seeing: Walter Benjamin and the Arcades Project* (Cambridge, Mass.: MIT Press, 1989), 253–86. In a footnote, Buck-Morss adds that Weber's analysis may well be reconciled with that of Benjamin. Citing an essay on Weber by Wolfgang Mommsen, she notes that Weber, in *Wissenschaft als Beruf* (1917), suggests that modernity sees the return of "the old and numerous gods," only that they are now "disenchanted and thus [take] the form of impersonal forces," who "climb out of their graves, strive for power over our lives and begin again their eternal struggle among each other" (454 n.4).

Balzac's writings, especially their stylistic fabric, reflect these historical circumstances, but—and this is Adorno's critique—they are ultimately unable to grasp the deeper historical forces at work. So it is that Adorno is able to argue that literary realism became obsolete, because "als Darstellung der Realität diese verfehlt" (147). That is to say: from the very beginning, realism was bound to fail, because "as a representation of reality, it did not capture reality" (128). Why? The rendering of concrete facts is one thing, the representation of processes quite another. Classical nineteenth-century realism, especially Balzacian realism, readily confuses one with the other. To capture reality, and to do it as adequately as possible: this, indeed, is the extraordinary challenge to which the modernist novel, especially in its formal dimensions, will attempt an answer.

Yet processes are impossible to depict, Adorno adds, and this helps explain why the realist novel, once so shockingly original in its hardheaded interest in the raw facts of everyday life, becomes antiquated and falls apart at the seams. To amplify his argument, Adorno cites Brecht with approval: a photograph of a modern factory—say, an AEG or a Krupp structure—may perhaps seem to reproduce an existing reality, and a decisive one at that, but the image is in effect utterly poor in information. It is a mere visual fact, a representation of a metaphor of modern life. No matter how much we pore over it, Brecht underscores, the image will tell us little or nothing about those processes that make the world go around: about, say, human relations, the organization of labor, means of production, the logic of commodification ... (147/128) In other words, we can look at the image of the AEG factory, but we cannot see through it. The economy is made visible, as it were, but it is not made intelligible; rather, it remains a cipher, obscure and mysterious.

Adorno's thesis—that storytelling is dying out because in the bourgeois era one can no longer shape the factors that are decisive for human experience into a coherent narrative whole—has a marked affinity with the argument in Benjamin's 1936 essay on Nikolai Leskov, "Der Erzähler," or "The Storyteller." Adorno alludes at least twice to this essay. Briefly, Benjamin argues that the art of storytelling has come to an end, and that this crisis—a crisis of narrative and of narratibility alike—is in the end also a social one. History, in short, has eroded the conditions of existence of genuine storytelling.

Yet the decline of storytelling is not a specifically modern phenomenon, although it has accelerated in our age. For Benjamin, genuine storytelling is always based in a face-to-face situation, a human skill that begins to deteriorate as early as the early modern age, coinciding with the printed book, the rise of the novel, and the literary market proper. From now on, storytelling ceases to turn around the collective and its way of exchanging experience by way of narrative. Instead, storytelling now centers on a historically new entity—the individual subject.

In the meantime, traditional narrative categories undergo a sea change, a formal development that in Benjamin's view reflects the fact that the very communicability of experience is decreasing as well. In other words, those same historical processes that helped make possible the modern reader and the printed book also brought about a gradual disintegration of "genuine experience." What this makes clear is that for Benjamin, the history of modern literature is intertwined with the history of human experience and the various forms it has assumed. In a word, Benjamin's theory of art is a theory of experience.[48]

If the communicability of experience is decreasing in the modern period, this is happening for at least two reasons.[49] First, experience has disintegrated, slowly but steadily, and become more or less impossible to narrate. Benjamin's key example are the soldiers who survived that methodical, systematic, and high-technological destruction known as the first world war, only to face a world that was no longer one.

> Eine Generation, die noch mit der Pferdebahn zur Schule gefahren war, stand unter freiem Himmel in einer Landschaft, in der nichts unverändert geblieben war als die Wolken und unter ihnen, in einem Kraftfeld zerstörender Ströme und Explosionen, der winzige, gebrechliche Menschenkörper.[50]

> The generation that had gone to school on a horse-drawn streetcar now stood under the open sky in countryside in which nothing remained unchanged but the clouds, and beneath these clouds, in a field of force of destructive currents and explosions, was the tiny, fragile human body.[51]

---

[48] See Jürgen Habermas, "Bewußtmachende oder rettende Kritik," in *Zur Aktualität Walter Benjamins,* ed. Siegfried Unseld (Frankfurt am Main: Suhrkamp, 1972), 201; "Consciousness-Raising or Rescuing Critique," in *Walter Benjamin: Critical Essays and Recollections,* ed. Gary Smith, trans. Frederick Lawrence (Cambridge, Mass.: MIT Press, 1991), 109.

[49] For a recent discussion of the concept of experience in Benjamin and Adorno, see Martin Jay, *Songs of Experience* (Berkeley and Los Angeles: University of California Press, 2005), 312–60.

[50] Walter Benjamin, "Der Erzähler," in *Illuminationen. Ausgewählte Schriften* (Frankfurt am Main: Suhrkamp, 1977), 386.

[51] Benjamin, "The Storyteller," in *Illuminations: Essays and Reflections,* trans. Harry Zohn (New York: Schocken, 1988), 84.

Like never before, the experience of war resisted narration, and traditional categories of narrative were in any case both antiquated and insufficient. Besides, that collective mode of processing and transmitting life experience that Benjamin thinks of as genuine storytelling—the old, originally oral tradition of exchanging stories, tales, legends, fairy tales, yarns, chronicles, and the like—had long since vanished, including those forms of social existence in which this tradition was embedded. What Benjamin has in mind is a crisis of narratibility.

Second, the communicability of experience has decreased because the media that set out to communicate human experience—for example, the novel and the newspaper—are inadequate to the task. The paradigmatic point of departure for the novel is the solitary individual. And what the newspaper communicates is not experience but rather information. This is a crisis of narrative forms.

Balzac's writings, for Adorno, testify to a historically determinate crisis of narrative and of narratibility alike. Adorno even suggests that the author of *La comédie humaine* is a failed realist writer. And yet Balzac's realism is nowhere as successful as when it fails. In an enigmatic yet crucial phrase, Adorno states, "Dessen eigener Begriff [des Realismus] ist keine konstante Norm: Balzac hat um der Wahrheit willen an ihr gerüttelt" [The very concept of realism is not a constant norm; Balzac undermined that norm for the sake of truth]" (152/132).

Anyone who reads Adorno's tightly packed essay, even readers well versed in Adorno's style, will be struck by its elliptical and fragmentary, even provisional, character. It not only appears unfinished; it is also eccentric in the extreme, which may be why Adorno hesitated to publish it. Also, it cannot be said that Adorno's method spends itself in in-depth stylistic analysis. He quotes Balzac only once, in passing, and so fails to offer passages that may substantiate his claims.

Yet I want to argue that this essay has important implications for the theory of literary realism. It merits our attention not least because Adorno insists, at one and the same time, and in one and the same critical move, that (1) realistic art contains a referential element and that it produces knowledge, albeit negatively; and that (2) realist practice is a product of aesthetic form. In Stephen Halliwell's terms, Adorno's notion of realistic representation builds on a "world-reflecting" model as well as on a "world-simulating" one.[52]

But can the one be reconciled with the other? The point, for Adorno, is not to reconcile two seemingly incompatible models but rather to tease

---

[52] Stephen Halliwell, *The Aesthetics of Mimesis: Ancient Texts and Modern Problems* (Princeton: Princeton University Press, 2002), 23.

out these conceptual tendencies within the realist project itself.[53] Indeed, the strong impulse to "reflect" the world coexists with the equally strong impulse to "simulate" the world. To put it differently, in Adorno's view, nineteenth-century realism is founded on a constitutive and irreducible contradiction, and this, indeed, is what makes the realist enterprise both historically significant and theoretically interesting.

In order to do justice to Adorno's argument, and especially to his reflections on Balzac's shortcomings, we have to register the fundamental ambivalence at the core of the essay: its twofold, ambiguous, equivocal character. What begins as an identification of a general weakness in Balzac—in particular, the obsessive interest in concreteness, including the unreflected assumption that a constellation of discrete facts may somehow conjure up the real—ends up as a celebration of the French realist. What is more, it is precisely the deficiencies that make Balzac a great writer. Adorno even goes so far as to suggest that Balzac's oeuvre tells us more about mid-nineteenth-century society than the most brilliantly conceived sociological treatise or learned historical account.

Adorno's approach is at once negative and positive, suspicious and affirmative. Few writers may have been as misguided in their stubborn pursuit of the realist detail as Balzac, and yet it is for this reason that Balzac is able to offer a highly relevant picture of the historical context that he sought to represent. Adorno's essay is a piece of literary criticism that offers not so much an interpretation as a critical assessment of Balzac's realism. Or to be more precise, it is an assessment of the adequacy—indeed, the truth content—of Balzacian realism.

But what we must then realize is that Adorno does not have an a priori model of realism; nor does he subscribe to a normative view.

---

[53] Fredric Jameson has suggested that what distinguishes the concept of realism from most concepts in the history of aesthetics is that it is not an exclusively aesthetic one. Inherent in the concept of realism is also a "cognitive" dimension. "The originality of the concept of realism," Jameson writes, "lies in its claim to cognitive as well as aesthetic status. A new value, contemporaneous with the secularization of the world under capitalism, the ideal of realism presupposes a form of aesthetic experience which yet lays claim to a binding relationship to the real itself, that is to say, to those realms of knowledge and praxis which had traditionally been differentiated from the realm of the aesthetic [...]. But it is extremely difficult to do justice to both of these properties of realism simultaneously. In practice, an over-emphasis on its cognitive function often leads to a naïve denial of the necessarily fictive character of artistic discourse [...]. At the other pole of this conceptual tension, the emphasis of theorists like Gombrich or Barthes on the 'techniques' whereby an 'illusion' of reality or '*effet de réel*' is achieved, tends surreptitiously to transform the 'reality' of realism into appearance, and to undermine that affirmation of its own truth—or referential—value, by which it differentiates itself from other types of literature. See Jameson, "Reflections in Conclusion," *in Aesthetics and Politics,* ed. Perry Anderson (London: Verso, 1980), 198.

Adorno's critique of Balzac's predilection for concreteness is anything but grounded in the idea that the great novelist could have conceived of his literary undertaking differently, that his "errors" and "misrecognitions" could have been "corrected," that his obsessive precision could have been "tempered," that he could have identified the "true" historical causes of those actions and phenomena that he so brilliantly describes in his works, and so on.

And it is on this point that Adorno's approach has important implications for the theory of realism. There is no "good" concreteness, for the simple reason that "genuine" concreteness does not speak its name. Concreteness can become visible as such only when it is already excessive. This is why no "healthy" concreteness can exist. And just as no "healthy" concreteness exists, so there is no "healthy," "sound," or "genuine" realism.

Balzac's penchant for the sensual, the detail, and specialized terminology is therefore not a stylistic "imbalance" to be redressed. Rather, Adorno approaches Balzac's ravenous appetite for those jumelles, frisquettes, tympans, and the like as a symptom, a clue, a trace, as something to be treated semiotically, that is, as a sign.[54] Ultimately, Balzac's appetite for the concrete is an index of a historical problem, one that Balzac both reflects and sets out to solve in one and the same gesture.[55]

The thrust of Adorno's essay is that nineteenth-century realism springs out of a loss of reality. The relation between the realist representation of reality and the world that occasions that same representation is far from an intimate one, much less immediate. On the contrary, it has never been more mediated—and nowhere more so than when realism seeks to conjure up the real by way of the concrete detail. Adorno's essay thus performs a subtle yet radical counterintuitive move, one that usefully throws open a set of fundamental questions at the heart of aesthetic debates over nineteenth-century realism.

Yet such a formulation—that realism is based in a fundamental loss of reality, and that epic representations of reality after Goethe can therefore only accomplish a derived form of realism—such a formulation clearly implies that a previous moment of epic plenitude must have existed and that realism somehow signifies a fall from a golden age of narrative rep-

---

[54] This points to a crucial difference between Barthes's reality effect and Adorno's critique of literary concreteness. Adorno's reality effects are signs, but they do not point to the essence of realism but to the historical specificity of some of its most characteristic moves, strategies, and solutions. For Adorno, the reality effects are not to be treated as purely rhetorical constructions.

[55] A fundamental weakness in Adorno: he never becomes more concrete and specific than this.

resentation. The problem with such conceptual designs is that they tend to encourage a nostalgia for plenitude that is then easily projected onto the historical past—as well as on to the future, as though future modes of representing the real should ideally be capable of restoring what has been lost. What is more, they readily obscure the utter heterogeneity and difference of the past—in this case, the prehistory of nineteenth-century realism.

In Adorno's view, there has never been a moment of plenitude. Realism has never known representational fullness, nor has it ever been capable of mimetic immediacy. Realism cannot be primary. In arguing that epic narrative in the nineteenth century is based on an essentially derived form of realism, Adorno is therefore not out to appeal to the idea that some more achieved form of realism existed before Balzac. He is not opposing Balzacian realism to some genuine kind of realism. If Adorno is opposing anything at all, then he is rather opposing the traditional, narrowly conceived mimetic view of realist discourse, according to which realism provides a picture intended to resemble the world about which it speaks. That is to say, Adorno's argument is in the end concerned not so much with the nature of realism as with theories of realism.

This is why Adorno argues that Balzac's realism is not to be seen as a *reproduction* of the real world but as an *evocation* of it. It is an antimimeticist argument that has much in common with the idea that Barthes puts forward in his essay "L'effet de réel." Flaubert's barometer may appear like an insignificant detail, as does perhaps also that little door in Michelet, but both are in fact carrying out an important job in that they are "reality effects." Perfectly negligible though they may seem, they serve to anchor the fiction—the representation—in the irreducible solidity of the real itself.[56] They endow the discourse with a sense of proximity and thinginess.

At the same time, however, there is an important difference between Adorno and Barthes. Unlike Barthes, Adorno also pays attention to the

---

[56] For a critical discussion of Barthes's reality effect, see Jameson, "The Ideology of the Text," in *The Ideologies of Theory: Essays, 1971–1986* (Minneapolis: University of Minnesota Press, 1988), 1:22–3: "It would be wrong, however, to conclude that this analysis, which so radically devalues the importance of content in realistic discourse, is for all that an example of some incorrigibly formalistic practice either; for the reality-effect would appear to be something more closely resembling a *by-product* of realistic discourse than a mark of its fundamental linguistic structure. And while Barthes does not go so far as to say that any type of discourse can on occasion, and as it were laterally, in passing, generate the *effet de réel*, it would seem implicit in his description that what has hitherto passed under the name 'realistic narrative' is at least a mirage to the degree that it has nothing structurally to distinguish it from narrative discourse in general."

very forms that *evocation* typically assumes. And he does so for the simple reason that he believes that these forms are historically significant in themselves. That is to say, they carry a certain historically determinate content and may therefore yield knowledge about the historical situation they seek to address. In other words, although Adorno elaborates an antimimeticist critique, this does not mean that realism does not signify.

The usefulness of Adorno's essay on Balzac, then, lies in its insistence that realism, even and especially as it sets out to provide a truthful, coherent, and essentially immediate reproduction of the world, is a historically specific product through and through. Nineteenth-century realism may aim at immediacy and verisimilitude, but that desire is as mediated as any other desire. There is nothing originary about literary realism. The realist impulse, in Adorno's account, can never be primary; it is always derived. Simply put, just as the penchant for concreteness is born in the age of abstraction, so realistic representation emerges as a historical response to a world that is becoming ever more difficult to grasp as a coherent whole, a world in which the gap between concrete experience and abstract knowledge has begun to split apart as never before.

This is what the frustrating experience of reading Balzac eventually led to: an essay on Balzac's exact imagination. The procedure reveals a great deal about Adorno's interpretive methodology. The attempt to master the opacity of Balzac's language did not end in transparency, as Adorno surely hoped when he first pulled out his French dictionaries, but in ever more opacity. And this opacity turned out to be that of history itself.

Chapter 2
The Image in Action: On *Madame Bovary*

In this chapter, I shall be proposing that *Madame Bovary* (1857) represents a turning point in the history of the novel, not because Flaubert breaks with the realist tradition that went before him, but because he allies himself so closely with a specifically realist preoccupation: the interest in the visible world. Flaubert takes the art of making things visible to extremes, so much so that we come to witness a clear split between impression and action, or between linguistic event and narrative event.[1]

The Look of Commodities

On a Monday afternoon in February, as the sun is setting, Emma Bovary receives a visit from a shopkeeper. The episode comes in the fifth chapter of the second part of *Madame Bovary* (1857). Emma has fallen in love with Léon, a mediocre young man born and bred in that provincial little town called Yonville, and she has just realized that Léon is in love with her.

Now monsieur Lheureux, as the shopkeeper is called, enters the Bovary residence in order to offer his services to the mistress of the house. He goes regularly to town, he explains to Emma as he unpacks his box, and he would be happy to supply her with fine clothes and fancy furniture, whatever she wants. He hands her a half-dozen embroidered

---

[1] That Flaubert was a visually oriented writer is well known. Yet this issue has received little sustained scholarly attention, especially in view of the overwhelming number of works on the French novelist. In recent years, however, the study of the visual dimension of Flaubert's style has been greatly facilitated by Adrianne Tooke's *Flaubert and the Pictorial Arts: From Image to Text* (Oxford: Oxford University Press, 2000). Tooke's contribution is, so far, the only book-length investigation of Flaubert and the visual. There exist, however, several inquiries into French realism that also feature discussions of Flaubert and the visual; see, for example, Henri Mitterand, *L'illusion réaliste. De Balzac á Aragon* (Paris: Presses Universitaires de France, 1994); Philippe Hamon, *Imageries. Littérature et image et image au XIXe siècle* (Paris: José Corti, 2001); Isabelle

collars. Emma looks at them, declaring that she is in need of nothing. The shopkeeper then spreads out a few other articles before her.

> M. Lheureux exhiba délicatement trois écharpes algériennes, plusieurs paquets d'aiguilles anglaises, une paire de pantoufles en paille, et, enfin, quatre coquetiers en coco, ciselés à jour par des forçats. Puis, les deux mains sur la table, le cou tendu, la taille penchée, il suivait, bouche béante, le regard d'Emma, qui se promenait indécis parmi ces marchandises. De temps à autre, comme pour en chasser la poussière, il donnait un coup d'ongle sur la soie des écharpes, dépliées dans toute leur longueur; et elles frémissaient avec un bruit léger, en faisant, à la lumière verdâtre du crépuscule, scintiller, comme de petites étoiles, les paillettes d'or de leur tissu.[2]

> Monsieur Lheureux delicately exhibited three Algerian scarves, several packets of English needles, a pair of straw slippers, and, finally, four eggcups delicately carved by convicts from coconut-shells. Then, his hands on the table, his neck outstretched, his back bent, his mouth gaping wide, he followed Emma's gaze, wandering undecided among his wares. Every so often, as though to get rid of the dust, he flicked a finger along the silk scarves, unfolded for display; and they rustled faintly, their woven flecks of gold gleaming out, in the green evening light, like little stars.[3]

It is in this seemingly insignificant episode that the reader is first introduced to Lheureux. And although Emma declines the merchant's gener-

---

Daunais, *Frontière du roman. Le personnage réaliste et ses fictions* (Montréal: Les Presses de l'Université de Montréal, 2002); and Aimée Israel-Pelletier, "Flaubert and the Visual," in *The Cambridge Companion to Flaubert,* ed. Timothy Unwin (Cambridge: Cambridge University Press, 2004), 180–95.

[2] Gustave Flaubert, *Madame Bovary,* ed. Philippe Neefs (Paris: Livre de Poche, 1999), 191. Further page references are given in the main text. In preparing this chapter, I have consulted the following bibliographies: "Gustave Flaubert," in *The Nineteenth Century,* ed. David Baguley, vol. 5 of *A Critical Bibliography of French Literature* (Syracuse: Syracuse University Press, 1994), 801–66; *Bibliographie der französischen Literaturwissenschaft,* ed. Otto Klapp (Frankfurt am Main: Klostermann, 1960–). D. J. Colwell, "Bibliography: Flaubert Studies, 1989–97," in *New Approaches in Flaubert Studies,* ed. Tony Williams and Mary Orr (Lewiston, N.Y.: Edwin Mellen Press, 1999), 207–34. For a valuable recent survey of Flaubert criticism, with a substantial bibliography, see Tony Williams, "Introduction: Flaubert Studies, 1983–96," in *New Approaches in Flaubert Studies,* 1–31.

[3] Flaubert, *Madame Bovary,* trans. Geoffrey Wall (London: Penguin, 1992), 82. Further page references are given in the main text. There are numerous excellent translations of *Madame Bovary,* and a note is in order here. I use Geoffrey Wall's translation because Wall makes a point of following Flaubert's idiosyncrasies as far as possible, especially when it comes to paragraph division, punctuation, and italicization. I have also consulted the translations of Margaret Mauldon (2004) and Lowell Bair (1959).

ous offers, Flaubert's narrator makes us understand that Lheureux is to be a crucial character in the novel. The shopkeeper's open mouth is a rich cipher: not only does it signify astonishment at Emma's promising delight in the goods he has brought along, but it is also prophetic of her tragic future.[4]

Before long, the cunning shopkeeper and his luxurious commodities will have triggered a process that slowly but steadily leads to the downfall of Flaubert's heroine, until she is trapped inside her inexorable fate. In this carefully staged drama, Lheureux is the evil genius par excellence. For Emma's nemesis is not so much the outcome of her having read too many romantic novels as her having accumulated debts of monstrous proportions. Flaubert's 1857 novel, as Franco Moretti has proposed, is "the tragedy of the consumer."[5] In this respect, too, Flaubert was a pioneering writer in that he was the first to narrate this story. For what makes Emma Bovary an eminently modern consumer is this: she

---

[4] Mouths are highly significant in Flaubert's thematic universe. See, for example, the famous scene toward the end of *L'éducation sentimentale,* where Flaubert uses the same expression, *béant*, to suggest Frédéric's utter stupefaction as he comes to witness how Dussardier is shot to death by a policeman who turns out to be Sénécal. The event makes Frédéric speechless, and Flaubert simply writes: "Et Frédéric, béant, reconnut Sénécal." Flaubert's choice of words was criticized by Maxime Du Camp, as Carlo Ginzburg has observed. He would have preferred a more straightforward and psychologizing expression. "*Béant* est bien faux à mon avis," Du Camp remarked when he had gone through the manuscript of *L'éducation sentimentale*. "C'est une épithète physique pour rendre une impression morale—avec un mot plus simple, épouvante—stupéfait—indigné, je ne sais quoi, tu feras plus d'effet" (quoted in Ginzburg, "Reflections on a Blank," in *History, Rhetoric, and Proof* [Hanover: University Press of New England, 1999], 105). Flaubert did not heed his friend's advice, a fact that reveals a great deal about his literary method: to say "béant" is to stick to an objective fact that, furthermore, can be seen; to say "indigné" is to psychologize, to spell out, to fill in, that is, to interpret. In Flaubert's view, it is not the writer but the reader who should decipher the potential meaning of bodily gestures and actions. What is more, the move from the succinct "bouche béante" to the minimal "béant" is also indicative of how Flaubert developed as a writer between *Madame Bovary* and *L'éducation sentimentale.* Flaubert, who already mastered the art of intimation, came to push his stylistic minimalism to extremes. It is also worth noting that the very last word that Flaubert uses to characterize Emma's visual appearance before she passes away is "béante." Through the window, Emma hears the blind beggar sing an ominous song, and within seconds, she exists no more: "Emma se releva comme un cadavre que l'on galvanise, les cheveux dénoués, la prunelle fixe, béante" (472). The long episode that began with Lheureux's gaping mouth is thus closed with Emma's death, two momentous moments bound together by way of a carefully chosen word.

[5] Franco Moretti, *The Way of the World: The "Bildungsroman" in European Culture* (London: Verso, 1987), 173. Lawrence Schehr similarly remarks that Emma Bovary "committed suicide because she had done nothing more dastardly than the nineteenth-century equivalent of maxxing out her credit card" (*Figures of Alterity* [Stanford: Stanford University Press, 2003], 103). On the "tragedy of the consumer," see also Eric Gans, *Madame Bovary: The End of Romance* (Boston: Twayne, 1989), 47–51, 54–5, 114–5.

has no actual need of the objects she procures.[6] This simple yet crucial fact, Moretti underscores, sets her apart from her predecessors in the history of literature.

Between Stendhal and Flaubert, the rise of a literary market proper has made itself felt, as has the full-fledged emergence of commodification. In Stendhal, there is not a single shop window. In Flaubert, there are many, especially in *L'éducation sentimentale.* In the same period, the number of newspapers and periodicals grow exponentially, as does the business of advertising. All these historical forces can be glimpsed in Flaubert's books, but they have been sedimented in the formal dimensions of his writings. It is not for nothing that Pierre Bourdieu, who devotes some five hundred pages to describing Flaubert's heroic conquest of autonomy, speaks of Flaubert's "realist formalism."[7]

One day it will dawn on Emma that she has reached a point of no return. Owing giant sums of money to Lheureux, bored to death by her husband, and abandoned by her lovers, she swallows a fistful of arsenic. Flaubert describes in excruciating detail Emma's death struggle over a dozen pages until, finally, her agonized body has come to rest and a film of mucus begins to cover her eyes.

But not much happens in the passage I quoted a moment ago. Lheureux displays a curious mix of wares; he looks at Emma; she looks at the goods; end of story. Yet these intricately crafted lines are remarkably dense. In fact, the paragraph is almost a distillation of everything that is typically associated with Flaubert. Consider the extraordinary precision that marks the description of the scattered objects on display; the cool detachment of the implicit narrator in relation to what is reported; and the emphatically visual nature of the scene, from Lheureux's oral cavity

---

[6] One day Emma decides to buy the most beautiful of the Algerian scarves. It is mentioned in passing. Léon has just moved to Paris to finish his legal studies, and his departure makes Emma desolate. It is at this point that she turns into a consumer, a willful, shameless, outrageous consumer. She buys a Gothic prie-dieu, spends an inordinate amount on money on lemons for the benefit of her nail care, and orders a luxurious dress from Rouen. She also decides to avail herself of Lheureux's services and thus selects the Algerian silk scarf she considers most pleasing. How does she wear it? Tied around her waist, over her dressing gown. When does she wear it? In the privacy of her home, when she withdraws to read books on her couch. The narrator says nothing more. All we need to know has been deposited in the image of Emma, and the carefully chosen facts speak for themselves. There she is, resting on her couch with a book in her hands and an exquisite accessory tied round her waist, a silent monument to vanity, excess, and delusion. We are now one third into the novel, and Emma is on the verge of being caught up in a historically new logic: the all-consuming desire to buy things for which one has no need.

[7] Pierre Bourdieu, *Les règles de l'art. Genèse et structure du champ littéraire,* 2d ed., rev. (Paris: Seuil, 1998), 182; *The Rules of Art: Genesis and Structure of the Literary Field,* trans. Susan Emanuel (Stanford, CA.: Stanford University Press, 1996), 107.

to the glistening gold threads in the scarves. What is more, multiple perspectives crowd the paragraph: first, Lheureux's point of view; second, that of Emma; and third, that of some unidentified authorial position.

What, exactly, is going on in these lines? Flaubert starts with a catalogue of the various articles Lheureux has brought along. The emphasis is on what they are, not on how they appear. It is a detailed enumeration of things that can be seen, but the narrator does not stress how they look. He notes, observes, records. Flaubert, one might say, seeks to conjure up the objects *per se*, as though language were a transparent veil. In true Flaubertian fashion, the objects are also highly particularized: not any needles, but *English* needles; not any slippers, but a *pair* of *straw* slippers, and so on.[8] In addition, Lheureux's articles are strikingly diverse. They seem haphazardly put together, as though he had thrown them into his box at the last minute. For all their apparent randomness, however, they have one thing in common. They address, and therefore confirm, Emma in her capacity as woman and as mistress of the house. The needles, the slippers, and the eggcups are useful objects and belong

---

[8] In *Drei Klassiker des französischen Romans,* 6th. ed. (Frankfurt am Main: Vittorio Klostermann, 1970), Hugo Friedrich brilliantly remarks: "Synonyma gibt es für Flaubert nicht" (132). Discussing Flaubert's will to style, Friedrich observes that the relentless search of the right word is no mere rhetorical game. In Flaubert, precision is always in the service of the real. As regards the status of objects in Flaubert, Friedrich notes a radical difference between Flaubert and his great predecessor. "[V]on Balzacs vertraulichem Verhältnis zwischen Mensch und Ding ist hier nicht mehr die Rede. Die Dinge haben hinsichtlich des Handelnden keinen Aussagewert, sie wohnen nicht in seinem Fluidum. Sie tauchen auch nicht auf als Zeugen früherer Geschlechter, als vergangenheitshaltige Wohnstätten, Kleider, Werkzeuge. Flaubert leitet sie nicht, wie Balzac, historisch her, er sagt nicht: dies Haus wurde von dem und dem dann und dann gebaut, bei seinem Erbauen geschah das und das, — sondern er sagt: dies Haus ist, und seine Teile sind; er bezeichnet nur das Dasein, nicht das Gewordensein. Die Dinge haben mit der Handlung nichts zu tun" (148). This, too, is an important observation. Between Balzac and Flaubert, a sea change has taken place. In Flaubert, things have been removed from their naturalizing contexts, and are presented exclusively in terms of being, their being there. In this sense, things resist narrative, Friedrich suggests. They are literally *Gegen-Stände*, or *Ob-jecta* (149). Yet there is something not quite right about this view. Things may be autonomous in Flaubert, but they often circulate within a commodity culture—consider Lheureux's silk scarves. Emma, after all, develops a mortal lust after things; and Frédéric Moreau takes over where Emma Bovary has left off. Janell Watson, in her discussion of material culture in the French nineteenth-century novel, goes so far as to suggest that Frédéric Moreau is "one of the most ardent consumers in French literature." As soon as Frédéric is faced with a new turn of events, he purchases new clothes, new furniture, and new *bibélots*. These objects, moreover, readily enter the space of the narrative text and become part of the plot. See Janell Watson, *Literature and Material Culture from Balzac to Proust: The Collection and Consumption of Curiosities* (Cambridge: Cambridge University Press, 1999), 53. For a comprehensive discussion of the importance of objects in Flaubert, with a particular emphasis on the sensuous materiality that they introduce into Flaubert's novels, see Pierre Danger, *Sensations et objets dans le roman de Flaubert* (Paris: Armand Colin, 1973).

to the feminine realm of the household. The Algerian scarves are the only exception. As we shall see, they have little to do with household needs and everything to do with desire.

Having provided a catalogue of Lheureux's wares, Flaubert supplies a visual impression of the man himself. With a few precise and speedy strokes, the shopkeeper appears as though in a snapshot. The narrator has already mentioned that Lheureux is a cunning, calculating, and scheming man; and the incisive sketch of his body posture and visual activity is meant to convey precisely these qualities.

But more is at stake. The passage revolves around seeing in the most fundamental sense, and it does so in several ways. On the one hand, Lheureux is represented as a visual impression—we can see him before us. On the other hand, he is also represented as a subject of perception: as someone who is busy looking. Indeed, Lheureux is studying Emma who, in her turn, is looking at the goods before her. Yet that is not what Flaubert actually writes, only what we deduce from his carefully chosen words: "il suivait, bouche béante, le regard d'Emma, qui se promenait indécis parmi ces marchandises."

A gaze that is wandering about on its own: we are now at a far remove from the notational and paratactic logic of the initial catalogue. This is the realm of spectacle. Emma's gaze has been turned into a syntactical agent—a subject—and is therefore free to take a verb, that is, to act. Having achieved autonomy, her gaze acts on its own.

The third and final sentence reports an action, first on the part of a human subject (the shopkeeper), then on the part of an object (the scarves). We can see before us how Lheureux's hands move over the scarves, arranging them, touching them, manipulating them. Before we know it, however, the emphasis is no longer on the wares as such, but on how they appear.

In the closing sentence, the scarves thus take on a life of their own, glistening in the evening light and producing delightful sounds. Whatever else a silk scarf may be and do, in Flaubert's hands it produces an aesthetic experience in the original Greek sense of the word—something for the eye and the ear to perceive, to sense, to feel. Having acquired a magical aura, Lheureux's commodity thus opens itself to libidinal investment. The narrator never says as much, but Emma's lust is clearly awakened. And so it is that Flaubert manages to make visible a phenomenon that, strictly speaking, cannot be seen—desire itself.

Who is looking at the scarves? Who is the author of the wondrous perceptual experience? I have already identified three possible points of view in the passage: that of Lheureux, that of Emma, and that of the implicit narrator. The sight of the scarf is related to all three of them, but it is not reducible to any one of them. And even if it is tempting to claim that Emma is the most likely perceiver of the three, it would be hard to make a case for it. Emma, after all, is the protagonist of Flaubert's tale, not the narrator.

What is more, throughout the novel she tends to be represented as an object of perception, not as a perceiving subject. No matter how hard we try, it is impossible to identify a clear-cut point of view, perceptual, narratological, or otherwise. In Flaubert, the boundaries between the realm of the implicit narrator and those of the protagonists are almost always blurred.[9]

All this is familiar. The narrative technique I have been alluding to is typically called "free indirect speech"— in French, *style indirect libre*; in German, *erlebte Rede*—and Flaubert is its unsurpassed master.[10] In making systematic use of this technique, Flaubert managed to take free indirect discourse to an entirely new level. Indeed, narratorial indeterminacy is a governing aesthetic principle in Flaubert, especially in his mature writings.[11]

In Flaubert, things, persons, or settings are perceived in a way that implies a particular point of view. Sights are related to seers, and everything that is seen is always perceived by someone. And yet the per-

---

[9] Victor Brombert has something similar in mind when he suggests that "Flaubert, even when his personal voice can be heard, tends to merge with his characters to the point of undifferentiation." Brombert speaks of fused points of view, "which allows for no distance while creating the illusion of distance," and concludes, interestingly, that with Flaubert objectivity is "a permanent state of immersion." See Brombert, *The Novels of Flaubert* (Princeton: Princeton University Press, 1966), 167, 168.

[10] See, for example, Albert Thibaudet, *Gustave Flaubert,* rev. ed. (Paris: Gallimard, 1935), 221–85; Claude Perruchot, "Le style indirect libre et la question du sujet dans *Madame Bovary*," in *La production du sens chez Flaubert,* ed. Claudine Gothot-Mersch (Paris: UGE, 1975), 253–86; Michal Peled Ginsburg, "Free Indirect Discourse: A Reconsideration," *Language and Style* 15 (1982): 133–49. For a more general treatment, see also Alain Rabatel, *La construction textuelle du point de vue* (Lausanne: Delachaux et Niestlé, 1998); Charles Bally, "Le style indirect libre en français I–II," *Germanisch-Romanische Monatsschrift 4,* no. 10 (1912): 549–56; no. 11 (1912): 597–606; and Gilles Philippe, *Sujet, verbe, complément. Le moment grammatical de la littérature française 1890–1940* (Paris: Gallimard, 2002), 67–84.

[11] Nathaniel Wing has usefully underscored that the essential "impersonality" that characterizes Flaubert's mature works derives not from a "distanced objectivity," but rather from "a mix of modes of presentation which prevent the reader from identifying a consistent pattern." In *Madame Bovary*, in particular, we never really know who speaks. As Wing notes, the narrative is articulated through a variety of points of view: now there is omniscient narration, now a limited perspective, now free indirect discourse. The result is narratological indeterminacy. See Nathaniel Wing, "Emma's Stories: Narrative, Repetition, and Desire in *Madame Bovary*," in *Emma Bovary,* ed. Harold Bloom (New York: Chelsea House Publishers, 1994), 133–64; quotation, 134.

spective implied is not reducible to any one character. For even if the perspective can be related to a particular character, it also issues from an impersonal space of narration. That is, the perspective cannot be wholly identified with the character in question. The result is that the seen comes before us "objectively," while at the same time also deriving from a "subjective" point of view. This is a general tendency in Flaubert's mature works, from *Madame Bovary* onward.[12] In fact, it is a systematic feature. As Michal Peled Ginsburg observes in her discussion of point of view in *Madame Bovary*, no categorical difference can be discerned between narrator and character.

> Every character is potentially a narrator to the extent that it sees something and that it allows what it sees to take its place of seer. But this structure also suggests that, in Flaubert, "spectacle"—what is seen—always takes the place of the eye-I that sees, replacing and thus eliminating the seer. The spectacle is finally the reality the novel represents and [...] this reality is generated by a particular point of view but can also exist as reality only if that point of view is suppressed and eliminated.[13]

This is why the scarves may take on a life of their own. Flaubert's narrator is sitting on Emma's shoulders, as it were, obliquely refracting the sight of the luxurious silk through her eyes. The point of view, however, is not hers alone. As a result, the scarves help constitute a new representational space. The image of the scarves acquires a nearly thing-like character. In fact, the entire scene emerges as a self-contained and self-isolating verbal artefact.

---

[12] In an essay on point of view in *Madame Bovary*, Jean Rousset emphasizes that the narrative perspective is constantly modulated, displaced, interlaced—and that Flaubert, at the same time, is able to craft a singularly homogeneous and fluid style, as though those perspectival transitions had never taken place, as though we were always in one and the same seamless narratorial space. "Dès le chapitre VI, Emma glisse au centre, et ne le quittera plus, si ce n'est pour de brèves interruptions. Rien là d'exceptionnel. Balzac, adepte du traitement global et panoramique, se sert d'un personnage central, Rastignac par example, et développe son action autour de lui. L'originalité de Flaubert sera dans la combinaison du point de vue de l'auteur et du point de vue de l'héroïne, leur alternance et leurs interférences, et surtout dans la prédominance accordée à la vision subjective du personnage en perspective. Dès lors, le problème sera d'assurer les déplacements de point de vue et les passages d'une perspective à une autre sans casser le mouvement, sans rompre le 'tissu de style.'" See Rousset, "*Madame Bovary* ou le livre sur rien," in *Forme et signification* (Paris: José Corti, 1962), 117–8.

[13] Michal Peled Ginsburg, "Vision and Language: Teaching *Madame Bovary* in a Course on the Novel," in *Approaches to Teaching Madame Bovary,* ed. Lawrence M. Porter and Eugene F. Gray (New York: The Modern Language Association of America, 1995), 62. For a more comprehensive discussion of the indeterminacy of voice as well as of point of view, see Ginsburg, *Flaubert Writing: A Study in Narrative Strategies* (Stanford: Stanford University Press, 1986), 82–107.

In this and many similar passages, the image readily declares its independence from its narratological context and turns into a thing of its own. What is more, the Flaubertian image has a strikingly protocinematic quality—decades before the advent of film. This has to do with the double-faced nature of observation in Flaubert. For while observation takes place in the here and now, and while it implies the perspective of an empirical observer present at the scene, it is also, and at the same time, highly impersonal, in the sense that the way in which the seen is actually seen can seldom be pinned down to a particular observer. And this rigorously staged perceptual indeterminacy is one of the keys to Flaubert's great invention: a new representational space that is his signal achievement and that breaks new ground in the history of the novel.

The Moving Sidewalk

Marcel Proust once wrote a critical article on Flaubert in which he drops a brilliant insight in passing: "Ce qui jusqu'à Flaubert était action devient impression."[14] What before Flaubert was action has now become impression. In Proust's view, Flaubert represents a radically new mode of writing in the history of French literature. He goes so far as to speak of a revolution, maintaining that with *L'éducation sentimentale* (1869) this revolution has been accomplished and is there for all to see.

In publishing this essay, Proust entered into a controversy with Albert Thibaudet, a leading literary critic, who had joined an ongoing debate concerning Flaubert's qualities as a stylist.[15] Did Flaubert know how to write? Could a novelist like Flaubert, who consistently made grammatical mistakes, be deemed a great writer? These questions ignited "la querelle sur le style de Flaubert," a largely forgotten yet highly interesting debate that raged in French newspapers and reviews for nearly three

---

[14] Marcel Proust, "A propos du 'style' de Flaubert," *La nouvelle revue française,* no. 76 (January 1920); reprinted in *Contre Sainte-Beuve précédé de Pastiches et mélanges et suivi de Essais et articles* (Paris: Gallimard, 1971), ed. Pierre Clarac and Yves Sandre 586–600; quotation, 588. For a discussion of Proust's analysis of Flaubert's style, see Gérard Genette, "Flaubert par Proust,"*L'Arc* 79 (1980), 3–17.

[15] In his polemic response to Thibaudet, Proust recycles some of the observations that he had made a decade earlier in an unfinished essay that was published posthumously, "A ajouter à Flaubert." Despite its fragmentary character, this early piece is instructive because here, too, Proust insists on the radical novelty of Flaubert's mode of writing, suggesting that syntax is a key element in Flaubert: "Comme il a tant peiné sur sa syntaxe, c'est en elle qu'il a logé pour toujours son originalité. C'est un génie grammatical" (299). In Proust's view, Flaubert is to the history of literature what Kant is to the history of philosophy and what Giotto and Cimabue are to the history of painting. See Proust, "A ajouter à Flaubert," in *Contre Sainte-Beuve,* 299–302.

years, from 1919 through 1921.[16] In Thibaudet's view, one should admit that "Flaubert n'est pas un grand écrivain de race et que la pleine maîtrise verbale ne lui était pas donnée dans sa nature même."[17] Thibaudet went on to claim that Flaubert lacked a sure ear for grammar, but he also underscored that great writers are not always great grammarians.[18]

Flaubert's mode of putting together words, clauses, and sentences was to find a perceptive defender in Proust. The article that ensued, "A propos du 'style' de Flaubert" (1920), is an extraordinary exercise in stylistic analysis, one of the best ever written on Flaubert. Yet Proust was anything but a wholehearted admirer of Flaubert. In fact, he did not particularly like his writings. One would be hard pressed to find a single beautiful metaphor anywhere in Flaubert, he claimed. And he found the vast correspondence nothing short of mediocre.[19]

---

[16] In recent years, this historical debate has attracted scholarly attention. For an incisive discussion of "la querelle sur le style de Flaubert," both with regard to its history and its implications, see Philippe, *Sujet, verbe, complément.* Not only does Philippe analyze the 1919–21 debate; he also traces its themes through the critical writings of Sartre and Barthes. In addition, Philippe has collected the major contributions to the debate, including the articles by Proust and Thibaudet, in *Flaubert savait-il écrire? Une querelle grammaticale* (1919–1921) (Grenoble: Ellug, 2002). On the exchange between Proust and Thibaudet, see also Ginzburg, "Reflections on a Blank."

[17] Albert Thibaudet, "Sur le style de Flaubert," *Nouvelle revue française,* no. 74 (November 1919), 942–53; quotation, 943. Thibaudet's rejoinder, "Lettre à M. Marcel Proust," appeared in *Nouvelle revue française* (March 1920), 426–37; see also Thibaudet's analysis of selected stylistic features in *Gustave Flaubert,* 438–41.

[18] In Thibaudet's defense, it must be said that his discussion was far more nuanced than Proust gave him credit for. Thibaudet suggests, for example, that Flaubert, because of his peculiar way with words, was able to reanimate a characteristic of the classical style—*le style parlé,* associated with the rhythm and space of the voice. He also proposes that Flaubert is the master of the cut, *la coupe:* "Dans l'intérieur de ses limites, un peu étroites, cette prose est d'une délicatesse de rythmes, d'une science et d'une variété de coupe incomparables. Avec La Bruyère et Montesquieu, Flaubert paraît dans la langue le maître de la coupe" ("Sur le style de Flaubert," 951). This last point must have resonated with Proust, who went on to celebrate Flaubert's cuts, arguing that the most beautiful element in *L'éducation sentimentale* was "not a sentence, but a blank." Two years later, in 1922, Thibaudet published a book-length study of Flaubert, parts of which explicitly refer to the 1919–21 debate, notably the exchange with Proust. In the final chapter, "Le style de Flaubert," Thibaudet offers a refined and significantly expanded analysis that teems with poignant observations, in particular, as regards the significance of the verb in Flaubert. For in Thibaudet's view, "le verbe est dans la phrase le mot essentiel, et un grand styliste se reconnaît à son emploi du verbe. Sur lui porte la partie la plus considérable de l'effort de Flaubert." See Thibaudet, *Gustave Flaubert,* 246.

[19] Proust, "A propos du 'style' de Flaubert," 595, 586, 592. In claiming that metaphor is the most important element of any style, Proust indirectly said a great deal about his own mode of writing, but he also expressed a standpoint that can be traced back to Aristotle's *Poetics.* For Aristotle, successful metaphors are a sign of genius: "[T]he greatest asset is a capacity for metaphor. This alone cannot be acquired from another, and is a sign of natural gifts: because to use metaphor well is to discern similarities." See Aristotle, *Poetics,* trans. Stephen Halliwell (Cambridge, Mass.: Harvard University Press, 1995), 115.

Even so, Proust considered the author of *Madame Bovary*, *L'éducation sentimentale,* and *Trois contes* a groundbreaking writer. Why? Primarily because of the way he handled grammar. Syntax, then, is at the heart of Flaubert's style. To understand Flaubert's singularity as a writer, one must understand how he treats syntax. It is a claim that should be grasped in the strongest sense possible. Proust is not arguing that grammar is pertinent to the understanding of Flaubert's project. His argument is a far more radical one: syntax founds Flaubert's style. In the end, Flaubert's originality is comprehensible only if connected to an analysis of his syntactical constructions. This is why Proust dwells on pronouns, verb forms, adverbs, prepositions, and conjunctions.[20]

If Flaubert did not always care about established rules of grammar, and if, indeed, he even committed linguistic errors, he did so for a simple reason: his syntactical idiosyncrasies were integral to his literary project. Not only did they give texture to his prose; they were an essential part of his narrative design. If one corrects Flaubert's systematically misplaced *et,* reconjugates his "eternal imperfect," removes his superfluous and strange-sounding adverbs, Flaubert's stylistic fingerprints will be erased. Flaubert will no longer be Flaubert.

In Proust's view, what is perhaps most characteristic of Flaubert's style is his predilection for turning objects into living entities. Things act in Flaubert. From a syntactical point of view, this means that inanimate objects are treated as subjects. "Les choses ont autant de vie que les hommes [Things have as much life as people]," Proust notes.[21] What is even more important is that this grammatical inversion is perfectly symmetrical, for the reverse is also true: in Flaubert, human subjects readily turn into objects. As we shall see, this is especially true of Flaubert's female characters, especially Emma Bovary.

In foregrounding Flaubert's tendency to turn inanimate objects into living beings, Proust was one of the first critics to analyze this stylistic feature in strictly syntactical terms. It is a feature that helps explain, in concrete and precise terms, the experience that numerous contempo-

---

[20] On how Proust's syntactical analysis can be applied to *Madame Bovary,* see Beryl Schlossman, "Flaubert's Moving Sidewalk," *in Approaches to Teaching Flaubert's "Madame Bovary,"* 69–76.

[21] Proust, "A propos," 588. The Goncourts were among the first critics to note this tendency in Flaubert. In *Madame Bovary*, they wrote in their diary, "les accessoires y vivent autant et presqu'au même plan que les gens. Le milieu des choses y a tant de relief autour des sentiments et des passions qu'il les étouffe presque." Quoted in Claudine Gothot-Mersch, *La genèse de "Madame Bovary"* (Paris: José Corti, 1966), 226. On how this tendency makes itself felt in Salammbô, see Bengt Landgren, "Salammbô – en roman om februarirevolutionen? Några perspektiv, problem och tolkningar i nyare Flaubertforskning," *Samlaren* (1983): 61–68, esp. 67.

rary readers had in reading Flaubert's novels, especially the later ones, namely, that they amount to little more than a series of precisely rendered images, tableaux vivants, or photographs.[22]

But there is more to Proust's analysis. Once objects have been turned into subjects, he observes, they need predicates; and this need, in its turn, necessitates a great variety on the level of the verb: "Cette activité des choses, des bêtes, puisqu'elles sont le sujet des phrases (au lieu que ce sujet soit les hommes), oblige à une grande variété de verbes."[23] A human character, after all, can do a great many things, and therefore the choice of verbs available when it comes to human subjects is, in principle, without limit. Not so when it comes to inanimate objects, immaterial phenomena, or even animals. From a conventional point of view, a fountain pen, a sunray, or a silk scarf are limited in what they can do. In Flaubert, however, this is no longer necessarily true. Consider, for example, the silk tissue before Emma's eyes: "[les] écharpes, dépliées dans toute leur longueur, […] frémissaient avec un bruit léger, en faisant, à la lumière verdâtre du crépuscule, scintiller, comme de petites étoiles, les paillettes d'or de leur tissu."

All this can be put a little differently. From a linguistic point of view, Flaubert systematically expands the lexical and semantic range inherent in a given object. More than anything else, it is a predicative expansion.[24] Indeed, if an object typically comes with a given cluster of potential verbs, then Flaubert is at pains to push the conventional limits of that predicative repertoire. An entire world of inanimate things and non-human phenomena is swept into motion, thus relativizing the anthropomorphic rules that typically tend to govern narrative, all the way down to the level of the sentence, and in this Flaubertian drama, the central device is the verb.

The result is an essentially leveled universe, one in which humans have no more, but also no less, agency than an Algerian silk scarf—at least as long as we limit the analysis to what Flaubert seeks to make visible.

---

[22] Jules Barbey d'Aurevilly, for example, likened *L'éducation sentimentale* to a magic lantern that was able to project images but utterly unable to tell stories: "Dans *L'Éducation sentimentale,* cette suite de tableaux à la file, tous pareils à une lanterne magique, il n'y a rien à raconter." See Barbey d'Aurevilly, review of *L'éducation sentimentale, Constitutionnel* (29 November 1869).

[23] Proust, "A propos," 589.

[24] I borrow this term from Philippe Hamon's "Qu'est-ce qu'une description?" *Poétique* 12 (1972): 465–85; "What Is a Description?" in *French Literary Theory Today,* ed. Tzvetan Todorov, trans. R. Carter (Cambridge: Cambridge University Press, 1982), 147–78.

The specific power of Proust's perspective resides in his intense attention to grammatical detail. He offers a series of brilliant stylistic observations based in analyses of typical sentence-patterns in Flaubert, demonstrating forcefully just how central syntax is. But he does not really venture into a more general attempt at describing the pragmatics of the Flaubertian style—this, of course, is a formidable task, as literary scholars have known for over a century.

What he does do, however, is furnish an image that manages to make visible the peculiar aesthetic effect produced by Flaubert's syntactic licence. Proust likens Flaubert's works to a giant "trottoir roulant," or "moving sidewalk," an unexpected yet singularly well-chosen metaphor that presides over the analysis.

> Et il n'est pas possible à quiconque est un jour monté sur ce grand *Trottoir roulant* que sont les pages de Flaubert, au défilement continu, monotone, morne, indéfini, de méconnaître qu'elles sont sans précédent dans la littérature.[25]

> And it is not possible for anyone who has ever climbed onto that great moving sidewalk of Flaubert's pages, with their continuous, monotonous, bleak, indefinite procession, to not realize that these pages are without precedent in literature.

Proust here refers to a technological invention that was first shown at the 1900 World Exposition in Paris, the largest World Fair that had taken place up until that point, with millions of visitors. A popular attraction at the Paris Expo, the moving sidewalk provided a new bodily and perceptual experience. Once you climbed onto the platform, you turned into a spectator. You stood still, watching the surroundings glide by—buildings, trees, parks, passers-by, and so on. You could do little else, and that was the point: this was an exclusively visual experience of a world in motion.

The moving sidewalk was part of a whole culture of turn-of-the-century fairground attractions that centered on perception and movement. It turned mobility and immobility upside down: hence the excitement. As soon as the sidewalk had gathered momentum, it seemed as though the environment was coming towards you. The attraction was a giant success. In fact, it was so popular that Anatole France used the "trottoir roulant" as a humorous point of departure for a political column on the front page of *Le Figaro* in the fall of 1900.[26]

---

[25] Proust, "A propos," 587.
[26] Anatole France, "Le trottoir roulant," *Le Figaro* (18 April 1900): 1.

A dazzling metaphor, Proust's sidewalk articulates a little-understood aspect of Flaubert's style. It manages to draw attention to two things at once—Flaubert's strong visual-perceptual penchant and the emphatically mobile, fluid, continuous dimension of those tableaux that crowd his writings from 1857. As in the moving sidewalk, the Flaubertian world is leveled, parading before the reader at a slow, steady, and never-ending speed; and the activity of the eye that watches that world is also leveled. The world simply glides by, there for all to see.

Proust was singularly well placed to appreciate these dimensions of Flaubert's style.[27] He was one of the first writers in France to explore the visual thrill inherent in automobile travel and how it defamiliarized habitual ways of looking at landscape, an exhilarating experience that he reproduced in an important episode in *A la recherche du temps perdu*.[28] Like Flaubert before him, Proust used devices of syntax to produce a sense of movement in the reader. Objects turned into subjects, the inanimate came to life, and the world was set in motion.[29]

This, then, is how Flaubert brings about a revolution in the history of French literature. It can no doubt be sensed in *Madame Bovary*, Proust suggests, but it is really only in *L'éducation sentimentale* that Flaubert truly becomes Flaubert. The revolution has taken place: "Ce qui jusqu'à Flaubert était action devient impression."[30]

It should be stressed that Proust writes not "image" but "impression"—it is the sensory impression, not so much the image, that is substituted for action. We have moved from the implicit notion of the transcendental and disembodied eye in Stendhal and Balzac, say, to the

---

[27] For an intertextual analysis of the Flaubertian presence in Proust's writings, especially on the formal level, see Annick Bouillaguet, *Proust lecteur de Balzac et de Flaubert. L'imitation cryptée* (Paris: Champion, 2000). Bouillaguet pays particular attention to Proust's article, "A propos du 'style' de Flaubert."

[28] See Marcel Proust, "Journées en automobile," in *Contre Sainte-Beuve*, 63–69. Proust's piece was originally published in *Le Figaro* on 19 November 1907, under the title "Impressions de route en automobile."

[29] On Proust and the rhetoric of speed, see Sara Danius, *The Senses of Modernism: Technology, Perception, and Aesthetics* (Ithaca, N.Y.: Cornell University Press, 2002), esp. 121–46.

[30] In a 1939 letter to Simone de Beauvoir, Jean-Paul Sartre made a similar observation as regards Flaubert's style. "Ce n'est pas par hasard que Flaubert est recherché dans ses substantifs et négligé dans ses verbes: ce parnassien soigne le *spectacle* et néglige l'*événement*. L'événement reste scandaleux pour lui: je hais le mouvement qui dérange ces lignes," in *Lettres au Castor et à quelques autres* (Paris: Gallimard, 1983), 1:305–6; quoted in Philippe, *Sujet, verbe, complément,* 181–2. Sartre was wrong on the first count: in fact, Flaubert's use of verbs has been much discussed (see, for example, Thibaudet's insightful discussion in *Gustave Flaubert*, 221–85); but he was right on the second count: that in Flaubert spectacle gains the upper hand over the event or, to use Proust's terms, that action is substituted for impression.

notion of the embodied eye in Flaubert. And Flaubert, I want to claim, is the first writer in the history of the novel to turn the embodied eye into an aesthetic means and structuring principle.

What does Proust have in mind when he suggests that in Flaubert impression is substituted for action? He does not dwell on this point, so let me do it instead. It is not that Flaubert does away with action. After all, a great many things happen in *Madame Bovary*, and dramatic things at that: Emma is married, gives birth to a daughter, commits adultery, accumulates debts, kills herself... Such is the stuff that narratives are made of. In Flaubert, however, novelistic action is organized according to a new and different mode. As numerous critics have underscored, Flaubert's writings mark the break-up from those narrative schemata inherent in the kind of realism typically associated with, say, Balzac.[31]

The representation of the character known as Emma is a particularly instructive example. On closer consideration, she exists on two separate levels of narrative reality simultaneously. On the one hand, Emma comes before us as a subject of actions, that is, a doer behind deeds—but we are not made to see her as she performs these acts; we are merely told that they have taken place, or else we infer that they have happened. On the other hand, Emma comes before us as an object of perception, that is, as a visual impression. We are now made to see her. And this typically means that we are invited to look at Emma in much the same way as one would approach a sculpture, a still life, or a floral arrangement.

In other words, there is a cleavage at the heart of *Madame Bovary*. This helps explain a vital part of the essential ambiguity of the portrait of Emma. Subject and object, active and passive, animate and inanimate: these two distinct modes of representing Emma vie for the reader's attention, and it is the second one—the pictorial representation of Emma—that gains the upper hand. More than anything else, it is Emma-as-image that shapes the reader's processing of Emma-as-character. Using Proust's distinction, we might say that the representation of Emma as visual impression absorbs the representation of Emma as a subject of actions.

More generally, what we witness in Flaubert is that the category of action and, therefore, of the event is undergoing change. Because there is a palpable discrepancy between action and impression, between plot and style, there is a widening gap between two distinct orders: between

---

[31] On how Flaubert performs a veritable de-Balzacification of the novel, see, for example, Jonathan Culler, *Flaubert: The Uses of Uncertainty* (Ithaca, N.Y.: Cornell University Press, 1974), 93–100; and Peter Brooks, *Reading for the Plot* (Cambridge, Mass.: Harvard University Press, [1984] 1992), 171–215.

the order of the narrative event and that of the linguistic event, that is, between events that take place in narrative and events that take place in language.[32]

The first stirrings of this historical development can be seen in early nineteenth-century writers, those early realists who display a radically new interest in the everyday world and, in so doing, pursue not so much the general as the particular, especially the visible particular: the look of a button, the shape of a collar, the texture of a cravat, the cut of a waistcoat, the length of a trouser pant.

I have dwelt at length on Proust's essay because it usefully connects the question of style to basic devices of syntax, and also because it offers a metaphor that is congenial with a central feature of the pragmatics of Flaubert's style. Proust does not say as much, but as I shall be proposing in the following pages, it is Flaubert's dexterity with verbs that enables what has so often been seen as Flaubert's proto-cinematic representation of the world.

This brings me to the heart of the problem. With Flaubert, we enter a new chapter in the history of literary visibility: the autonomy of the seen. We witness the emergence of a new representational space. For once we reach Flaubert in the history of the novel, the art of making things and persons visible in the way that, say, Stendhal and Balzac had perfected, has been replaced by the production of more or less autonomous images. Such image production has little or nothing to do with embellishment, nor with illustration.

In introducing the notion of "representational space," I am alluding to Fredric Jameson's work on modernism, more specifically, to his analysis of Joseph Conrad's "aestheticizing strategy." And what Jameson means by "aestheticizing strategy" is the "designation of a strategy which for whatever reason seeks to recode or rewrite the world and its own data in terms of perception as a semi-autonomous activity."[33]

In Conrad's works, Jameson suggests, two narratological paradigms coexist, and both are concerned with the relation between the implied reader and narrative content. The first paradigm points back to the nineteenth century; the second anticipates the twentieth century and high-

---

[32] The distinction I am introducing here is inspired by Fredric Jameson's discussion of a single sentence in Vladimir Nabokov, a witty and elegant sentence describing how a human hand enters a freezer. In this way, Nabokov turns an utterly unsignificant event into an extraordinary linguistic event; and the sentence, moreover, acquires autonomy. See Jameson, *A Singular Modernity: Essay on the Ontology of the Present* (London: Verso, 2002), 205.

[33] Jameson, *The Political Unconscious: Narrative as a Socially Symbolic Act* (Ithaca, N.Y.: Cornell University Press, 1981), 229–31; quotation, 230.

modernist aesthetics. Thus on the one hand, Conrad urges on the reader a "theater-goer's position with respect to the content of the narrative." Addressed as a spectator, the reader is invited to approach what is taking place in the novel as though it happened on a "scene." Terms like "tableau" and "spectacle" have a similar function and occur frequently in Conrad as in most nineteenth-century writers.

On the other hand, there is in Conrad a proto-modernist impulse. Not only does Conrad place the emphasis on *how* things are seen; he also has a predilection for rewriting appearance in terms of highly particularized modes of perception, notably visual ones. Things and persons and sights are thus subject to a certain "aestheticization" in the original sense of the word. In the end, Jameson suggests, the unity of the theatrical metaphor is undermined by Conrad's will to style, as he tends to rewrite the phenomenal world in terms of perception for perception's sake. The relation between the implied reader and narrative content is therefore transformed into "a matter of sense perception, into a virtually filmic experience."[34]

What I now wish to suggest is that the "aestheticizing strategy" that makes itself felt in writers from Conrad to Proust, from Joyce to Nabokov, can be traced back to Flaubert. My point is not that Flaubert can be seen as a proto-modernist writer, which he surely can. Nathalie Sarraute's essay, "Flaubert le précurseur" (1965), remains the most eloquent and perceptive elaboration of this argument.[35] Rather, the argument that I wish to put forward is that Flaubert's narratological technique—in particular his systematic use of free indirect discourse—does important work in the domain of the visible, from which he manages to extract a whole new and complex order.

We have seen that the kind of narratorial indeterminacy that governs Flaubert's mode of telling stories readily translates into perceptual indeterminacy, and that this fact, in its turn, helps create a new kind of literary image. So it is that Flaubert's mode of treating the visible, and especially his predilection for self-contained images, opens a new representational space in the history of the novel. The visual texture of Flaubertian narration resembles nothing that came before it.

---

[34] Jameson, *Political Unconscious,* 232.
[35] Nathalie Sarraute, "Flaubert le précurseur," *Preuves* (February 1965): 3–11.

Emma As Image

In the summer of 1856, after four and half years of dogged labor, Flaubert finished *Madame Bovary*. It is estimated that he rewrote every page five to six times.[36] The novel was first published in serialized form in *Revue de Paris* in the fall of 1856. Before long, Flaubert was prosecuted for having offended public morality and religion.[37]

And yet this was a story that he had originally thought of as being about nothing. In 1852, just as he was about to start work on *Madame Bovary*, Flaubert explained in a letter to Louise Colet that he wanted to write a novel "about nothing." Unhappy with his previous literary attempts, he told Colet that he had two options, either to succeed as a writer or to throw himself out of the window. He continued:

> Ce qui me semble beau, ce que je voudrais faire, c'est un livre sur rien, un livre sans attache extérieure, qui se tiendrait de lui-même par la force interne de son style, comme la terre sans être soutenue se tient en l'air, un livre qui n'aurait presque pas de sujet ou du moins où le sujet serait presque invisible, si cela se peut. Les oeuvres les plus belles sont celles où il y a le moins de matière; plus l'expression se rapproche de la pensée, plus le mot colle dessus et disparaît, plus c'est beau. Je crois que l'avenir de l'Art est dans ces voies.[38]

> What seems beautiful to me, what I should like to write, is a book about nothing, a book dependent on nothing external, which would be held together by the internal strength of its style, just as the earth, suspended in the void, depends on nothing external for its support; a book which would have almost no subject, or at least in which the subject would be almost invisible, if such a thing is possible. The finest works are those that contain the least matter; the closer expression comes to thought, the closer language comes to coinciding and merging with it, the finer the result. I believe the future of Art lies in this direction.[39]

This statement is a famous one, but it should not be grasped too literally. Flaubert's projected book about nothing certainly had a subject. Nathalie Sarraute, in her essay on Flaubert's significance in the history

---

[36] Gothot-Mersch, *La genèse de "Madame Bovary,"* 279.

[37] The trial, including the speech of Flaubert's defense lawyer, is to be found as an appendix in Flaubert, *Oeuvres,* ed. Albert Thibaudet and René Dumesnil (Paris: Gallimard, 1951), 1:615–83. For an account of the trial and its historical context, see Geoffrey Wall, *Flaubert: A Life* (London: Faber and Faber, 2001), 227–37.

[38] Flaubert to Louise Colet, 16 January 1852, *Correspondance,* ed. Jean Bruneau (Paris: Gallimard, 1973–98), 2:31.

[39] *The Letters of Gustave Flaubert,* ed. Francis Steegmuller (London: Picador, 2001), 213.

of the novel, argues that an entirely new literary content emerges in the pages of *Madame Bovary*. Flaubert manages to articulate a new aspect of the world, she suggests, to the effect that a "new psychological substance" irrupts into the history of the novel: images, perceptions, reveries, dreams, fantasies, illusions, clichés, ideologies … Hence the radical novelty of Flaubert.[40]

What is more, Flaubert's chosen protagonist fails to adhere to a time-honored pattern. Emma Bovary is not only a woman but also of middle-class origins, which was still relatively unusual in modern serious realism.[41] But the true difference is that Emma is a splendidly non-exemplary character. No sooner is she married than she begins to excel in adultery, deception, and fraud; and on her deathbed, as her body fights the arsenic, she shows no signs of remorse.

What is still more scandalous is that the narrator, in lavishing detailed attention on her many bad deeds, willfully suspends moral judgment, apparently rejecting to uphold ideals of right conduct. We could not be further removed from the ideals of neoclassicism; indeed, Flaubert's tragedy vigorously refuses the idea of exemplum. This is why Thomas Pavel, in his history of the Western novel, speaks of Flaubert's rigorously worked out anti-idealism.[42]

In several ways, then, Flaubert's materials were "low" ones, but as he wrote Colet, he saw no reason to distinguish between high and low subject matters. Style was everything. Style, Flaubert suggested, was to be liberated once and for all from the age-old dictatorship of subject matter. He envisioned a new formal ideal, beyond generic doctrines and aesthetic norms: "La forme, en devenant habile, s'atténue; elle quitte toute liturgie, toute règle, toute mesure; elle abandonne l'épique pour le roman, le vers pour la prose [Form, in becoming more skilful, becomes attenuated; it leaves behind all liturgy, rule, measure; the epic is discarded in favor of the novel, verse in favor of prose]."[43]

A novel about nothing? Exactly what Flaubert may have meant is unclear. "Il me faudrait tout un livre pour développer ce que je veux dire [I should need an entire book to develop what I want to say]," he explained in the same letter to Louise Colet. "J'écrirai sur tout cela dans ma vieillesse, quand je n'aurai rien de mieux à barbouiller [I'll write about all

---

[40] Sarraute, "Flaubert le précurseur." See also Victor Brombert, "Flaubert and the Status of the Subject," in *Flaubert and Postmodernism,* ed. Naomi Schor and Henry F. Majewski (Lincoln: University of Nebraska Press, 1984), 100–115.
[41] See Erich Auerbach, *Mimesis* (Tübingen: Francke, [1946] 2001), 422–59; *Mimesis,* trans. Willard R. Trask (Princeton: Princeton University Press, 1957), 454–92.
[42] Thomas Pavel, *La pensée du roman* (Paris: Gallimard, 2003), 281–90.
[43] Flaubert to Colet, 16 January 1852, *Correspondance,* 2:31; *Letters,* 213.

that in my old age, when I'll have nothing better to scribble]."[44] But one thing is clear: *Madame Bovary* explodes traditional notions of action. It initiates a process that will culminate with *L'éducation sentimentale* (1869): the dissolution of the event.

If we know that Flaubert's protagonist is Emma Bovary, we also know that *Madame Bovary* is not Emma's story, but the story about Emma. What is more, the story neither begins with her, nor ends with her. Two other narratives frame Emma's story. The opening pages of the book revolve around Charles Bovary and his background, while the closing pages deal with Homais, the man of the future who, right at the very end, receives the Legion of Honour.

When Emma is introduced into the narrative, she enters it as a set of visual impressions refracted through the gaze of her future husband.[45] Unlike Charles Bovary, Mademoiselle Emma carries very little history and almost no biography; all she carries is a name that attaches her to her father—and a fine blue merino-wool dress with three flounces. It is as though she existed only in the present.

In making her first appearance, the narrative entity called "Emma" is a bundle of discrete visual details. Charles Bovary is tending to Emma's father and his fractured leg; Emma, meanwhile, is busy making pads—she sews, pricks her finger tops, sucks them, continues to sew. The sight produces something like an aesthetic experience in the country doctor, whose eyes are immediately drawn to her finger tops:

> Charles fut surpris de la blancheur de ses ongles. Ils étaient brillants, fins du bout, plus nettoyés que les ivoires de Dieppe, et taillés en amande. (72)

> Charles was surprised at the whiteness of her nails. They were lustrous, tapering, more highly polished than Dieppe ivories, and cut into an almond shape. (11)

Having bandaged Père Rouault's leg, the country doctor is invited to a small meal. Charles strikes up conversation with the young woman. Flaubert tells us that they talk, but we do not hear what they say. We hardly ever hear them speak in the novel, except for some utterly insignificant phrases. Flaubert wants to make us see, and what we are made

---

[44] Flaubert to Colet, 16 January 1852, *Correspondance,* 2:31; Letters, 213.

[45] For a detailed stylistic analysis of how Emma is introduced into the novel, see Bernard Masson, "Le corps d'Emma," in *Flaubert, la femme, la ville* (Paris: Presses universitaires de France, 1983), 13–22. Masson argues that the images of Emma in the second chapter serve to focalize Charles's newly awakened desire. Flaubert, in other words, speaks by way of the image, that is, he seeks to show rather than to tell.

to see, now that the conversation comes to a temporary halt, is what Charles sees.

> Son cou sortait d'un col blanc, rabattu. Ses cheveux, dont les deux bandeaux noirs semblaient chacun d'un seul morceau, tant ils étaient lisses, étaient séparés sur le milieu de la tête par une raie fine, qui s'enfonçait légèrement selon la courbe du crâne; et, laissant voir à peine le bout de l'oreille, ils allaient se confondre par derrière en un chignon abondant, avec un mouvement ondé vers les tempes, que le médecin de campagne remarqua là pour la première fois de sa vie. Ses pommettes étaient roses. Elle portait, comme un homme, passé entre deux boutons de son corsage, un lorgnon d'écaille. (73)

> Her neck rose out of a white collar, turned down. Her black hair, brushed so smooth that each side seemed to be in one piece, was parted in a delicate central line that traced the curve of the skull; and, just revealing the tip of her ear, it coiled at the back into a thick chignon, with a rippling pattern at the temples, something that the country doctor now observed for the first time in his life. Her cheeks were touched with pink. She had, like a man, tucked into the front of her bodice, a tortoiseshell lorgnon. (12; translation amended)

Very little happens in the scene. Charles and Emma exchange a few predictable phrases, meanwhile having something to eat and drink. So where is the action? The overall plot may have come to a halt, but a crucial subplot is about to take shape. The action is right here: in Charles's gaze as it moves from one physical feature to the next, scanning Emma's neck, her hair, her cheeks, all discrete and detachable elements that form an odd portrait of the young woman.

Emma herself recedes into the background, while her neck acquires syntactical agency and a linguistic life of its own.[46] The phrase, "son cou sortait d'un col blanc," may seem innocent enough, but the second sentence follows up and amplifies the syntactical pattern. Soon Emma's coiffure, too, begins to act. Indeed, the central event in the passage is the conduct of Emma's hair. Flaubert uses sixty words to describe the shape of her hairdo, a carefully crafted description that, within the space of a

---

[46] Jean Rousset rightly notes that in these early scenes, Emma appears as an object, not as a subject. Nothing is said about what she thinks, feels, or experiences; there is also no exchange, no communication. Charles looks at her, she lets herself be looked at, nothing more, nothing less. Rousset aptly characterizes Emma and Charles as "monads." See Rousset, *Leurs yeux se rencontrèrent. La scène de première vue dans le roman* (Paris: Corti, 1981), 37–40. To Rousset's analysis, I want to add that this tendency is a structural one, persisting throughout the novel. Whenever Emma is looked at, she turns into an image. As we shall see, the representation of Emma is marked by a fundamental cleavage between impression and action.

single sentence, reproduces the visual impression of her coiffure: not so much hair as rather meticulously styled pieces.

The thinglike character of the hairdo is even echoed in the patterning of the sentence. Just as Emma's hair detaches itself from the visual appearance of which it is a part, so Flaubert's sentence liberates itself from its narrative context and acquires autonomy. And just as the parting divides Emma's hair into two distinct volumes, so the semi-colon bisects Flaubert's sentence into two separate yet related propositions.

The portrait already speaks of Emma as a potential object of desire. Charles, without really realizing it, has fallen in love. Before long, he finds himself making regular trips to the farm under the pretext of making sure that Père Rouault's leg is healing well. A routine begins to develop, even as Emma and Charles bid each farewell on the doorstep and then, during a moment of delicious silence, wait for his horses. The scene is focalized through Charles, assisted by the eloquent narrator:

> On s'était dit adieu, on ne parlait plus; le grand air l'entourait, levant pêle-mêle les petits cheveux follets de sa nuque, ou secouant sur sa hanche les cordons de son tablier, qui se tortillaient comme des banderoles. (75)

> They had said goodbye, they had no more to say; the fresh air wrapped all about her, fondling the stray locks of hair at the nape of her neck, or tugging on the strings of the apron around her hips, fluttering them like streamers. (13)

Emma is on the doorstep, and if she appears like a still life, as a *nature morte,* it is because the narrator so emphatically presents her as an object of an action. It is the wind that acts, not Emma. Syntactically speaking, the wind is the subject, acting now on her hair curls, now on her apron strings. In Flaubert, such moments of predicative expansion are semiotically coded: we have entered the sexual field of vision.

The wind scene serves as a prelude to the final part of the passage that artfully suggests how Charles comes to experience a quiet epiphany as he looks at Emma. They wait for his horses, as usual, but this new version of the farewell scenario is even more deeply immersed in the world of particulars.

> Une fois, par un temps de dégel, l'écorce des arbres suintait dans la cour, la neige sur les couvertures des bâtiments se fondait. Elle était sur le seuil; elle alla chercher son ombrelle, elle l'ouvrit. L'ombrelle, de soie gorge de pigeon, que traversait le soleil, éclairait de reflets mobiles la peau blanche de sa figure. Elle souriait là-dessous à la chaleur tiède; et on entendait les gouttes d'eau, une à une, tomber sur la moire tendue. (75)

> One day, when it was thawing, the trees in the yard were oozing damp from their bark, the snow on top of the sheds was melting. She was at the door; she went to fetch her parasol, she opened it. The parasol, made of marbled silk, as the sun came shining through it, spread shifting colours over the whiteness of her face. There she was smiling in the moist warmth of its shade; and you could hear the drops of water, one by one, falling on the taut fabric. (13)

On this beautiful day in early spring, the snow is melting away, and Charles's senses are wide open. He experiences something like a profane epiphany, a compelling moment of aesthetic plenitude, and Emma is its locus. The scene is made visible and audible, nothing more, nothing less. It is true that Emma herself acts here, but as so often, that action of hers is unimportant, even trivial.

The true action is to be found elsewhere in the passage, for as soon as Emma has fetched her parasol, she is stripped of syntactic agency and becomes the backdrop of a perceptual drama. Flaubert places her on the threshold and turns her into an object of sensory perception, into something to see and to hear—for Charles, for the narrator, for the reader.[47] She is motionless, caught as though in a freeze-frame. The sunlight acts on her face, just as the water drops act on the parasol fabric. Emma's facial skin, one might say, is to the sunlight as the parasol is to the droplets. Emma's skin and the parasol thus have the same status within Flaubert's economy of description: they are surfaces to which things happen. Emma, in any case, has literally become an aesthetic object. The marker "une fois" signals that a narrative event is to be expected, but this is an event that takes place in language.

Every time the country doctor is in Emma's presence, his experience of her being is represented in aestheticizing terms, especially visual ones. And every time the narrator sets out to report that experience, the diegetic speed slows down and comes to a halt. In the meantime,

---

[47] As so often in Flaubert, the seen cannot be pinned down to a particular observer. The passage is focalized through Charles, that much is clear, but it is of course unlikely that the country doctor would be capable of such eloquence. Adrianne Tooke, in her wide-ranging discussion of Flaubert's pictorialism, underscores the essential artfulness of the parasol scene, while at the same time noting the independence of such descriptions from the surrounding narrative: "The fact that the description of Emma beneath her parasol is like a painting adds a dimension to the scene, giving the reader a sense of beauty and making her believe that this echoes something of what Charles may be experiencing. In these descriptions art is all around, giving value. These visions 'hang in the air', so to speak, unattached, as if they are an intrusion from another world—or genre! This is a privileged moment, thematically and stylistically—description evokes an *ailleurs* which narrative almost cannot contain." See Tooke, *Flaubert and the Pictorial Arts: From Image to Text* (Oxford: Oxford University Press, 2000), 203.

the precious moment begins to expand as though it had been put under a magnifying glass. Emma and Charles are now newly married; he is passionately in love with his wife, but he utterly fails to realize that her feelings are not mutual. In fact, Emma herself has not yet discovered just how bored she is, but it will soon dawn on her. It sometimes happens that Charles spends a few blissful moments in the early morning just looking at his sleeping wife, until she shows signs of waking up:

> Au lit, le matin, et côte à côte sur l'oreiller, il regardait la lumière du soleil passer parmi le duvet de ses joues blondes, que couvraient à demi les pattes escalopées de son bonnet. Vus de si près, ses yeux lui paraissaient agrandis, surtout quand elle ouvrait plusieurs fois de suite ses paupières en s'éveillant; noirs à l'ombre et bleu foncé au grand jour, ils avaient comme des couches de couleurs successives, et qui, plus épaisses dans le fond, allaient en s'éclaircissant vers la surface de l'émail. Son oeil, à lui, se perdait dans ces profondeurs, et il s'y voyait en petit jusqu'aux épaules, avec le foulard qui le coiffait et le haut de sa chemise entr'ouvert. (94–5)

> In bed, in the morning, close together on the pillow, he gazed at the sunlight playing in the golden down on her cheeks, half hidden by the scalloped edges of her bonnet. So very close, her eyes seemed even bigger, especially when she first awoke and her eyelids fluttered into life. Black in the shadows, and deep blue in full daylight, as if the colours were floating layer upon layer, thickest in the depths, coming clear and bright towards the surface. His eye drifted away into the deep, and there he saw himself in miniature, head and shoulders, with his nightcap on his head and his shirt unbuttoned. (25–6)

Charles's gaze traces how the sunlight moves over Emma's cheeks as she lies resting on her pillow, an aesthetic event if there ever was one. Such moments are necessarily as fragile as they are short-lived, however, for Flaubert has put a taboo on the sublime, so when Charles's farcical nightcap comes into view, we know that we have been plunged back into the sad facts of the quotidian real.

We are only forty pages into the first part of the book, but this much is clear: this caricatural morning scene, a mere fragment of an extended passage that speaks of Charles's newfound marital happiness, is designed to give a foretaste of the absolute incompatibility between husband and wife. Charles devours the sight of his beloved; he even looks deeply into her wide-open eyes, but Emma does not return his gaze—just as surely as she fails to reciprocate his feelings. From now on, the abyss between Charles and Emma will only grow, and the careening plot of the novel thrives on the irreducible discrepancy between his world and hers.

Yet this is not what makes this passage interesting. It is a comic snapshot of Charles's universal mediocrity, to be sure, and an effective anticipation of the ennui that will soon come crashing down on Emma, but there is more to it. Once again we are presented with a scene in which the act of looking is thematized. It offers, in allegorical form, the model according to which visual perception tends to operate in Flaubert. In fact, it is a passage in which Flaubert's visual poetics is encapsulated. Things may be seen, but no knowledge is derived from the seen. The perceptual datum is mute. What is more, the gaze is almost never returned. Humans, objects, landscapes: all are immersed in themselves.

In the Lheureux episode that I discussed at the outset of this chapter, Flaubert described how the shopkeeper was following the gaze of Emma who, in her turn, was looking at the commodities before her. Emma's eyes were said to "wander" among the wares; Lheureux himself was made visible too. Moments like this recur constantly in Flaubert. What is more, they come with a gendered division of visual labor.

The stuff of Emma is permanently made visible, at least as a cluster of part-objects, some moving, some at a standstill, but where is the totality of her existence? Where is the substance of Emma herself in that bundle of discrete visual particulars, when we have been made to see her perfectly shaped finger nails, her golden facial hair, her fluttering eyelids, her translucent nose tip, her curly neck hair, her ravishing profile?[48] When Charles looks into Emma's eyes, he discovers not her soul. He discovers nothing, for there is nothing: no consciousness, no interior, no depth. Emma's eyes are mere reflecting devices.

It is not that Flaubert has failed to give us Emma's truth, denying her a subjectivity of her own, or an identity, or an inner being. It is also not that Charles is utterly unable to understand who Emma is. My argument is a different one. Eyes, in *Madame Bovary,* are never treated as mirrors of the soul. In Flaubert, that powerful metaphor is long since dead. Eyes are simply things—to be exposed, to be looked at, to be pored over. They may be admired for their beauty, as often happens in this narrative about

---

[48] For a perceptive analysis of the representation of faces in Madame Bovary, with a focus on its lexical, technical, and thematic aspects, see Claudine Gothot-Mersch, "La description des visages dans *Madame Bovary*," Littérature 15 (October 1974): 17–26. Gothot-Mersch usefully underscores that woman, in Flaubert, is always an object of visual contemplation. She also points out that a classic description typically presents characters the first time they appear, whereby the characterization is set once and for all; in Flaubert, by contrast, descriptions tend to be disseminated and distributed throughout the narrative, and this is particularly true for Emma. The description of Emma as she first enters the plot is restricted to a small number of discrete physical details; these visual data, furthermore, are pieced out over several pages. For this reason, Gothot-Mersch argues, "la description proprement flaubertienne n'a rien de systématique" (24). But as I shall be proposing in the following pages, even though the visual representation of Emma may be fragmented, dispersed, and given over to details, it nevertheless follows a highly recognizable pattern, especially when analyzed in syntactical terms.

sentimental education, but they are never indicative of some meaning, personal or otherwise. Eyes may do things but they say precious little. Eyes are surfaces. They carry no depth and therefore no hermeneutics.[49] By the same token, the perceived engenders little knowledge. Perception, in Flaubert, seldom yields insights into the reality of the object in question. If Charles discovers anything at all, he discovers only himself; or to be more precise, he discovers only the image of himself as reflected in the eye of the other. And what he discovers is surely disconcerting.

Emma herself can never be known, in and of herself, except in a strictly empirical and therefore rather trivial sense, as in the following episode, when Charles and Emma have arrived at the Vaubyessard château to attend a ball given by the Marquis. As Emma puts the finishing touches on her attire, Charles catches a glimpse of her image as mediated by the mirror:

> Il la voyait par-derrière, dans la glace, entre deux flambeaux. Ses yeux noirs semblaient plus noirs. Ses bandeaux, doucement bombés vers les oreilles, luisaient d'un éclat bleu; une rose à son chignon tremblait sur une tige mobile, avec des gouttes d'eau factices au bout de ses feuilles. Elle avait une robe de safran pâle, relevée par trois bouquets de roses pompon mêlées de verdure. (118)

> He saw her in the mirror, from behind, between two candles. Her dark eyes seemed even darker. Her hair, billowing smoothly around her ears, had a blue sheen; the rose in her chignon was quivering on its fragile stem, with artificial dew-drops on the tips of the leaves. She wore a dress of pale saffron yellow, trimmed with three bouquets of pompon roses mixed with green. (38–9)

This is a record, but of what? Not of Emma, but of Emma-being-looked-at. Charles is infatuated with his dazzlingly beautiful wife, and it would seem natural that he looks at her with a libidinally charged gaze, especially during their courtship and the early days of marriage. Yet this is a systematic tendency in *Madame Bovary*. Emma is made visible in this way throughout the novel, and not only when Charles is the implied beholder. The visual experience of her appearance is overwhelmingly refracted through the lens of desire, and in Flaubert that means being

---

[49] In Proust, too, the visual apparatus itself becomes an object of sight. As Malcolm Bowie has observed, the Proustian eye is anything but a window of the soul; it is, rather, a physiological surface to be pored over and decoded, a transmitter of obscure and unstable meanings. See Bowie, *Proust Among the Stars* (London: HarperCollins, 1998), 13–16. For a perceptive comparison of the figuration of the gaze in Proust and Joyce, see Reinhard Baumgart, "Blicke und Berührungsverbote," in *Addio. Abschied von der Literatur* (Munich: Hanser, 1995), esp. 156–65.

presented as an image. Whether Emma is looked at by Charles, or by Léon, or by Rodolphe, the representational mode is more or less the same. Emma's appearance is rarely described in any other way. Indeed, we never really get to know who she is—that, of course, is part of her tragedy, and in Flaubert, such knowledge is structurally impossible anyway—but we get to know all the more about how she appears in the eyes of others, especially male others.[50] And these descriptions have a striking tendency to be cast in one and the same stylistic mold.

For this reason, *Madame Bovary* emerges not so much as a story about Emma as rather about the men who perceive her, desire her, and make her the object of their gazes. Add to this that we seldom hear her speak, except for a handful of splendidly trivial utterances, and the overall picture becomes clear: Emma is an image, and remains an image. And if Emma is an imaginary phenomenon, then *Madame Bovary* ultimately tells the story of so many male subjects who are, and remain, subject to the imaginary.[51]

If Emma is always already an image in the narrative, and if, furthermore, she is perceived as an image by the men around her, it follows that no qualitative distinction is to be made between real Emma and imaginary Emma, between the "original" and the "copy." Indeed, if Emma belongs in the imaginary, it seems appropriate that the mental representation of her being would differ very little from her pictorial representation. Consider the episode when Rodolphe, having broken up with Emma, looks at the miniature portrait she once gave him. In a rare moment of contemplation, Rodolphe conjures up the memory of his former mistress—but what he recalls is not Emma-as-lived-reality, nor Emma-as-the-subject-of actions, but rather Emma-as-image:

> [P]uis, à force de considérer cette image et d'évoquer le souvenir du modèle, les traits d'Emma peu à peu se confondirent en sa mémoire, comme si la figure vivante et la figure peinte, se frottant l'une contre l'autre, se fussent réciproquement effacées. (313)

---

[50] See Gothot-Mersch, "La description," 24–5.

[51] Frederik Tygstrup, for example, has called attention to the fragmented and essentially imaginary nature of Emma's body, but like a majority of critics, he stops short of an analysis of the rigorously gendered aspect of the visual dynamics in which the representation of Emma's body is implicated. Indeed, the perception of Emma's body is always refracted through the sexual field of vision. The only exception is her corpse, of which I shall have more to say shortly. See Frederik Tygstrup, "Realisme som symbolsk form," i *På sporet af virkeligheden. Essays* (Copenhagen: Gyldendal, 2000), 51. On Emma and fragmentation, see also Peter Brooks, *Realist Vision* (New Haven: Yale University Press, 2005), 54–70.

> [F]rom dwelling on this image and from calling up the memory of the original, Emma's features gradually blurred in his mind, as if the living and the painted faces, rubbing one against the other, were both being obliterated. (162)

Similarly, when Charles tries to evoke the memory of his deceased wife, he desperately grapples after her image. To think of Emma is, for Charles, to visualize her image, and when he realizes that her image has begun to dissolve, all that remains is nothingness:

> Une chose étrange, c'est que Bovary, tout en pensant à Emma continuellement, l'oubliait; et il se désespérait à sentir cette image lui échapper de la mémoire au milieu des efforts qu'il faisait pour la retenir. Chaque nuit pourtant, il la rêvait; c'était toujours le même rêve: il s'approchait d'elle; mais, quand il venait à l'étreindre, elle tombait en pourriture dans ses bras. (496–7)

> It was peculiar, that Bovary, though he thought continually of Emma, began to forget her face; and he was in despair as he felt the image slipping from his memory no matter what he did to keep hold of it. Every night, he dreamed about her; always it was the same dream: he came nearer; but when he went to embrace her, she turned to putrid flesh in his arms. (283)

Anyone who subjects Flaubert's novel to close textual analysis will notice the utter asymmetry between Emma's mode of looking at the men to whom she feels attracted and the way in which she is looked at by the men who feel attracted to her. In both cases we are dealing with objects of desire, yet the difference is striking. Emma readily turns into image, whereas the men in the novel do not, not even when she, in fact, desires them.

It is true that Emma, the primary image-maker in the novel, sometimes makes images of her two lovers, Léon and Rodolphe, and she is also represented in the act of looking at them, but her visualizations are almost never reproduced; and when they are, her impressions are not subject to aestheticization. Consider the scene in which Emma conjures up images of Léon in his absence—he has just moved out of town, and Emma is desolate. The image of Léon is mentioned, but his appearance, the memory image itself, is not made visible.

> [E]lle avait une mélancolie morne, un désespoir engourdi. Léon réapparaissait plus grand, plus beau, plus suave, plus vague; quoiqu'il fût séparé d'elle, il ne l'avait pas quittée, il était là, et les murailles de la maison semblaient garder son ombre. Elle ne pouvait détacher sa vue de ce tapis où il avait marché, de ces meubles vides où il s'était assis. (216)

> [S]he felt a dull melancholy, a lethargic despair. Léon reappeared, taller, more beautiful, more charming, less distinct; though far away from her, he had not left her, he was there, and the walls of the house seemed to carry his shadow. And she could not take her eyes from that carpet where he had walked, from those empty chairs where he had sat. (98)

And when Rodolphe first enters the plot, we see him through Emma's curious eyes. As so often, Emma is at the window, an architectural element that mediates between interior and exterior, private and public, serving as a powerful metaphor of the eye. Jean Rousset has underscored the structural importance of the window in *Madame Bovary*.[52] Flaubert's narrator even supplies a miniature sociology of the window: "elle s'y mettait souvent," he states and then goes on to explain that, "la fenêtre, en province, remplace les théâtres et la promenade [the window, in the provinces, replaces theatres and promenading" (221/101). And so it is that Emma catches sight of a stranger. Crossing the street a few yards away, he turns out to be approaching the Bovary residence:

> [E]lle aperçut un monsieur vêtu d'une redingote de velours vert. Il était ganté de gants jaunes, quoiqu'il fût chaussé de fortes guêtres; et il se dirigeait vers la maison du médecin, suivi d'un paysan marchant la tête basse d'un air tout réfléchi.
> – Puis-je voir Monsieur? demanda-t-il à Justin, qui causait sur le seuil avec Félicité.
> Et, le prenant pour le domestique de la maison:
> – Dites-lui que M. Rodolphe Boulanger, de la Huchette, est là. (221–2)

> [S]he noticed a gentleman in a frock-coat of green velvet. He was wearing yellow gloves, though shod in heavy gaiters; and he was heading towards the doctor's house, followed by a peasant walking with head bent and a rather thoughtful look.
> – Can I see the doctor? he asked Justin, who was on the doorstep, talking to Félicité.
> And, taking him for the doctor's servant:
> – Tell him that Monsieur Rodolphe Boulanger de la Huchette is here. (101–2)

In this scene, Emma's future lover enters the plot. Rodolphe quickly emerges into view, along with his bold green coat and his equally bold yellow gloves, but he disappears just as quickly, well before an image proper has even begun to congeal, for the visual impression of Rodolphe is not treated as the occasion for a prolonged meditation on the sensuous immediacy of the moment.

---
[52] Rousset, "Madame Bovary," esp. 123–31.

Unlike Emma in the passages I discussed a moment ago, Rodolphe is not only a grammatical subject (he moves through space; he makes assumptions), but he is also a speaking subject (he addresses strangers). In fact, he even speaks his name, a name that attaches him to a property and therefore also to a given social identity.[53] In other words, as seen by Emma, Rodolphe is more than a mere image. Emma, by contrast, when looked at by the men around her, emerges as an image and little else.

Yet, why should Emma's manner of gazing at the men to whom she feels attracted follow the same representational pattern that shapes that of the men looking at her? My point is not that such symmetry ought to exist. My point is also not that Flaubert's writings display characteristically patriarchal elements. What I want to suggest, rather, is this: the difference between male and female—between the representation of male and female objects of desire, and between the representation of male and female gazes—takes us to the heart of a gendered division of labor, a gendered representational economy that the narrative both presupposes and reinforces. Ultimately, Flaubert's image of Emma is inscribed in an old art-historical tradition. Emma is the artist's model, the very vehicle of aesthetic experimentation, both its end and its means.

When Léon Dupuis, the young clerk I mentioned at the beginning of the chapter, first catches sight of Emma, the representation of his experience has much in common with Charles's mode of perceiving Emma during those first months of courtship—and with the way in which Rodolphe, too, will soon be looking at Emma. The description thus focuses on her visual appearance and is marked by an almost photographic precision—but then one should note that in Flaubert's "photographic" descriptions, there is always something that moves.

In the farewell episode, we saw how the sunlight illuminated Emma's cheeks, turning her into a sensory spectacle before Charles's wide-open eyes. In the following scene, when Léon sets his eyes on Emma for the first time, glowing flames cast light on her physical appearance, transforming her yet again into a dazzling object of visual perception.

---

[53] In fact, Flaubert's narrator hastens to fill out the picture, providing the reader with relevant information regarding Rodolphe's social status: "Ce n'était point par vanité territoriale que le nouvel arrivant avait ajouté à son nom la particule, mais afin de se faire mieux connaître. La Huchette, en effet, était un domaine près d'Yonville, dont il venait d'acquérir le château, avec deux fermes qu'il cultivait lui-même, sans trop se gêner cependant. Il vivait en garçon, et passait pour avoir *au moins quinze mille livres de rentes*" (222); "It was not out of territorial vanity that the newcomer had added *de la Huchette* to his name, but merely to make himself known. La Huchette was an estate near Yonville, where he had just bought the château, along with two farms he was working himself, though without putting himself to any great trouble. He was a bachelor, and said to have at least *fifteen thousand a year*" (102).

> Madame Bovary, quand elle fut dans la cuisine, s'approcha de la cheminée. Du bout de ses deux doigts, elle prit sa robe à la hauteur du genou, et, l'ayant ainsi remontée jusqu'aux chevilles, elle tendit à la flamme, par-dessus le gigot qui tournait, son pied chaussé d'une bottine noire. Le feu l'éclairait en entier, pénétrant d'une lumière crue la trame de sa robe, les pores égaux de sa peau blanche et même les paupières de ses yeux qu'elle clignait de temps à autre. Une grande couleur rouge passait sur elle, selon le souffle du vent qui venait par la porte entr'ouverte.
>
> De l'autre côté de la cheminée, un jeune homme à chevelure blonde la regardait silencieusement. (159)

> Madame Bovary, once she was in the kitchen, made for the fireplace. With the tips of her fingers, she took hold of her dress at the knee, and, lifting it just to her ankle, held out to the fire, above the leg of mutton on the spit, a foot clad in a small black boot. The flames lit every inch of her, a harsh brilliance penetrating the weave of her dress, the fine pores of her white skin and even her eyelids that she blinked repeatedly. Vivid reds washed over her, driven by the wind that blew in through the open door.
>
> From the other side of the fireplace, a young man with blond hair was watching her in silence. (63)

Focalized through Léon, the description of Emma is emphatically visual and tremendously detailed, moving from one visible particular to the next, from those two fingers lifting that dress to those blinking eyelids and that half open door. The paragraph presents the seen as an autonomous visual event, and the young man with blond hair serves as its narrative pretext.[54]

Who is the protagonist here? It is neither the subject looking (Léon) nor the subject being looked at (Emma). If we examine the paragraph more closely, we realize that there is really only one protagonist: the fire. Acting on Emma, it illuminates, animates, inscribes. The fire makes things visible. The firelight, one might say, writes the image of Emma.[55]

---

[54] As so often in Flaubert, the autonomy of the visual event is matched by the autonomy of the paragraph. In the final version of the manuscript, the so-called *manuscrit définitif autographe*, Flaubert separates the seen (Emma) from the implied seer (Léon) by inserting a paragraph sign immediately before "De l'autre côté," thus making clear that he wants to start a new paragraph when Léon is to emerge into view. See "Madame Bovary," Flaubert Papers, Institut des textes et des manuscrits modernes (CNRS-ENS), Paris, Mme B. g 221, fol. 155.

[55] Wherever Emma appears, there is light: sunlight, moonlight, firelight. Light has an important pictorial role: it acts, shapes, inscribes. Indeed, in Emma's presence light solidifies, turning into a benevolent force that writes her image. Light, in *Madame Bovary*, is thus both agent and author; and the image of Emma is photographic in the original sense of the word: as an instance of the writing of light.

The scene takes place at the Yonville inn; and Emma, in a bold move that exposes her ankle, keeps her foot close to the fire to stay warm.[56] Léon devours her appearance with his eyes in much the same way as the people at the inn will soon devour that roasting mutton leg. The leg of Emma and the leg of mutton: Flaubert's sardonic irony is plain. The parallel is surely designed to pre-echo Emma's fate in the novel, but the juxtaposition of images also bespeaks a more general tendency: the predilection for thingification. Just as Emma is subject to syntactical objectification, so the paragraph itself turns into a linguistic thing, a verbal artefact. Or (and why not?) into the textual equivalent of a mutton leg.

Clearly, the description of Emma is more than a mere description because it presupposes a beholder that perceives her as image.[57] Indeed, Léon already apprehends Emma as image, as an essentially pictorial and therefore flattened representation. And once she is seen as a two-dimensional visual phenomenon, she may well appear as though in a relief, as when Léon, a few moments later, takes delight in observing how her collar stands out boldly against the surface of her face.

> Léon avait posé son pied sur un des barreaux de la chaise où madame Bovary était assise. Elle portait une petite cravate de soie bleue, qui tenait droit comme une fraise un col de batiste tuyauté; et, selon les mouvements de tête qu'elle faisait, le bas de son visage s'enfonçait dans le linge ou en sortait avec douceur. (166)

---

[56] In her classic study of the genesis of *Madame Bovary*, Gothot-Mersch has shown that Flaubert recycled much material from his earlier works, both from the so-called *Oeuvres de jeunesse* and *Le dictionnaire des idées reçues*. The fireplace passage thus recycles a passage from an early work: "Elle fit deux pas pour s'avancer vers le milieu de la cheminée, elle étendit un pied, puis le second, et y chauffa tout debout la semelle de ses bottines noires" (quoted in Gothot-Mersch, *La genèse*, 209).

[57] I have suggested that Emma is overwhelmingly represented as an image and, which ultimately amounts to the same thing, as an object of desire. The examples could be multiplied. Interestingly enough, the male characters in the novel seldom appear as aestheticized objects, much less as objects of desire, not even when Emma in fact feels attracted to them. Here, however, is an exceptional moment, partly focalized through Emma: "Emma reprit le bras de M. Léon. Elle marcha rapidement pendant quelque temps; puis elle se ralentit, et son regard, qu'elle promenait devant elle, rencontra l'épaule du jeune homme, dont la redingote avait un collet de velours noir. Ses cheveux châtains tombaient dessus, plats et bien peignés. Elle remarqua ses ongles, qui étaient plus longs qu'on ne les portait à Yonville. [Emma took Monsieur Léon's arm again. She walked along quickly for some time; she slowed down, and her gaze came around from the path ahead and happened upon the shoulder of the young man, whose frock-coat had a black velvet collar. His auburn hair tumbled down over it, smooth and well combed. She noticed his fingernails, which were longer than was usual in Yonville]" (179/75). Interestingly enough, however, Emma's visual impressions of Léon's appearance do not amount to an image.

> Léon had put his foot on one of the bars of the chair in which Madame Bovary was sitting. She was wearing a little cravat made of blue silk, that made her tube-pleated batiste collar stick up like a ruff; and, whenever she moved her head, half her face was screened by the fabric or else was pleasingly revealed. (67)

Emma, I want to propose, is always already an image in the narrative, and as such she is only intermittently lost from view. Consider the episode when Rodolphe, the competent womanizer, is walking down the streets of Yonville with Emma on his arm on the day of the agricultural show. They know each other only superficially and have yet to become lovers—that delicious moment in the woods, when Emma gives in to his will, is six weeks into the future. For now they are merely cruising the busy streets of Yonville. Rodolphe looks at Emma from the corner of his eye:

> Son profil […] se détachait en pleine lumière, dans l'ovale de sa capote qui avait des rubans pâles ressemblant à des feuilles de roseau. Ses yeux aux longs cils courbes regardaient devant elle, et, quoique bien ouverts, ils semblaient un peu bridés par les pommettes, à cause du sang, qui battait doucement sous sa peau fine. Une couleur rose traversait la cloison de son nez. Elle inclinait la tête sur l'épaule, et l'on voyait entre ses lèvres le bout nacré de ses dents blanches. (232)

> Her profile […] stood out in the strong light, in the oval of her bonnet fastened with pale ribbons that looked like strands of river-weed. Her eyes, with their long curving lashes, were looking straight ahead, and, though wide open, they looked slightly constricted, because the blood in her cheeks was pulsing softly beneath the delicate skin. A pink color penetrated the flesh between her nostrils. She was leaning her head to one side, and you saw between her lips the pearly crowns of white teeth. (109; translation amended)

This is one of many meticulously crafted representations of how Rodolphe's gaze scans Emma's face and head, and of what he fastens on to—in this case, her facial profile and how it is brought out by the oval of her hat. The description also dwells on her well-shaped eye lashes, her blood veins, her nostrils, her lips, her white teeth. It is as though an invisible frame surrounded her head. Again, this is not so much a description of Emma's appearance as rather a description of a female creature who is already perceived as image. And this image, moreover, is not only flattened but also framed. In fact, there is double framing, because in Rodolphe's eyes, Emma's profile is framed by the oval of her bonnet. Generally speaking, Emma's face, profile, or appearance is remarkably often reported to "stand out" against this or that background.

The activity of looking in Flaubert is almost always spatially defined. It is also body-based. The implied spectator is a physiological entity, present in the here and now. A frame presupposes a perspective; one might even say that a frame produces a perspective. And if the image of Emma is surrounded by a frame—be it visible or invisible—the perspective thus produced is not of the kind that one finds in, say, a painting by the eighteenth-century artist Canaletto but rather of the kind that one finds in a photograph or in a film still. A painting by Canaletto has depth and investigates perspective for its own sake. The image in Flaubert is flat. The aesthetics of the image in Flaubert is an aesthetics of flatness. I shall have more to say about this feature in the chapter on *L'éducation sentimentale*.

That Flaubert has a striking predilection for placing his female characters within a frame has been noted by numerous critics. Pierre Danger, in particular, has observed that such framed images very often emerge, not as portraits of the person in question, but rather as the pure objectification of desire or dreams.[58] What I would like to underscore here, however, is that in Flaubert female objects of desire are not only represented as images. They are also perceived as such. And if, furthermore, Emma is always already an image, then the experience of Emma belongs in the imaginary realm, in the literal sense of the word as well as in the metaphorical one.

> Puis, cent pas plus loin, elle s'arrêta de nouveau; et, à travers son voile, qui de son chapeau d'homme descendait obliquement sur ses hanches, on distinguait son visage dans une transparence bleuâtre, comme si elle eût nagé sous des flots d'azur. (262)

> A hundred yards further on, she stopped again; and, through her veil, which hung obliquely from her man's hat to her hips, you could make out her face, in a slight blue haze, just as if she were swimming beneath the waves of the sea. (128)

The image is an odd one. Perhaps Proust was right after all: perhaps Flaubert did not have much talent for metaphors. What is clear, at any rate, is that Flaubert has an overwhelming predilection for placing the emphasis on *how* things are seen. Furthermore, he tends to rewrite appearance—and so far I have discussed Emma's appearance—in terms of highly particularized modes of perception, especially visual ones. As these extraordinary passages make plain, Emma is repeatedly subject to "aestheticization" in the original sense of the word (from *aistheta,*

---

[58] Danger, *Sensations et objets dans le roman de Flaubert,* 144–6.

things perceptible by the senses, from *aisthesthai,* to perceive). Emma's appearance is infinitely open to writing and rewriting—to allegorization, objectification, and autonomization:

> Et [...] Léon, du coin de l'oeil, épia sa physionomie.
> Ce fut comme le ciel, quand un coup de vent chasse les nuages. L'amas de pensées tristes qui les assombrissaient parut se retirer de ses yeux bleus; tout son visage rayonna. (359)

> And [...] Léon, from the corner of his eye, watched her expression.
> It was just like the sky, when a puff of wind sweeps away the clouds. The burden of sadness that dimmed her blue eyes seemed to be lifted; her whole face was shining. (190)

Emma is Flaubert's canvas: she is the prime means of Flaubertian aesthetics, as well as its end. At the same time, Emma is the formal pretext that serves to motivate the aesthetic program for which the novel serves as a vehicle—I shall return to this point.

What is remarkable about the images of Emma I have been discussing here is not so much that they are utterly stylized, rhetorically complex, and visually elaborate, which they certainly are, nor that they emerge as self-contained entities existing outside of narrative time, which they no doubt do. What is remarkable is that these images are so much alike. Whether Emma is looked at by Charles, or by Léon, or by Rodolphe, makes little difference. Who sees is unimportant, as long as it is someone who finds her attractive, for what Flaubert offers by way of these spectacular scenes are variations on a single theme. This is why we may speak of the image of Emma in the singular. Even if her visual appearance is infinitely open to writing and rewriting, that appearance of hers tends overwhelmingly to be inscribed in more or less the same way.

Leo Bersani, in a discussion of those stylistic idiosyncrasies that give Flaubert's prose its distinct flavor, underscores the French writer's predilection for things that come in threes, the non-connective "and" to introduce a final clause, and the adverb at the end of the phrase. "The high priest of style," Bersani concludes, "is thus the master of the rhythmical tic."[59]

To this, I want to add that the high priest of style is also the master of the visual tic. For what is the image of Emma if not a cliché in the literal sense of the word? Flaubert's mode of making Emma visible follows a stylistic pattern that is highly recognizable, even predictable: no sooner has she emerged into view than she turns into an object of perception to

---

[59] Leo Bersani, introduction to *Madame Bovary,* trans. Lowell Bair (New York: Bantam, 1981), xviii.

which things happen; and as we have seen, this stylistic tendency can be studied, in concrete detail, on the level of the predicate.

As She Lies Dying

The episode devoted to the death of Emma Bovary is a syntactical triumph. In the course of a dozen pages, the narrator records Emma's final hours of agony, from that initial foul taste in her mouth to her chattering teeth and rolling eyes. If Flaubert appears to excel in crisp cruelty, it is simply because he mobilizes all those syntactical resources he has been refining throughout the story of Emma Bovary in order to make this the most ultimate event stand out in bold relief. Flaubert, in short, wants to make us see; and what we are made to see is how Emma turns into a spectacle of death.

So far I have been proposing, among other things, that *Madame Bovary* is a monument to predicative expansion, and nowhere more so than in the visual representation of Emma. And now, as she lies dying, Flaubert is simply doing what comes naturally. He takes the predicative expansion to its logical conclusion. For what we are witnessing here is an action without an agent, that is, a predicate without a subject. You can kill yourself, to be sure, and thus be the subject of the action, but the dying as such has no subject. It happens to you; you are being acted upon; you are the object of an impersonal action.

>Puis elle se mit à geindre, faiblement d'abord. Un grand frisson lui secouait les épaules, et elle devenait plus pâle que le drap où s'enfonçaient ses doigts crispés. Son pouls, inégal, était presque insensible maintenant.
>
>Des gouttes suintaient sur sa figure bleuâtre, qui semblait comme figée dans l'exhalaison d'une vapeur métallique. Ses dents claquaient, ses yeux agrandis regardaient vaguement autour d'elle, et à toutes les questions, elle ne répondait qu'en hochant la tête; même elle sourit deux ou trois fois. Peu à peu, ses gémissements furent plus forts. Un hurlement sourd lui échappa; elle prétendit qu'elle allait mieux et qu'elle se lèverait tout à l'heure. Mais les convulsions la saisirent; elle s'écria:
>
>—Ah! c'est atroce, mon Dieu! (460)

>Now she began to groan, feebly at first. A great shudder ran through her shoulders, and she turned whiter than the sheet she was clutching with her rigid fingers. The irregular pulse was almost imperceptible.
>
>Drops of sweat were trickling down her face, which was turning blue and looked as though it had been coated in the fumes from some metallic compound. Her teeth were chattering, her bulging eyes stared vaguely around the room, and to every question she replied with merely a shake

of the head; she even smiled two or three times. Little by little, her groans became louder. A stifled scream escaped her lips; she said she was feeling better and would be getting up soon. But she was seized by convulsions; she cried out:
– Oh, my God, it's horrible! (258–9)

The passage is committed to pregnant detail, the focal point being Emma's body. We are offered a carefully crafted catalogue of so many discrete physical features and detachable body parts: Emma's skin, eyes, teeth, shoulders, and fingers. The narrator also dwells on her bodily secretions, movements, and gestures. Emma's fragmented body is the canvas upon which Flaubert's narrator traces her destiny. All this should be familiar by now. We have seen the tendency before, in one episode after the next, yet there is an essential difference in that Emma Bovary, that primary object of desire, has now utterly lost her desirability. Once she stood on that threshold smiling at Charles while the shifting light played on her cheeks, but now she is an abject creature in pain, undergoing a slow yet relentless process of physical disfiguration.

But if Emma is subject to disfiguration, Flaubert's sentences are not. They are as exquisitely shaped as ever. They press ahead, mercilessly and forcefully, intent on one thing only, to capture how death goes to work on Emma as the poison spreads through her body. Emma may sweat and groan, but the discourse does not. On the contrary, it thrives on the discrepancy between Emma's torment and the detached way in which her suffering is recorded. The hideous details are rendered with clinical precision, and the episode speaks with the authority of medical discourse. The medical gaze, one might say, has replaced the gaze of desire.

The deathbed episode culminates in the representation of Emma's mortal remains. It appears when Charles, returning to Emma's room a few hours after her passing away, opens the curtains around the bed to look at his deceased wife. Homais, the pharmacist, and Bournisien, the priest, are keeping vigil over the corpse. Focalized through Charles, the description begins at Emma's head and zigzags its way down to her toes, thus seeking to reproduce how Charles's gaze travels over her body. The passage dwells on what can be seen, and that alone; and this is what meets Charles's eye:

Emma avait la tête penchée sur l'épaule droite. Le coin de sa bouche, qui se tenait ouverte, faisait comme un trou noir au bas de son visage, les deux pouces restaient infléchis dans la paume des mains; une sorte de poussière blanche lui parsemait les cils, et ses yeux commençaient à disparaître dans une pâleur visqueuse qui ressemblait à une toile mince, comme si des araignées avaient filé dessus. Le drap se creusait depuis ses seins jusqu'à ses genoux, se relevant ensuite à la pointe des orteils; et il semblait à Charles que des masses infinies, qu'un poids énorme pesait sur elle. (477)

Emma had her head resting on her right shoulder. The corner of her mouth, set open, looked rather like a black hole in the lower part of her face; her thumbs were curved across the palms of her hands; a sort of white powder besprinkled her eyelashes; and her eyes were beginning to blur under a pale film of mucus that was like a soft web, just as if spiders had been at work upon them. The sheet curved across smoothly from her breasts to her knees, making another peak at the tips of her toes; and to Charles it seemed as if an infinite mass, en enormous weight, lay pressing upon her. (270)

This scene is remarkable for its rigorously dry tone: it is as though death, now that it has done its job, has absorbed Emma's characteristic features. An alien force has descended on her and ruthlessly carried out its depersonalizing task.

In the meantime, Flaubert's discourse, too, has been evacuated. For what style can reproduce what death has left behind? Only a notational logic. There is no irony here. Not even the subtle simile—the metaphorical spiders—manages to break out of the facticity of the description and its happy empiricism: the spiders invite thoughts of dusty corners and mildewed objects, thus adding to the macabre atmosphere enveloping the spectacle of the dead body, but they do not introduce a secondary level of signification. Emma has moved out; spiders move in—that's all.

What we see is what we get, and what we see is dead organic matter, nothing more, nothing less. Remove that final clause—"et il semblait à Charles que des masses infinies, qu'un poids énorme pesait sur elle"—and it becomes apparent that the sight of Emma's corpse could belong to anyone. Nothing connects it to Charles in particular; anyone could have authored it. We might put this a little differently and say that Charles serves as the formal pretext for this final peek at Emma in her entire being. Just as Charles opens the bed curtains, so Flaubert opens a description that quickly turns into an autonomous image, sealing itself off from the narrative flow in which it is embedded.[60]

This is the last whole-length portrait of Emma. All preceding descriptions of Emma as she lies dying come together in this final pictorial rep-

---

[60] The visual autonomy of the paragraph is clearly marked in the final version of Flaubert's manuscript; see "*Madame Bovary*," Flaubert Papers, Institut des textes et des manuscrits modernes (CNRS-ENS), Paris, Mme B g 221, 467–8.

resentation. Emma is gone, and her image sets, congeals, freezes. All is quiet, and we hear, retroactively, the echo of her sighing, groaning, and screaming. And we also see, retrospectively, how she once used to look. We recall that delightful moment in the spring when she was standing beneath the parasol and the sunrays were playing on her face, or when she was relaxing in that armchair and it seemed as though a golden halo surrounded her head, or when she was traveling in that boat with Léon late at night and the moon illuminated her appearance as she emerged from under those willow branches, or when she was walking down the street with Rodolphe and he perceived how her profile emerged out of her bonnet and how the veins were beating under her skin, as though carrying a promise of things to come.

What could be further removed from the sight that awaits Charles as he approaches the deathbed? All these desire-laden scenes stand out in grotesque contrast against the representation of Emma's corpse.

Yet there is no categorical difference. Whether Emma is dead or alive, Flaubert's visual representations of her appearance are informed by the same logic. Ante mortem versus post mortem: semiotically things are very different, but syntactically they are not. It is true that the deathbed episode comes with a new lexicon, one that revolves around disease and disfiguration. As we have seen, the description of Emma is cast in the sobering language of death, and her features have changed beyond recognition: with that gaping black hole in her face, that film of mucus over her eyes, that dark liquid leaking out of her mouth, she is a monument to the uncanny.

To be sure, the narrator never once says that the sight of Emma is disgusting, appalling, or nauseating, but Flaubert's lexical choices, and their associational fields, force the reader in the direction of such a semantic register. And this inbuilt interpretive framework is brought to the surface when the narrator drops a metaphor—a *comparatio*—to make visible what Emma looks like when, seconds before the end, she suddenly hears the voice of the blind beggar and his sinister song.

> Emma se releva comme un cadavre que l'on galvanise, les cheveux dénoués, la prunelle fixe, béante. (472)
>
> Emma roused herself, like a cadaver being galvanized, her hair unfastened, her eyes fixed wide open. (266)

Semantically speaking, the portrait of Emma that comes before us in these final pages is an elaborate study in horror, all the more so because the narrator stubbornly sticks to the visible evidence.

Syntactically, however, little has changed. Dead Emma is very much like Emma alive.[61] But if there is a kinship, even a likeness, between the one and the other, what then does death mean? It means that the gaze of desire has withdrawn and that there is nothing to animate the image of Emma. Gone is the wind that used to play with her hair curls and apron strings, gone is the sunlight that used to flicker over her face, gone is the stone floor that made the lining of her silk dress rustle deliciously.

Take away desire, and Emma becomes what she always was: a *nature morte*, a still life, an inanimate object, a two-dimensional image. Every time she used to enter the libidinally charged field of vision, the narrative flow came to a standstill and her appearance was caught as though in a freeze-frame; yet there was always a peripheral detail that moved and thus animated the still life, typically a body part, a piece of clothing, or a part object; or else the image of Emma was set in motion by a light source—the sun, the moon, the fire. Now that she is dead, the way in which her visual appearance is represented follows more or less the same syntactical pattern as when she was alive. Emma is de-subjectified, de-personalized, de-humanized. In short, she is subject to de-anthropomorphization. What sets dead Emma apart is that the syntactic tendency is irreversible. She has been turned into an object once and for all, forever denied the possibility of taking a predicate. This is what death means and, as we have seen, it makes little difference in the end.

Two Scenes of Writing

Now that Emma is dead, desire too is gone. And when desire is gone, the force field of the aesthetic necessarily dissolves into nothing. The stage has thus been set for the grand finale, the social triumph of Homais.

So far I have been dwelling on a particular aspect of Flaubert's novel, a complex of problems that revolves around the visible, especially the image. I have sought to demonstrate just how strongly the will to make things visible makes itself felt in *Madame Bovary*. In focusing on the visual representation of Emma, I have discussed the Flaubertian image both on the level of content and on that of form. It is true that the domain

---

[61] That there is no essential difference between the image of dead Emma and that of the living version may perhaps seem like an outrageous proposal. But consider two phrases, both being part of detailed visual representations of Emma's appearance, both serving to open the description in question. The first refers to dead Emma; the second, to living Emma: "Emma avait la tête penchée sur l'épaule […]"; "Elle inclinait la tête sur l'épaule […]." Syntactically speaking, no qualitative difference is to be had. In both cases, she is the subject of an—inessential—action: leaning her head to one side, that's all.

of the image also encompasses other objects, especially landscape, but Emma is the most important content of the image form. Take away the desire-laden images of Flaubert's protagonist, and the plot would collapse. But the image of Emma is important for yet another reason: it is the prime vehicle of the artistic program that emerges implicitly in the pages of *Madame Bovary*. Emma is both the means and the end of the Flaubertian aesthetics of perception. The narrative stands or falls with its female protagonist.

But the analysis can also be turned around. To write a book about nothing, a novel in which style is everything—why not take Flaubert's odd ambition seriously? We might then be alerted to the possibility that Emma is the content that serves to motivate the form. Emma, indeed, is the pretext for the image—and for that new representational space designed by Flaubert. In the preceding pages, I have sought to show that the pictorial representations of Emma that run through the novel from beginning to end are remarkably alike. Carefully crafted and stylistically elaborate though they are, they display precious little variety. They are all of the same order. They read as a string of similar images, shaped by a syntactical and rhetorical pattern that remains very much the same—indeed, it even informs the image of dead Emma, the difference being that things no longer move.

I do not mean to say that these repetitions lessen Flaubert's artistic achievements, nor that Flaubert fails to produce a lifelike portrait of Emma when she emerges into the force-field of male desire and turns into spectacle. The point I wish to make, rather, is that the striking similarity of these images might alert us to the possibility that we have entered a different realm altogether: the realm of aesthetics. In other words, the image of Emma has little to do with the character known as Emma; it has all to do with that new space of representation engineered by Flaubert. The image of Emma is a text within the text, coherent, insistent, forming a pattern of its own. Emma is the motivation of the device. Or, to put it differently, Emma is not the content of her image, but rather its form.

I now want to move the focus of attention and discuss the question of writing. It is an issue that Flaubert's novel thematizes from beginning to end, in a number of different ways, and it pertains in significant ways to the art of making things visible.

Naomi Schor, in a shrewd analysis of *Madame Bovary*, has exposed a hidden thematics in Flaubert's 1857 novel by uncovering a constellation of structuring themes that concern the issue of writing. Read literally, *Madame Bovary* tells the tale of a voracious and ultimately deluded female consumer of romantic novels. In a commonly accepted view,

99

Flaubert's book is about reading: about what happens when one reads too much fiction, surrendering oneself to the work of the signifier, that is, to "nonsense," "idleness," and "poison," as Emma's mother-in-law would have it.

Read thematically, however, quite a different story emerges. *Madame Bovary* is not so much about reading as about writing. What is more, Flaubert's protagonist turns out to be anything but a foolish consumer of books. In fact, not only does Emma want to become a writer, she even becomes one. Examined more closely, Flaubert's novel brings into play two economies of writing, one female-coded, the other male-coded, and they coexist uneasily throughout the narrative. These two economies of writing are represented by Emma and Homais. Writing and sexual difference: in Schor's view, this is the pivotal hermeneutic matrix of *Madame Bovary*. To uncover such layers, one has to approach Flaubert's narrative by way of a critical hermeneutic partly inspired by structuralism, partly by thematic criticism. What will then become apparent is that Emma and Homais are structural opponents.

Indeed, if there is a central drama in the novel, it is not Emma versus Charles, nor Emma versus Rodolphe. The paradigmatic opposition is that between Emma and Homais; it is "half-expressed, half-concealed by their names, which should be read "Femm(a) vs. Hom(ais)"—*Femme* (woman) vs. *Homme* (man)."[62] Geoffrey Wall, Flaubert's translator and biographer, makes a similar point.[63]

Both Emma and Homais want to become writers; in fact, both want to publish and to make a name for themselves. In the case of Homais, this is abundantly clear. He announces time and again that he is the author of a seventy-two-page memorandum on the production of cider, *Du cidre, de sa fabrication et de ses effets,* as well as other works written for the benefit of the public good, among them, a pharmaceutical thesis.

Homais is also a local journalist of sorts. He has taken upon himself to report on events of social interest taking place in Yonville and its vicinity, and contributes articles to *Le Fanal de Rouen*. Towards the end of the novel, Homais has been so successful in his journalistic endeavors that he dreams of becoming an author proper, with a work to his name.

---

[62] Naomi Schor, "For a Restricted Thematic: Writing, Speech, and Difference in *Madame Bovary*," in *Breaking the Chain: Women, Theory, and French Realist Fiction* (New York: Columbia University Press, 1985), 3–28.

[63] See Geoffrey Wall, introduction to *Madame Bovary,* (London: Penguin, 1992), xvii–xviii: "Emma and Homais—in French the two names suggest *femme* and *homme*—woman and man. Homais is the gross comic ballast to Emma's yearning but not-quite-tragic sublimities. Homais and Emma, masculine and feminine, they stand for the contrary energies that Flaubert himself awkwardly encompassed."

> Cependant, il étouffait dans les limites étroites du journalisme, et bientôt il lui fallut le livre, l'ouvrage! (495)

> Yet he felt stifled within the narrow limits of journalism, and soon he was yearning for a book, for authorship! (282)

Emma, too, wants to become an author, with a work to her name. Early in the novel, when she has begun to suffer under the weight of provincial boredom, she waits for something to happen. In the meantime, she reads, daydreams, takes the odd walk. She also decides to acquire writing instruments:

> Elle s'était acheté un buvard, une papeterie, un porte-plume et des enveloppes, quoiqu'elle n'eût personne à qui écrire [...]. (131)

> She had bought herself a blotting-pad, a writing-case, a pen-holder and envelopes, though she had nobody to write to [...]. (47)

Bored by her sluggish marital life, Emma dreams of taking a lover, as she wants to become the heroine of a romance novel. Yet, Schor argues, there is another and more important reason why Emma wants a lover, which is that she wants to write and therefore needs someone to write to. What Emma lacks is not so much a lover as a receiver, an addressee, a reader. But there is more to Emma's half-expressed, half-concealed dreams. Not only does she want to author a romantic novel, she also desires literary prestige, including all the material signs that typically come with success.

> Elle aurait voulu que ce nom de Bovary, qui était le sien, fût illustre, le voir étalé chez les librairies, répété dans les journaux, connu par toute la France. (133)

> She would have liked this name of Bovary, the name that was hers, to be famous, to see it displayed in the book-shops, quoted in the newspapers, known all over France. (48)

On one page, we read that Emma acquires writing instruments; on the following, we read that Emma wants her surname to gain national glory. Schor suggests that these two enunciations, seemingly inconspicuous in their respective contexts, must be read together, as part of one and the same underlying phantasmatic structure. On the literal level, Emma speaks of her husband, the good country doctor, and of the fame she foolishly desires on his behalf, that sorry figure who has not even cared to cut his copy of the *Dictionnaire des sciences médicales.* This wish-fulfillment phantasy, however, is a thinly disguised displacement of a more fundamental one. For on the thematic level, the narrative entity known as "Emma" articulates a far more deep-seated and heretical fantasy, one that can surface only in a fragmentary, incoherent, and essentially distorted form.

Who is speaking here? Who, or what, is expressing the desire to become a famous writer? Emma, of course, provided that we see her as a personification, but speaking here is in some sense also Flaubert himself, Schor suggests. In her view, the novel is inscribed in a familiar genre, one that is perhaps best known under the Joycean rubric, "Portrait of the Artist as a Young Man." The vital difference is that Flaubert's bold appropriation of the genre portrays not the young man but the young *woman.* "Madame Bovary—c'est moi": Flaubert's peculiar statement should not only be taken seriously, Schor insists. It must be taken literally.

When Emma seeks consolation in the company of Rodolphe, everything falls into place. She begins her apprenticeship in the art of writing. She does not publish, that is true, but she writes profusely on a daily basis. She writes letters: lengthy, eloquent, and poetic love epistles. Emma's secret work of art is thus an epistolary novel—this is the only generic model available to her, brought up as she is on eighteenth-century literature. This is why Emma needs a lover. She now becomes what she always wanted to be: the heroine of a romantic work of fiction.

Emma's epistolary novel has a natural sequel in lover number two, Léon. Even when her passion for the lawyer begins to cool, she continues to write. Her epistolary writings take on a life of their own, now liberating themselves fully from the reality—that is, the lover—to which they were always attached. They may be addressed to Léon, but the pragmatics of Emma's writings now transcends such trivialities. Her letters conjure up imaginary worlds that are as compelling and evocative as any successful literary representation, and Emma has finally become a writer proper. Writing for the sake of writing, producing for the sake of producing, Emma Bovary has happened upon the pleasure of the text:

> Elle n'en continuait pas moins à lui écrire des lettres amoureuses, en vertu de cette idée, qu'une femme doit toujours écrire à son amant.
> Mais, en écrivant, elle apercevait un autre homme, un fantôme fait de ses plus ardent souvenirs, de ses lectures les plus belles, de ses convoitises les plus fortes; et il devenait à la fin si véritable, et accessible, qu'elle en palpitait émerveillée, sans pouvoir néanmoins le nettement imaginer, tant il se perdait, comme un dieu, sous l'abondance de ses attributs. Il habitait la contrée bleuâtre où les échelles de soie se balancent à des balcons, sous

le souffle des fleurs, dans la clarté de la lune. Elle le sentait près d'elle, il allait venir et l'enlèverait tout entière dans un baiser. (429)

None the less she continued to write love-letters to him, by virtue of the following notion: a woman should always write to her lover.
But, as she was writing, she beheld a different man, a phantom put together from her most ardent memories, her favourite books, her most powerful longings; and by the end he became so real, so tangible, that her heart was racing with the wonder of it, though she was unable to imagine him distinctly, for he faded, like a god, into the abundance of his attributes. He lived in the big blue country where silken rope-ladders swing from the balconies, scented by flowers and lit by the moon. She felt him so near, he was coming and he was about to carry her away quite utterly with a kiss. (236-7)

This helps explain why Emma's structural opponent is Homais. If Emma writes for pleasure, Homais is an emphatically goal-oriented writer. If Emma's texts aim at producing reality effects, those of Homais aim at changing the real itself. The construction of the plot comes as a confirmation of this basic tension of the novel. Emma, after all, is survived not by Charles but by Homais. Indeed, if Emma's life ends in disaster, that of Homais is a parable of social triumph; and Flaubert's tale ends only when Homais's social ascension has been detailed and brought to conclusion, culminating with the Legion of Honor.[64] What we have in this rivalry between Emma and Homais is a competition between two gendered economies of writing.

But if authorship is what Emma really wants, why does the text not say so? Why does her desire to become a writer remain a wishful substratum? Why can it be glimpsed only in the interstices of narrative? And why is her craving for literary fame displaced onto Charles, her superbly sluggish husband? This repression, Schor argues, "results from Emma's sex."[65] For what Emma ultimately envies in a man is what she can never have: a phallus, that is, access to the symbolic order. Schor points out that Emma's apprenticeship in the art of writing runs parallel to her repeated attempts at changing her sex and therefore her destiny.

In Freudian language, Emma seeks to reverse "castration." Baudelaire was the first critic to note that the portrait of Emma is remarkable for its androgyny. In fact, Emma is not only represented as a "masculin-

---

[64] That Emma and Homais are indeed the main characters of the novel, their fates as intertwined as those of Don Quixote and Sancho Panza, was underscored by Albert Thibaudet as early as in 1922: "S'il y a deux figures centrales dans *Madame Bovary,* comme dans *Don Quichotte,* Emma et Homais, le roman est à deux versants: la défaite d'Emma, l'épanouissement et le triomphe d'Homais" (*Gustave Flaubert,* 116).
[65] Schor, "For a Restricted Thematic," 17.

ist" woman ("she had, like a man, tucked into the front of her bodice, a tortoiseshell lorgnon"), but anyone who reads Flaubert's novel closely will discover that her impatience with all the constraints that typically come with the female sex is thematized on numerous occasions, all the way from her wish to have a male child to her attack on Rodolphe when he refuses to help her in a time of desperate need. This, Schor suggests, is the subversive desire that must be repressed: Emma's scandalous desire to enter the symbolic order.

In Schor's analysis, Emma thus practices a form of writing that is vigorously opposed to that of Homais. Yet this is only part of the picture, for what Schor also argues is that Emma's relationship to writing comes very close to Flaubert's. *Madame Bovary—c'est moi.*[66] This means that there is a significant divide *within* the economy of writing on which the novel builds.[67] To grasp the precise nature of this divide, and to understand its rich implications for the aesthetic it helps to shape, we need to take a closer look at Homais.

The Indestructible Scribbler

The Homais episodes are singularly rewarding for the analysis of a central preoccupation in Flaubert—the question of writing. In addition to being a successful pharmacist, a true pillar of society, and an upwardly mobile bourgeois of a particularly shameless kind, Homais is a man of words.[68] He is a linguistic machine, by turns learned and colloquial, now showing off Latin, now English, now slang. He thrives on the proliferation of discourse. He is a dexterous rhetorician, an unstoppable talker, an indestructible scribbler. He is a walking encyclopedia of readymade

---

[66] On Flaubert's identification with Emma, both in the process of writing *Madame Bovary* and as manifest in the novel itself, see Charles Bernheimer, "The Psychogenesis of Flaubert's Style," in *Emma Bovary,* ed. Harold Bloom, 81–90. See also Dacia Maraini, *Searching for Emma: Gustave Flaubert and 'Madame Bovary,'* trans. Vincent J. Bertolini (Chicago: University of Chicago Press, 1998).

[67] Schor, preface to *Breaking the Chain,* xii.

[68] On Homais as a site of discourse, see Philippe Dufour, *Flaubert et le pignouf. Essai sur la représentation romanesque du langage* (Saint-Denis: Presses Universitaires de Vincennes, 1993), "Le langage d'épicier d'un apothicaire," 15–63. In Dufour's view, Homais is above all a man of the spoken word; and he devotes particular attention to the character's rhetorical modes and linguistic registers. He remarks, for example, that Homais's language is a second degree language, entirely made up by quotations. In the following pages, however, I want to show that there are excellent reasons for taking seriously Homais's scriptural performances as well, especially his journalistic writings. As we shall see, Homais's newspaper pieces occupy a highly strategic and, therefore, significant place within the textual economy of the novel itself.

phrases and an inexhaustible fund of clichés. He has the right phrase for every occasion and, in his universe, less can never be more. Homais, in short, is everything that Flaubert is not.

Every time Homais appears on the narrative scene, there is an element of voluptuous sadism in the narrator's irony. Any reader will notice that the narrator takes pleasure in ridiculing this ambitious little man of letters. Yet we should not let the irony deceive us, no matter how malicious and biting it may be. We are now at the core of Flaubert's novel to the extent that it is at all possible to speak of a core in such a decentered and self-undermining narrative construct as *Madame Bovary*. The Homais episodes form a highly charged cluster of themes that revolve around the question of writing: text, style, rhetoric, print, media, representation, discourse, publishing, public culture, the relation between world and language, the relation between private and public, and so on. This is especially true when it comes to Homais's journalistic activities. For Flaubert's narrator is not content merely to tell us about Homais's contributions to the local paper, *Le Fanal de Rouen*. He even proceeds to quote Homais's texts at length.

Homais is cited on three separate occasions, first, when he covers the agricultural show, a lengthy report full of rhetorical artifice; second, when Homais, in equally stylized phrases, celebrates Charles Bovary's clubfoot surgery; and third, when Homais persecutes the blind beggar in a series of notices written in the *pluralis majestatis*. These texts are reproduced in whole or in part. The only exception is Emma's death. Homais does write a short notice about her passing away for *Le Fanal de Rouen,* but the piece itself is not quoted—all we are informed is that Homais is at pains to explain the cause of her death, as it must not be publically known that Emma killed herself using arsenic that she was able somehow to obtain from Homais's own pharmacy.[69]

If we look more closely at Homais's contributions to *Le Fanal,* we see that these texts deal with those very public events, those *actualités,* which also happen to be key episodes in the novel itself: the agricultural show, the surgical operation, the expulsion of the village ostler.

---

[69] "Il avait à écrire deux lettres, à faire une potion calmante pour Bovary, à trouver un mensonge qui pût cacher l'empoisonnement et à le rédiger en article pour le *Fanal*, sans compter les personnes qui l'attendaient, afin d'avoir des informations; et, quand les Yonvillais eurent tous entendu son histoire d'arsenic qu'elle avait pris pour du sucre, en faisant une crème à la vanille, Homais, encore une fois, retourna chez Bovary" (473). "He had two letters to write, a sedative to make up for Bovary, a story to concoct so as to explain the poisoning and an article to put together for *Le Fanal*, not to mention the people waiting to ask him questions; and, once the whole village had heard his account of how she had mistaken arsenic for sugar when she was making a vanilla custard, Homais, yet again, went back to see Bovary" (267).

This means, too, that one and the same event in the life of the Yonville community is rendered twice, first in Flaubert's version, then in that of Homais. We might put this a little differently and say that the novel, in citing Homais's journalistic texts, in effect reiterates events that have been narrated already. But why does the novel quote itself? Why this repetition, this duplication?

Interestingly enough, the narrator is not bothered with Homais's scientific writings, if I may call them that. The pharmaceutical thesis, the memorandum on cider, and the statistical treatise are brought up many times, not least by Homais himself, but they are never cited. Homais the writer is Homais the journalist. This circumstance is a significant one, and it deserves closer scrutiny. And as we shall see in a moment, Homais's stories in *Le Fanal* are excessive verbal performances that contain all one might expect in the way of stylistic commonplaces and rhetorical ornamentation.

In short, Flaubert pits his own narrative discourse against that of Homais. One may, of course, approach such a juxtaposition of discourses—the novelistic and the journalistic—as yet another feature of the proliferation of linguistic codes that Flaubert's novel both reflects and reproduces.[70] Anna Ahlström, in an early, lexicological inquiry into Flaubert's style, shows just how immersed his writings are in local dialect, foreign languages, neologisms, and so on.[71]

But there is more to the Homais episodes. It is not simply a question of linguistic variety. As I have intimated already, Homais is a singular

---

[70] No other French novel displays as much linguistic variety as does *Madame Bovary*, Albert Thibaudet remarked in 1922. It contains "la langue parlé" as well as "la langue écrite," and takes both to extremes. What is more, each character speaks in his or her own style. In fact, Homais has two registers: "Homais a deux styles, aussi admirablement individualisés l'un que l'autre: son style parlé, et son style écrit du *Fanal*, un style écrit dont le ridicule consiste précisément à ne rien conserver de la parole" (*Gustave Flaubert*, 276).

[71] See Anna Ahlström, *Etude sur la langue de Flaubert* (Mâcon: Protat Frères, 1899). Ahlström deserves more than a citation: not only was she the first woman to receive a doctoral degree in Romance languages at a Swedish university; she also wrote one of the first book-length studies of Flaubert's entire oeuvre. As Gilles Philippe notes, Ahlström's study ("although brief, authored by a foreigner, and of mediocre quality") was in fact reviewed on the front page of *Le Temps*, the largest daily newspaper in France; see Philippe, *Sujet, verbe, complément*, 49. For a Bourdieu-inspired sociological account of Ahlström's professional career (in Swedish), see Annika Ullman, *Stiftarinnegenerationen. Sofi Almquist, Anna Sandström, Anna Ahlström* (Stockholm: Stockholmia, 2004), esp. 55–61, 76–88. See also Sigbrit Swahn, "Omkring Anna Ahlströms avhandling om Flaubert 1899," in *Anna Ahlström. Vår första kvinnliga doktor i romanska språk år 1899,* ed. Kerstin Jonasson and Gunilla Ransbo (Uppsala: Acta Universitatis Upsaliensis, 2000), 41–5; and Kerstin Jonasson, "Anna Ahlström som språkvetare och romanist," in *Anna Ahlström,* 47–53.

figure in *Madame Bovary* in that he represents the printed word. In his capacity as pharmacist turned amateur journalist, he chronicles life in Yonville, that is to say, he emplots events of general interest and reproduces them in that nineteenth-century mass medium par excellence, the newspaper. Homais is more than a mere man of letters; he is also a narrator. All of which brings me to the heart of the matter: Homais the journalist is Flaubert's double even as he is also structurally opposed to Flaubert. Homais is the not-Flaubert, the un-Flaubert, even the anti-Flaubert. This, then, is the Homais whom Flaubert proceeds to expose by means of citation.

Homais's discourse enters Flaubert's text in two major ways: by way of quotation marks and by way of italicization. Italics are a typographic detail that plays a crucial role in the pages of *Madame Bovary.* In fact, Homais is the most italicized character in the narrative. Why does Flaubert italicize? Traditionally speaking, italicization is chiefly used to indicate emphasis or to set off a foreign word. It separates the weighty from the non-weighty, translating into the medium of the printed word a feature that comes naturally with oral delivery. Not so in Flaubert. He mobilizes the slanted letter not as a means of emphasis but as a vehicle of alienation: it is a graphic gesture that signals distance, difference, deviation. It is anything but a question of prosodic stress, for the simple reason that Flaubert's project revolves not around voice but around discourse.

In *Madame Bovary,* italicization creates a textual space reserved for alien speech. This is a kind of speech that belongs to all and therefore to nobody in particular. It is a genuinely collective linguistic phenomenon and therefore an anonymous one, circulating everywhere and irrupting always into any level of social life, including the private sphere. It precedes the individual speaker whose speech it inflects, refracts, and modulates.

The Flaubertian italic, of course, has an emphatic function in that it serves to call attention to a subtle change of gear, but above all its function is a semiotic one. When letters begin to slant to the right, we know that we have entered the endless empire of the stereotype. Italicization, in Flaubert, is therefore no mere typographic device. It always conveys meaning. It frames the signifier, installing a hermeneutic horizon that structures the reader's processing of the text. Tones overlay each other, creating a fundamental dissonance that resounds through the entire narrative. It is as though the narrator were a ventriloquist.

Encoded early on in the novel, italicization appears in the very first sentence ("Nous étions à l'Étude, quand le Proviseur entra, suivi d'un *nouveau* habillé en bourgeois…"). Within a few pages, italicization has been encoded so successfully that it acquires a semiotic function and begins to produce significance, serving in particular as an ironic means of expression. The italic typeface says: you are now in the stifling realm of jargon and sociolects and doxa, of formulaic expressions and received ideas, of sclerotic idioms and fashionable phrases, all imposed by petit bourgeois culture. It also says: unfortunately, there is no exit.

Flaubert uses italicization where others might have used quotation marks—in this sense, he has an heir in the Austrian writer Thomas Bernhard, in whose writings italicization also serves as a crushingly effective means of irony.[72] Perhaps Flaubert, in dispensing with quotation marks in favor of the italic, had already understood what Adorno was to point out in an essay on punctuation, "Satzzeichen" (1956), that quotation marks should not be used as an ironic device.

> Anführungszeichen soll man nur dort verwenden, wo man etwas anführt, beim Zitat, allenfalls wo der Text von einem Wort, auf das er sich bezieht, sich distanzieren will. Als Mittel der Ironie sind sie zu verschmähen. Denn sie dispensieren den Schriftsteller von jenem Geist, dessen Anspruch der Ironie unabdingbar innewohnt, und freveln an deren eigenem Begriff, indem sie von der Sache trennen und das Urteil über diese als vorentschieden hinstellen.[73]

> Quotation marks should be used only when something is quoted and if need be when the text wants to distance itself from a word it is referring to. They are to be rejected as ironic device. For they exempt the writer from the spirit whose claim is inherent in irony, and they violate the very concept of irony by separating it from the matter at hand and presenting a predetermined judgment on the subject.[74]

To use quotation marks is to suggest a difference in kind. Here is the one, there is the other, and they are not to be confused. To move from the roman to the italic, however, is to suggest a difference in degree—the proximity between the one and the other explains why the slanted letter is uncanny.

The question thus becomes, what is the "matter at hand" (*die Sache*) in Flaubert, as Adorno puts it? In some ways, it is inconsistent to speak of "alien speech" in *Madame Bovary,* because in Flaubert all speech

---

[72] See, for example, Thomas Bernhard, *Auslöschung. Ein Zerfall* (Frankfurt am Main: Suhrkamp, 1986).
[73] Theodor W. Adorno, "Satzzeichen," in *Noten zur Literatur,* ed. Rolf Tiedemann (Frankfurt am Main: Suhrkamp, 1981), 109–10.
[74] Adorno, "Punctuation Marks," in *Notes to Literature,* trans. Shierry Weber Nicholsen (New York: Columbia University Press, 1991), 1:94.

is in the final analysis alien speech.[75] It can be exposed, orchestrated, distanced, squeezed, mocked, debunked, and thoroughly ridiculed—the effects are often hilarious, even devastating—but it cannot be subverted. Why? Because in Flaubert there is no locus from which such a critique can ever be launched. And this, in the end, is precisely why Flaubert needs to italicize.

Claude Duchet, in an article on italicized discourse in *Madame Bovary*, proposes that the totality of italics in the novel be considered as a text within the text, as a systematic network or even as a textual isotope.[76] Italicization is the great equalizer in the novel, Duchet suggests, hence also the great banalizer. For as soon as the italic has been encoded as a semiotic marker, as that which identifies a given utterance as originating not in the speaker but in that vast, powerful, all-encompassing discursive system called dominant ideology, then virtually any word or phrase, no matter how insignificant, may undergo modulation and acquire unexpected shades of meaning. The italicized linguistic unit thus talks in two registers all at once: speech and alien speech. In this way, Flaubert puts into play what Duchet calls a perversion of meaning, as when he first pens a perfectly innocent phrase—"Le jeune homme avait beaucoup de mémoire"—and then, in going through the proofs, proceeds to underline *jeune homme*.[77] Because of this simple typographic mechanism, we hear how the voice of that nameless other resounds eerily through the trivial sentence, altering it from within.

I have discussed the use of italics in Flaubert, and I have sought to show that the Flaubertian italic, by its sheer presence, keeps alive a prom-

---

[75] For a discussion of the citational structure in Flaubert, see Christopher Prendergast, "Flaubert: The Stupidity of Mimesis," in *The Order of Mimesis: Balzac, Stendhal, Nerval, Flaubert* (Cambridge: Cambridge University Press, 1986), 180–211. At the heart of Flaubertian mimesis, Prendergast suggests, is not so much representation as rather repetition and imitation. Flaubert's version of realist mimesis thus turns around the copy. To the extent that Flaubertian mimesis seeks to reproduce, it does so by way of citation. Flaubert's realism originates, Prendergast argues, not in the real but in the copy.

[76] Claude Duchet, "Signifiance et in-signifiance. Le discours italique dans *Madame Bovary*," in *La production du sens chez Flaubert,* ed. Claudine Gothot-Mersch (Paris: UGE, 1975), 358–78: "Il semble donc légitime de considérer ensemble les italiques de *Madame Bovary* comme un texte dans le texte, comme un réseau qui fait système ou encore comme une isotopie du texte" (366). Duchet goes so far as to argue that all italicized linguistic units in *Madame Bovary*—snippets of speech as well as book titles, names of establishments as well as Latin phrases—help create a vast textual space of collective linguistic practice, the manifestations of which are mediated by dominant bourgeois ideology. In mobilizing the italic, Flaubert is thus able to expose the textualization of social meaning as well as the reverse: the social text itself. On Flaubert's use of italics, see also Henry H. Weinberg, "The Function of Italics in *Madame Bovary*," *Nineteenth-Century French Studies 3,* no. 1–2 (fall-winter 1974–1975): 97–111.

[77] Duchet, "Signifiance," 374.

ise that can never be fulfilled: the promise of authentic, non-estranged, non-contaminated speech.[78] I have also stressed that Homais is the most thoroughly italicized character in the novel. Indeed, Flaubert's italic discourse tends powerfully toward Homais, just as it also flows incessantly from the pharmacist.

With Homais's journalistic texts, however, things are very different. To be sure, they are the epitome of alien speech, the culmination of clichéd language, the emblem of current perceptions. But they are not part of the italicized discourse that comes before us in the novel. Flaubert encloses Homais's journalistic texts within quotation marks. They form a textual entity of their own. Indeed, when it comes to Homais's written discourse, Flaubert emphatically marks a difference in kind. This is the one, this is the other, and they are not to be confused.

The most prominent of Homais's journalistic pieces is the account of the agricultural show, to which he brings an unmistakable pathos. It is the kind of pathos that comes with the willful attempt at writing in the high style. He covers a special event in the life of Yonville—an occasion that elevates itself over the humdrum reality of everyday life—and it is as though it needs to be matched by an equally elevated style. Here is Homais and his representation of the village festivities, right at the end of the celebrated agricultural show episode. Note how carefully embedded Homais's text is within the narrative discourse. In quoting Homais, Flaubert's narrator cannot refrain from intervening into the article, now summarizing, now paraphrasing, now anticipating, even interspersing the odd commentary on its stylistic characteristics ("dithyrambic"):

> Deux jours après, dans le *Fanal de Rouen,* il y avait un grand article sur les comices. Homais l'avait composé, de verve, dès le lendemain:
> "Pourquoi ces festons, ces fleurs, ces guirlandes? Où courait cette foule, comme les flots d'une mer en furie, sous les torrents d'un soleil tropical qui répandait sa chaleur sur nos guérets?"
> Ensuite, il parlait de la condition des paysans. Certes, le gouvernement faisait beaucoup, mais pas assez!
> "Du courage! lui criait-il; mille réformes sont indispensables, accomplissons-les." Puis, abordant l'entrée du Conseiller, il n'oubliait point "l'air martial de notre milice", ni "nos plus sémillantes villageoises", ni les vieillards à tête chauve, "sorte de patriarches qui étaient là, et dont quelques-uns, débris de nos immortelles phalanges, sentaient encore bat-

---

[78] Although italicization is a highly significant typographic device in *Madame Bovary,* it is only sparingly used in Flaubert's subsequent writings. Claudine Gothot-Mersch has observed that from *Salammbô* onward, quotation marks gain in importance and serve a similar function as does the italic; in *L'éducation sentimentale,* finally, quotation marks have replaced the italic. See Gothot-Mersch, "La parole des personnages," in *Travail de Flaubert,* ed. Gérard Genette and Tzvetan Todorov (Paris: Seuil, 1983), esp. 212–5.

tre leurs coeurs au son mâle des tambours." […] Quand il arrivait à la distribution des récompenses, il dépeignait la joie des lauréats en traits dithyrambiques. "Le père embrassait son fils, le frère le frère, l'époux l'épouse. Plus d'un montrait avec orgueil son humble médaille, et sans doute, revenu chez lui, près de sa bonne ménagère, il l'aura suspendue en pleurant aux murs discrets de sa chaumine.

Vers six heures, un banquet, dressé dans l'herbage de M. Liégeard, a réuni les principaux assistants de la fête. La plus grande cordialité n'a cessé d'y régner. Divers toasts ont été portés: M. Lieuvain, au monarque! M. Tuvache, au préfet! M. Derozerays, à l'agriculture! M. Homais, à l'industrie et aux beaux-arts, ces deux soeurs! M. Leplichey, aux améliorations! Le soir, un brillant feu d'artifice a tout à coup illuminé les airs; on eût dit un véritable kaléidoscope, un vrai décor d'opéra, et un moment notre petite localité a pu se croire transportée au milieu d'un rêve des *Mille et une Nuits.*

Constatons qu'aucun événement fâcheux n'est venu troubler cette réunion de famille."

Et il ajoutait:

"On y a seulement remarqué l'absence du clergé. Sans doute les sacristies entendent le progrès d'une autre manière. Libre à vous, messieurs de Loyola!" (254–6)

Two days later, in *Le Fanal de Rouen,* there was a long article on the show. Homais had composed it, extempore, the very next morning.

"Whence these festoons, these flowers, these garlands? Whither hastens this crowd, like the surges of an angry sea, beneath a torrential tropical sun pouring forth its heat upon our furrows?"

Next, he mentioned the condition of the peasants. Certainly, the government was doing a great deal, but not enough! "Fear naught," he cried to it; "a thousand reforms are indispensable, let us bring them to pass." And dealing with the arrival of the councillor, he did not omit "the martial air of our militia," nor "our sprightliest maidens," nor "the old men with bald heads, latter-day patriarchs, some of whom, the remnants of our immortal phalanxes, felt their hearts beating once again to the manly sound of the drum." […] When he reached the prize-giving, he portrayed the joy of the winners in dithyrambic terms. "Fathers embracing their sons, brothers brothers, husbands their wives. Many a one showed his humble medal with pride, and no doubt, once home again, at his fair wife's side, will he hang it, weeping the while, upon the plain walls of his cottage.

About six o'clock, a banquet, served in Monsieur Liégard's meadow, assembled the principal persons at the show. The utmost cordiality reigned there throughout. Divers toasts were proposed: Monsieur Lieuvain, to the King: Monsieur Tuvache, to the Prefect: Monsieur Derozerays, to Agriculture! Monsieur Homais, to Industry and the Arts, those twin sisters! Monsieur Leplichey, to Progress! In the evening, brilliant fireworks suddenly illumined the skies. 'Twas a veritable kaleidoscope, a true scene from the opera, and, for a moment, our little locality could have fancied itself transported into the midst of a scene from the Thousand and One Nights.

>Let it be stated that no untoward incident occurred to disrupt this family occasion."
>
>And he added:
>
>"Only the clergy were remarked to be absent. No doubt the sacramentals have a different idea of progress. As you wish, apostles of Loyola!" (123–4)[79]

This is Flaubert at his comic best. The comedy is a savage one: it thrives on the clash between rhetoric and reality, between Homais's ornate stylistic performance and the dull-witted world he seeks energetically to transform. Flaubert holds up Homais's stylistic performance to ridicule. Pigs and peasants do not easily fit into the grand manner, he demonstrates, not to speak of *les petits bourgeois*. Unless, of course, you are Virgil and master the *stilus mediocris*—and Homais does not. For this comedy of discrepancy is above all of a linguistic kind, deriving from the undeterred fervor with which he approaches his journalistic task. In his zeal to celebrate the village and its inhabitants, as well as law and order, agriculture, progress, reason, and enlightenment, all at the same time, he manages to commit nearly every stylistic vice against which classical rhetoricians used to caution. Homais's style is thus characterized by excess not grandeur, rashness not strength, dullness not gravity, abandon not joy, pomposity not greatness.[80] What is perhaps even more remarkable is that he manages to cramp so many vices into such a small space.

Ultimately, however, the point is not that Homais's article is bad, or amateurish, or ostentatious, or opportunistic, nor that it is an exercise in empty verbal embellishment. Writing like Homais's has a comedy of its own, to be sure, but it would not be nearly as hilarious if it were not for the narrative environment in which it is embedded. Using Plato's terms, we might say that Homais is to Flaubert as *diegesis* to *mimesis*.

---

[79] Flaubert's English translator, Geoffrey Wall, has italicized the quotations from Homais's newspaper account, but for the sake of argument, I have restored the original quotation marks. I should add that in Flaubert's final version of the manuscript, Homais's article is enclosed within quotation marks. See "Madame Bovary," Flaubert Papers, Institut des textes et des manuscrits modernes (CNRS-ENS), Paris, Mme B. g 221, fol. 282.

[80] See Quintilian, *The Orator's Education*, trans. Donald A. Russell (Cambridge, Mass.: Harvard University Press, 2001), bk. 12, ch. 11, 80. Quintilian praises moderation and ease; the safest route is down the middle, he stresses. See also Umberto Eco, "A Portrait of the Artist as Bachelor," in *On Literature,* trans. Martin McLaughlin (London: Secker & Warburg, 2005), 96–7. Indeed, Homais's piece would have been a wonderfully instructive example in Quintilian, demonstrating that there can be too much of a good thing. Too many metaphors obscures language and wearies the audience, Quintilian warns (*Orator's Education,* bk. 8, ch. 6, 14).

The sheer presence of Homais's piece transforms Flaubert's description of the show into the raw material (mimesis) on which Homais's article then draws (diegesis). Flaubert's rendering of the show thus becomes the "reality" in relation to which Homais's article emerges as a "representation." Every time Flaubert quotes Homais, this is the effect produced.

At the same time, however, Homais's piece also serves to push Flaubert's account into the foreground, so that Flaubert's stylistic performance, too, slides into view. Indeed, Homais's piece produces a textual juxtaposition of the highest interest, and the contrasting effect works both ways. We are confronted with two different textual regimes, two different linguistic orders, two different modes of representing the real. As soon as Homais's text intervenes into that of Flaubert, the master text too stands out in bold relief. And this is the very discrepancy that produces the formidable comedy of these pages.

It is interesting to note that when Flaubert was working on the episode about the agricultural show, he appears to have begun with Homais's newspaper article and to have completed it rather quickly, only then proceeding to produce a draft of the show itself—this part of the episode, however, was all the more challenging and time-consuming. In fact, it took Flaubert several months of gruelling labor to complete the first draft of the scene. In a letter to Louise Colet, written on 15 July 1853, Flaubert gave a detailed account of the state of the manuscript. The finale of the episode—Homais's account of the agricultural show—was already finished. What remained to be written was the scene of the show itself.

> J'ai été fort en train cette semaine. J'ai écrit huit pages qui, je crois, sont toutes à peu près faites. Ce soir, je viens d'esquisser toute ma grande scène des Comices agricoles. Elle sera énorme; ça aura bien trente pages. Il faut que, dans le récit de cette fête rustico-municipale et parmi ses détails (où *tous* les personnages secondaires du livre paraissent, parlent et agissent), je poursuive, et au premier plan, le dialogue continu d'un monsieur *chauffant* une dame. J'ai de plus, au milieu, le discours solennel d'un conseiller de préfecture, et à la fin (tout terminé) un article de journal fait par mon pharmacien, qui rend compte de la fête en bon style philosophique, poétique et progressif. Tu vois que ce n'est pas une petite besogne. Je suis sûr de ma couleur et de bien des effets; mais pour que tout cela ne soit pas trop long, c'est le diable![81]

> I have been in excellent form this week. I have written eight pages, all of which I think can stand pretty much as they are. Tonight I have just sketched my entire big scene of the Agricultural Show. It will be enormous—thirty pages at least. Against the background of this rustico-municipal celebration, with all its details (all my secondary characters

---
[81] Flaubert to Colet, 15 July 1853, *Correspondance*, 2:386.

will be shown talking and in action), there must be continuous dialogue between a gentleman and the lady he is "warming up". Moreover, somewhere in the middle I have a solemn speech by a councillor from the Prefecture, and at the end (this I have already done) a newspaper article written by my pharmacist, who gives an account of the celebration in fine philosophical, poetical, progressive style. You see it is no small chore. I am sure of my local colour and of many of my effects; but it's a devilish job to keep it from getting too long.[82]

Close to two months later, on 7 September 1853, Flaubert wrote to Colet that he was still hard at work on the agricultural show:

> Voilà depuis lundi cinq pages d'à peu près faites; *à peu près* est le mot, il faut s'y remettre. Comme c'est difficile! J'ai bien peur que mes *comices* ne soient trop longs. C'est un dur endroit. J'y ai *tous* mes personnages de mon livre en action et en dialogue, les uns mêlés aux autres, et par là-dessus un grand paysage qui les enveloppe. Mais, si je réussis, ce sera bien symphonique.[83]

Five days later, Flaubert informed Colet that his writing had come to a halt, a recurrent leitmotif in his voluminous correspondence. Flaubert had been toiling away at his sentences, doggedly trying to produce new ones, connecting them, disconnecting them, reconnecting them, changing the word order, rewriting, rewording, revising, then trying anew, again and again, but to no avail. He was so exhausted that all he could muster, in the breathless opening of the letter, was an anguished prose filled with exhortations, interjections, and exclamation marks:

> La tête me tourne d'embêtement, de découragement, de fatigue! J'ai passé quatre heures sans pouvoir faire *une* phrase. Je n'ai pas aujourd'hui écrit une ligne, ou plutôt j'en ai bien griffonné cent! Quel atroce travail! Quel ennui! Oh! l'Art! l'Art! Qu'est-ce donc que cette chimère enragée qui nous mord le coeur, et pourquoi? Cela est fou de se donner tant de mal! Ah! la *Bovary*, il m'en souviendra! J'éprouve maintenant comme si j'avais des lames de canif sous les ongles, et j'ai envie de grincer des dents. Est-ce bête! […] Ce à quoi je me heurte, c'est à des situations communes et un dialogue trivial. Bien écrire *le médiocre* et faire qu'il garde en même temps son aspect, sa coupe, ses mots même, cela est vraiment diabolique, et je vois se défiler maintenant devant moi de ces gentillesses en perspective pendant trente pages au moins. Ça s'achète cher, le style! Je recommence ce que j'ai fait l'autre semaine. Deux ou trois effets ont été jugés hier par Bouilhet ratés, et avec raison. Il faut que je redémolisse presque toutes mes phrases.[84]

---
[82] *Letters*, 265.
[83] Flaubert to Colet, 7 September 1853, 2:426.
[84] Flaubert to Colet, 12 September 1853, 2:428–9.

Nine days later, on 21 September, Flaubert was no less gloomy. He was still at work on the agricultural show, trying to perfect a passage in which a villager lights some Chinese lanterns.[85] Although he had rewritten the paragraph numerous times, it was still not done. He told Colet that he hoped to be midway through the agricultural show by the end of the following week.[86]

The next day, the tone was very different. Flaubert reported that he was pleased with his day-work and that things looked good indeed: "J'ai bien travaillé aujourd'hui. Dans une huitaine, je serai au milieu de mes Comices que je commence maintenant à comprendre. J'ai un fouillis de bêtes et de gens beuglant et bavardant, avec mes amoureux en dessus, qui sera bon, je crois."[87]

Such contentment never lasted very long. Two weeks later, on 7 October 1853, he wrote to Colet that it was all a never-ending task, excruciating, torturous, dull. "Mais je voudrais tant avoir fini ce roman! Ah! quels découragements quelquefois, quel rocher de Sisyphe à rouler que le style, et la prose surtout! *Ça n'est jamais fini.*"[88] Nevertheless, Flaubert had now reached the core of the scene—the dialogue between Emma and Rodolphe that serves as a prelude to the celebrated seduction scene in the woods.

Toward the end of October, after several more bouts of verbal impotence—"J'ai passé aujourd'hui toute la journée [...] sans pouvoir non seulement écrire *une* ligne, mais trouver une pensée, un mouvement! Vide, vide complet"—Flaubert figured that he would need six more weeks to finish the first draft of the episode.[89] Even so, he added, he would of course have to rewrite it all, as he considered the style to be somewhat fussy. "Ainsi, j'aurai été depuis le mois de juillet jusqu'à la fin de novembre à écrire *une scène*! [So it will have taken me from July to the end of November to write *one scene*!]"[90]

When those six weeks had passed, he had made progress. The agricultural show was finished.[91] He had even begun work on the love scene

---

[85] See also Gothot-Mersch, *La genèse,* 248–9.
[86] Flaubert to Colet, 21 September 1853, 2:434.
[87] Ibid., 2:437.
[88] Flaubert to Colet, 7 October 1853, 2:447.
[89] Flaubert to Colet, 17 October 1853, 2:452; Flaubert to Colet, 25 October, 2:457–8.
[90] Flaubert to Colet, 25 October 1853, 2:458.
[91] On 9 December 1853, Flaubert wrote: "Je suis très fatigué ce soir. (Voilà deux jours que je fais *du plan,* car enfin, Dieu merci, mes comices sont faits, ou du moins ils passeront pour tels, jusqu'à nouvelle révision.)" Flaubert to Colet, 9 December 1853, 2:476. It is also interesting to note that the following episode—the love scene in the woods, the *baisade,* as Flaubert used to call it in his letters to Colet and Bouilhet—was comparatively easy to write. At the end of December, Flaubert wrote to Colet that the scene was

in the woods, where Emma, swooning, surrenders to Rodolphe. In a letter to Louis Bouilhet, a close friend of his who had critiqued numerous drafts of the agricultural show and other episodes, Flaubert explained that he had decided to reread the second part of the book. He found the writing thin, he told Bouilhet, not just stylistically but also structurally.[92] Yet there was one exception, one piece of writing that found favor in Flaubert's eyes, however minimal, and that was Homais's newspaper article.

> J'ai relu, hier, toute la seconde partie. Cela m'a semblé *maigre*. Mais ça marche (?). Le pire de la chose est: que les préparatifs psychologiques, pittoresques, grotesques, etc., qui précèdent, étant fort longs, *exigent*, je crois, un développement d'action qui soit en rapport avec eux. Il ne faut pas que le Prologue emporte le Récit (quelque déguisé et fondu que soit le Récit), et j'aurai fort à faire, pour établir une proportion à peu près égale entre les Aventures et les Pensées. En délayant tout le dramatique je peux y arriver, à peu près? Mais il aura donc 75 mille pages, ce bougre de roman-là! Et quand finira-t-il?
>
> Je ne suis pas mécontent de mon article de Homais (indirect et avec citations). Il rehausse les comices, et les fait paraître plus courts, parce qu'il les résume.[93]

Within the chapter about the agricultural show, as Flaubert here explicitly states, Homais's article comes as a summary—a summary that makes the show seem both shorter and grander than it actually was. Where Flaubert needs some twenty pages to carry out his version, Homais needs less than two. This may seem obvious enough. Homais, after all, has authored a newspaper piece, not a chapter in a novel. Why should we even bother to compare these versions, aimed as they are for very different media contexts, each with its own reading rationale and rhetorical repertoire? Because the juxtaposition itself is an invitation to comparison. Flaubert has put down a flag. Look, he says, this is how things should be done, and this is how they should not be done. Put differently: Homais's article performs the function of an inbuilt instruction on how to approach Flaubert's text. It is a hint at how to read *Madame*

---

done: "Du reste, la *Bovary* avance. La baisade est faite" (Flaubert to Colet, 28 December 1853, 2:490).

[92] Work on the agricultural show was thus painfully slow. But as Gothot-Mersch has shown, there is nothing exceptional about this chapter. In fact, some episodes and passages required even more work (*La genèse,* 179). What I have sought to foreground here is the marked contrast between Flaubert's own account of the show and that of Homais; Flaubert put a lot of work into the former, whereas Homais's version of the show came easy—remarkably enough, Flaubert was even pleased with it.

[93] Flaubert to Bouilhet, 8 December 1853, 2:472–3.

Bovary precisely because it is a hint at how not to read it. It is a clue that reveals a great deal about Flaubert's literary method.

And this method turns above all around the art of making things visible. I shall confine my comments to the way in which Flaubert and Homais open their respective pieces. Both begin their accounts with exposition in the classical sense, both turning to the sensuous immediacy of the scene itself: the village of Yonville and its preparations for the show. Both, furthermore, seize on more or less the same things, on the decorations (the garlands) and how the village is quickly filled with people from the locality (the crowd). But where Flaubert, in elaborating an anatomy of the scene, amasses a wealth of concrete detail, Homais is emphatically selective.

Here is Flaubert:

> Ils arrivèrent, en effet, ces fameux Comices! Dès le matin de la solennité, tous les habitants, sur leurs portes, s'entretenaient des préparatifs; on avait enguirlandé de lierres le fronton de la mairie; une tente dans un pré était dressée pour le festin, et, au milieu de la Place, devant l'église, une espèce de bombarde devait signaler l'arrivée de M. le préfet et le nom des cultivateurs lauréats. [...]
>
> La foule arrivait dans la grande rue par les deux bouts du village. Il s'en dégorgeait des ruelles, des allées, des maisons, et l'on entendait de temps à autre retomber le marteau des portes, derrière les bourgeoises en gants de fil, qui sortaient pour aller voir la fête. (227–9)

> It had actually come, the day of the great show! From early on that solemn morning, all the inhabitants, at their doors, were discussing the preparations; garlands of ivy had been hung above the main door of the town hall; a tent, in a meadow, had been put up for the banquet, and, in the middle of the square, in front of the church, a kind of bombard was to mark the arrival of the Prefect and the naming of the prizewinners. [...]
>
> The crowd came into the main street from both ends of the village. They poured out of the lanes, out of the alley-ways, out of the houses, and from time to time there came the bang of a door-knocker falling, behind ladies in thread gloves, on their way out to see the festivities. (105–6)

In setting the stage for the agricultural show, Flaubert offers description pure and simple. The narrator's gaze sweeps over the village and its streets, as though from afar. There are no metaphors, only notations—the only exception is the word "dégorgeait" that turns the crowd into a liquid mass flooding the streets of Yonville. Apart from this solitary image, Flaubert's passage is cast in a literalist language, sticking to what can be heard and seen. This, then, is how Flaubert treats the morning scene.

Here is Homais's take on the same subject matter:

> Pourquoi ces festons, ces fleurs, ces guirlandes? Où courait cette foule, comme les flots d'une mer en furie, sous les torrents d'un soleil tropical qui répandait sa chaleur sur nos guérets?

> Whence these festoons, these flowers, these garlands? Whither hastens this crowd, like the surges of an angry sea, beneath a torrential tropical sun pouring forth its heat upon our furrows?

In a sense, Homais is merely doing what Flaubert does: applying beautiful language to a mediocre reality. "Write the mediocre well!" Flaubert urged. So what is the difference?

The real, in Homais, is a mere pretext for doing style—and, as the remainder of his piece makes clear, for propagating ideas. No sooner has the real been evoked—those flowers, those garlands, those visitors—than it is evacuated, emptied out by Homais's will to style. And style, for Homais, means eloquence, and eloquence means formulas. Within the space of two sentences, he mobilizes a veritable parade of time-honored rhetorical devices. He opens with two rhetorical questions, both serving to introduce the topic at hand. The first question is *asyndetic* in character, while the second builds on a *comparatio* between the people and the sea, a splendidly conventional metaphor that then finds company in an equally worn image—that of the furious sea, "la mer en furie." To top things off, Homais has elaborated an artfully constructed pattern of alliterations and assonances: *f*estons, *f*leurs, *f*oule, *f*lots, *f*urie; *p*ourquoi, *o*ù, *c*ourait, *s*ous, *f*oule; *c*omme, *t*orrents, *s*oleil, *tr*opical. It is hard to imagine an opening denser in rhetorical strategies.

Homais's account of the show is an exercise in ritualistic application of rhetoric, especially when it comes to metaphors and similar figurative language. It is surely no coincidence that he begins his piece by speaking of embellishment—part of the sublime parody is that those festoons, flowers, and garlands also have a metacritical function: they serve, on the formal level, as a pre-echo of the pharmacist's flowers of speech.

This is, of course, not to suggest that Flaubert does not make use of time-honored rhetorical devices too. On the contrary, Flaubert is a cunning rhetorician. But the difference should be obvious by now: in Flaubert, rhetoric is a means; in Homais, it is an end. Or put a little differently: for Flaubert, rhetoric is a question of form; for Homais, it is a question of formulae.[94]

---

[94] Which does not mean that a classical rhetorician like, say, Quintilian would not have found fault with Flaubert's rhetoric, especially his metaphors. In *The Orator's Educa-*

But things are not quite that simple, because there is a peculiar elective affinity between Flaubert and his pharmacist turned amateur journalist. A central character in the novel, Homais figures largely in its second and third parts, and he also gets the last word. Yet the ambitious pharmacist, for all his importance, was not part of the so-called first scenario for *Madame Bovary*. As Claudine Gothot-Mersch has shown in her classic study of the genesis of *Madame Bovary*, Homais entered the writing process only later.[95] Gothot-Mersch has also demonstrated that Flaubert, in revising his manuscript, systematically removed as many metaphors and tropes as possible.[96] In fact, the first version of the crowd scene at the beginning of the agricultural show chapter relies heavily on metaphor. What is more, these images were of a truly conventional kind—just as worn as those employed by Homais. In this early description of the crowd and how it fills the streets of Yonville, Flaubert thus originally wrote: "[La foule] circulait dans la grande rue, comme une rivière indolente dans son lit naturel, recevant les affluents des allées et des ruelles [et elle] faisait lac devant la mairie." In the process of revising, Flaubert decided that the metaphors had to go. As Gothot-Mersch emphasizes, in the definitive, slimmed-down version of the scene, only a single figurative word remains: "il s'en *dégorgeait* des ruelles, des allées, des maisons."[97]

Where did the metaphors go? They ended up in Homais's piece. Indeed, what is Homais's newspaper article, if not the receptacle of Flaubert's refuse? And there they serve as the characterizing mark of a truly bad writer. This is why Homais is the not-Flaubert, the un-Flaubert, even the anti-Flaubert. In other words, Homais is much closer to Flaubert than one might think.

But what is at issue here is difference, for us as well as for Flaubert, and it lies on a different plane. Homais, unlike Flaubert, does not seek to make the reader see. The flowers are not flowers, the garlands are not garlands: they are signifiers. Things in themselves are not enough for Homais; they must be endowed with a secondary level of meaning, and so it is that his elaborate metaphors promptly soak up the very reality that motivated them in the first place. Indeed, no sooner have the flowers, or the garlands, or the people been mentioned, than they are pressed into the service of

---

tion, Quintilian underlines that metaphor should always be more impressive than that which it replaces (bk. 8, ch. 6, 18). This helps explain the weakness that Proust perceived in Flaubert; consider, for example, the famous passage in *Madame Bovary* where Flaubert likens "the islands in the river" to fish – to "de grands poissons noirs arrêtés."
[95] Gothot-Mersch, *La genèse,* 119.
[96] Ibid., 258.
[97] Ibid.

signification. They mean something other than themselves, and what they mean is ultimately this: *I am literature.*

What Flaubert, by contrast, wants to achieve is not literature but literality. He is attempting to elaborate something like a zero degree of literary language, as Barthes once suggested, an absolute language untainted by preconceived ideas.[98] He wants to deliver up the thingness of the world by way of language, and in this bold enterprise, his privileged ally is the visible. The difference between Homais and Flaubert is that in the former, the visible generates meaning; in the latter, the visible puts an end to meaning.

Are we to conclude that *Madame Bovary* is a vast allegory of writing? That it is a book preeminently concerned with its own linguistic activity, playing off various modes of representing the world against one another? That it is a text in which language constantly turns back on itself? That the novel, as a piece of writing, stages its own scene of production?

It is true that *Madame Bovary*, this most bookish of books, is a splendidly self-conscious, self-reflexive, and self-referential literary artefact. But to conclude that it is an allegory of writing seems to me both reductionist and gratuitous. Yet if we stretch that term—writing—and conceive of it in the largest possible sense, so that it comes to include not only literary writing but also letters and above all journalism and advertising, the picture immediately becomes a great deal more complex and the proposal begins to make sense. We may then glean how *Madame Bovary* lends itself to a historicizing reading, how Flaubert's commitment to form is also, on a deeper level, informed by a specific historical context whose contours I have begun to delineate.

For a gloss on this context we only need to go to the remarkable passage that serves to introduce Homais into Flaubert's 1857 novel. It is a richly textured paragraph in which, furthermore, nearly all the themes I have been discussing so far come together. The scene is embedded in the exposition of Yonville that opens the second part of the book. Emma and Charles Bovary are about to move to this quiet market-town, so small that it has one street only. In introducing Homais, Flaubert's narrator makes visible one of the most significant characters in the novel by putting him in his proper place: we thus see Homais in the pharmacy, writing away at his desk in the middle of the night, basking in the light of a burning oil-lamp. This is the office from which he produces coverage for *Le Fanal de Rouen*; and Flaubert will cite him no less three times,

---

[98] Barthes, *Le degré zéro de l'écriture* (1953), in *Oeuvres complètes,* ed. Eric Marty (Paris: Seuil, 1993), 1:139–66.

allowing generous space for Homais's accounts of significant events in the life of the Yonville community. And as I have suggested, Flaubert thereby duplicates three key episodes in the novel itself: the agricultural show, the surgical operation, and the expulsion of the village ostler.

Meanwhile, Homais the writer is surrounded by signs of all kinds—sign boards, name plates, and door plates as well as advertisements. These signs may not carry much meaning, but they are dense with significance, not only because they serve to characterize Homais and to prefigure his narrative function in the novel, but also, and above all, because they inscribe the narrative in the contemporary historical context to which it is a reaction—that corrupt empire of signs, that world of fallen language, that universe of alien speech. When it comes to Homais, the writing is literally on the wall:

> Mais ce qui attire le plus les yeux, c'est, en face de l'auberge du *Lion d'or*, la pharmacie de M. Homais! Le soir, principalement, quand son quinquet est allumé et que les bocaux rouges et verts qui embellissent sa devanture allongent au loin, sur le sol, leurs deux clartés de couleurs; alors, à travers elles, comme dans des feux de Bengale, s'entrevoit l'ombre du pharmacien, accoudé sur son pupitre. Sa maison, du haut en bas, est placardée d'inscriptions écrites en anglaise, en ronde, en moulée: "Eaux de Vichy, de Seltz et de Barèges, robs dépuratifs, médecine Raspail, racahout des Arabes, pastilles Darcet, pâte Regnault, bandages, bains, chocolats de santé, etc." Et l'enseigne, qui tient toute la largeur de la boutique, porte en lettres d'or: *Homais, pharmacien*. Puis, au fond de la boutique, derrière les grandes balances scellées sur le comptoir, le mot *laboratoire* se déroule au-dessus d'une porte vitrée qui, à moitié de sa hauteur, répète encore une fois *Homais*, en lettres d'or, sur un fond noir.
>
> Il n'y pas ensuite rien à voir dans Yonville. (149)

> But what particularly catches the eye, just across from the Golden Lion, is the pharmacy of Monsieur Homais! In the evening, particularly, when his oil-lamp is lit and the red and green jars that adorn his window cast forth, on the street, their two coloured beams; then, behind them, as though in Bengal lights, you get a glimpse of the pharmacist's shadow, bent at his desk. His house, from top to bottom, is plastered with inscriptions written in longhand, in copperplate, in block capitals: VICHY, SELTZER & BARÈGES WATERS, PURGATIVE SYRUPS, RASPAIL'S ELIXIR, ARABIAN SWEETMEATS, DARCET'S PASTILLES, REGNAULT'S OINTMENT, BANDAGES, BATHS, MEDICINAL CHOCOLATE... And the sign, taking up the whole width of the shop, says in gold letters: HOMAIS, PHARMACIST. There, at the back of the shop, behind the big scales screwed down on the counter, the word *Laboratory* unfurls above a glass door, which, half-way up, announces once again HOMAIS, in letters of gold, on a black ground.
>
> There is nothing further to see in Yonville. (57)

Once more an expansive image unfolds before our eyes. Caught in the act of writing, Homais is turned into spectacle—just like Emma before him. As so often in Flaubert's 1857 novel, the passage offers a complete, self-contained, and autonomous visual event, and it has a paragraph to itself. Homais himself is nowhere to be seen, only his shadow, but his world—the pharmacy—is all the more visible, delivered up to us in compact form, as a consumable visual artefact. I have discussed several such self-sufficient word-images in the preceding pages, focusing in particular on the visual representation of Emma. Yet the difference is crucial. Homais, unlike Emma, is not subject to aestheticization; nor is he an object of desire. In fact, we can hardly discern his appearance; he is a mere digit on the screen. What is going on here?

The scene appears at first glance to be a pure description of what will meet the eyes of Charles and Emma Bovary when they first enter Yonville. The passage turns around the visible and that alone. As the narrator underscores not once but twice, it is the eye-teasing aspect of Homais's pharmacy, including its many ostentatious signs, that explains its singular presence in Yonville and turns it into a glaring anomaly. In fact, the edifice emerges like a giant lantern, emitting light in the nocturnal darkness in which the little town is shrouded. Indeed, what is Homais's pharmacy if not *le fanal de Yonville*?

But the passage is no mere description. It is a text about other texts—about texts that have been turned into things. In duplicating the inscriptions surrounding Homais, the passage thematizes a central concern in Flaubert, the commodification of the letter, the reification of the word, the commercialization of the text. And it does so in the most graphic mode possible.

In the end, the image of Homais's pharmacy belongs to a radically different narrative order: it represents an Ur-scene. For what Flaubert puts forth here is the scene of writing itself. But not any scene, and certainly not a timeless, abstract, and ahistorical one. It is, quite specifically, Homais's scene of production, to be sure, but it is also a fictional recreation of the scene of writing circa 1850. It is, in short, an allegorization of Flaubert's own scene of writing.

The Utopia of the Image

I have come to the end of this chapter, and it is time to gather together some of the threads I have laid out. We have seen that Flaubert's novel is centrally concerned with other forms of writing, particularly journalism. This means that *Madame Bovary* incorporates within itself other media and modes of representation, including those with which the mid-nineteenth-century novel increasingly competes. This means, too, that Flaubert's novel incorporates into its own discourse those phenomena that help constitute that vast social domain known as the bourgeois public sphere, that newly emerged social space that owes its existence to newspapers, periodicals, and other kinds of print media, including advertising.

That the early nineteenth century saw the advent of modern journalism is well known. The press now began to expand at a pace previously unseen. In 1824, as Marc Angenot notes, there were twelve daily newspapers in Paris, with a total print run of 55,000 copies; in 1870, the number of Parisian newspapers had tripled, and the total print run amounted to close to 1,200,000 copies.[99] A similar expansion marked the provinces, and it continued up until the outbreak of the Great War in 1914.

If, as Angenot suggests, nineteenth century France was a culture of print, the single most important phenomenon was not the book but the newspaper.[100] Why? Because the expansion of the press helped destabilize the culture of print, introducing a whole new notion with wide-ranging consequences: evanescence. "L'imprimé, que ce soit le livre, le quotidien, la brochure de colportage ou la feuille-réclame, est dans son omniprésence banale un objet autonome, pourvu d'une identité, immuable et indéfiniment réutilisable. C'est cette image que le Journal, comme imprimé-qui-se-jette et don't l'intérêt s'évanouit en quelques heures, est venu gravement déstabiliser."[101] As a result, Angenot stresses, an anguished conflict arose between the durable and the ephemeral, between the eternal and the obsolescent.

Flaubert's lifelong obsession with clichés, commonplaces, and received ideas would be unthinkable without the existence of this immate-

---

[99] Marc Angenot, *1889. Un état du discours social* (Québec: Préambule, 1989), 79. What is true for Paris is true for the provinces as well; in 1889 more than 130 French towns could boast with having at least three so-called *feuilles* (80). For a discussion of *1889*, see Fredric Jameson, "Marc Angenot, Literary History, and the Study of Culture in the Nineteenth Century," *Yale Journal of Criticism* 17, no. 2 (2004): 233–53.

[100] Angenot reminds his reader that the print item includes more than just the book and the periodical, and this is why one is entitled to term the nineteenth century as a print culture. "Ce sont les billets d'enterrement, les effets de commerce, les lettres de deuil, les prospectus publicitaires, papillons, affichettes, affiches, cartes de visite, cartes à jouer, faire-part divers, factures, effets bancaires, billets, tickets, invitations à diner, menus, bons-primes, brevets et diplômes, images de piété, guides et itinéraires, canards, ronds de bock, cartes-postales…" (*1889*, 60).

[101] Angenot, *1889*, 60.

rial yet highly significant space of social discourse and public opinion. For most of his adult life, Flaubert kept a file that served as an outlet for his maniacal pursuit of received ideas. He had plans for compiling a *Dictionnaire des idées réçues*, but that vast attempt at erecting a satirical monument to the universal stupidity of his age never became more than a torso.[102] But if, in *Madame Bovary*, there is a character who personifies this projected dictionary, it is Homais.[103] Flaubert himself scribbled in the margins of his manuscript that a single newspaper article by Homais would be enough for future attempts at reconstructing scientifically "all the ineptitude of a bourgeois."[104]

All speech in Flaubert is in the end alien speech, I suggested above in discussing Flaubert's italics. But it is not quite that simple. Much in Flaubert revolves around discourse, but not all. There is a representational realm in which the spiraling irony is arrested, if only for a moment, and that is the realm of the image. The reason I have spent much time discussing the Flaubertian image is that it is the only space in Flaubert's writings that is virtually exempt from the all-pervasive narrative irony that cuts everywhere. If there is anything like redemption in Flaubert, it is located in the visible, especially in the image.[105] The image is a utopian enclave in the midst of that proliferation of discourse on which Flaubert's irony thrives. It is a safe haven in a world of fallen language, a moment of truth in a universe of clichés and commonplaces. But I have also dwelt on the Flaubertian image because, in the final analysis, its logic—its form, its aesthetics, its rationale—is inseparable from those very historical phenomena that his writings expose with such relentless and hard-headed irony.

Autonomous, framed, detachable: Flaubert's images, in all their syntactical and rhetorical complexity, come before the reader like poems for the eye. *Un poème pour les yeux*—that's Balzac's phrase. Yet what Balzac had in mind in devising this suggestive metaphor was not literary images but something else completely, namely, advertisements—those advertising posters that Parisian booksellers in the 1820s used to place in the shop window or on the sidewalk in order to promote a certain book.

---

[102] For a critical discussion of Flaubert's lifelong obsession with the commonplace, see Jean-Paul Sartre, "La conscience de classe chez Flaubert II," *Les temps modernes* 21, no. 241 (June 1966), 2113–53. See also Avital Ronell, *On Stupidity* (Urbana, Ill.: University of Illinois Press, 2002), 11–15.

[103] See also Gothot-Mersch, *La genèse,* 139.

[104] A single article by Homais, Flaubert thus wrote, "suffirait dans l'avenir aux Cuviers de la psychologie, à pouvoir reconstituer toute l'ineptie d'un bourgeois, si la race n'en était impérissable." Quoted in Gothot-Mersch, *La genèse,* 207.

[105] Peter Brooks makes a similar point with regard to *L'éducation sentimentale.* See Brooks, *Reading for the Plot,* 182.

To Balzac, these posters were like a poem for the eye: typographically advanced, quaintly colored, and beautifully illustrated.[106] In mobilizing Balzac's designation, I wish to stress not only the artfulness of the Flaubertian image but also, and above all, its emphatically thinglike character. It is marked by the very logic it seeks to overcome. As such, the Flaubertian image represents a new object in the history of the novel.

---

[106] Honoré de Balzac, *Illusions perdues,* ed. Philippe Berthier (Paris: Flammarion, 1990), 361.

Chapter 3
The Aesthetics of the Colon: On *L'éducation sentimentale*

To turn the glorious tradition of the French nineteenth-century novel into rubble, all the way from Stendhal and Hugo to Sand and Balzac, and to erect a spectral ruin in its place—that may not be what Flaubert intended to do when he began work on *L'éducation sentimentale* (1869), but that is what he had accomplished when he was done.

It took him five years of tireless labor. And that labor, painstakingly documented in Flaubert's vast correspondence, yielded not only one of the most important literary works of the nineteenth century. It also yielded one of the most exasperating novels of any time.

The novel is a monument to ennui, passivity, and petrification. It tells the story of a bourgeois male who achieves nothing, gets nowhere, and fails always. Covering the period from 1840 through 1867, the narrative begins when the protagonist Frédéric Moreau is eighteen. It ends twenty-seven years later, when he has reached the age of forty-five.

Frédéric Moreau is a person of considerable resources: he inherits a large sum of money, enough to make him a man of independent means; and, no less important, he teams up with strategically placed women. But it makes little difference, because his destiny is mediocrity. A post-Balzacian hero utterly lacking in ambition, Frédéric even fails to regret his shortcomings when, at the end of the narrative, he sits down to reflect on his life.

On the face of it, the novel is little more than an ironic version of the Bildungsroman. A young middle-class man falls in love with a married woman, but fails in his feeble attempts at seducing her; in the meantime, he tries to make his way in the world, only to arrive at disillusionment, that nineteenth-century theme par excellence.[1] Yet the novel resembles nothing that came before it.

---

[1] On how Flaubert explodes the paradigm of the Bildungsroman, see Franco Moretti, *The Way of the World: The "Bildungsroman" in European Culture* (London: Verso, 1987), esp. 167–79.

In 1864, when he had just begun work on *L'éducation sentimentale,* his most ambitious undertaking, Flaubert wrote a letter to an admirer, a Mlle Leroyer de Chantepie, in which he explained what he was aiming at.

> Me voilà maintenant attelé depuis un mois à un roman de moeurs modernes qui se passera à Paris. Je veux faire l'histoire morale des hommes de ma génération; "sentimentale" serait plus vrai. C'est un livre d'amour, de passion; mais de passion telle qu'elle peut exister maintenant, c'est-à-dire inactive. Le sujet, tel que je l'ai conçu, est, je crois, profondément vrai, mais, à cause de cela même, peu amusant probablement. Les faits, le drame manquent un peu; et puis l'action est étendue dans un laps de temps trop considérable.[2]

Yet although Flaubert wanted to write the moral history of the men of his generation, with Frédéric Moreau as the principal scene of action, *L'éducation sentimentale* is anything but a case study. To be sure, the reader will recognize the generic contours of the Bildungsroman, but the irony is devastating. Flaubert turns *Wilhelm Meister* inside out, along with the entire tradition issuing from Goethe's paradigmatic story. Why? Because Flaubert's novel refuses to teach a lesson. It rejects the idea that it should reflect on the experiences it recounts. It vigorously resists allegorization. It seeks immanence, not transcendence. The tale about monsieur Frédéric Moreau is a tale about Frédéric Moreau, period.

At the same time—and this is one of the mind-boggling paradoxes on which Flaubert's masterpiece feeds—the main part of the novel takes place during the 1840s, that is, the years leading up to the 1848 revolution in Paris, a historical event if there ever was one.[3] Flaubert even proceeds to depict the February revolution and the June insurrection with his sluggish hero as witness, sometimes placing him in the midst of the gun smoke, sometimes having him arrive too late, sometimes placing him at a window.

Critics tend to agree that the book is a boring one. When the novel was first published, the reviewer in *Le Gaulois* exclaimed: "Oh, quel ennui! quel ennui!"[4] The writer was none less than Francisque Sarcey, a leading literary critic at the time.

---

[2] Flaubert to Mlle Leroyer de Chantepie, Croisset, 6 October 1864, in Flaubert, *Correspondance,* ed. Jean Bruneau (Paris: Gallimard, 1991), 3:409.
[3] See Edward Said, *Beginnings* (New York: Columbia University Press, 1985), 147.
[4] Francisque Sarcey, review of *L'éducation sentimentale, Le Gaulois,* 4 December 1869. Sarcey's article was published in two installments, the first on December 3, the second, on December 4. Like a majority of critics, Sarcey considered Flaubert's 1869 novel a failure. Not only was it pompous, cold, and empty; it was also utterly boring.

Critics also tend to agree that the book is boring because of its protagonist and his singular mediocrity. Henry James once famously asked why Flaubert had to choose such an inferior, even "abject," human specimen to serve as the major character.[5] As James saw it, Frédéric is at once too weak and too privileged for the reader to be able to sympathize with him.

For Jonathan Culler, however, this explanation is insufficient. It is not merely Frédéric's mediocrity that exasperates the reader. "It is rather the obstacle this mediocrity poses to intelligibility," Culler remarks. "For if Frédéric's mediocrity explains his failure it does so in a way that is peculiarly uninteresting and that closes rather than opens thematic perspectives."[6]

How are we to approach this exasperating, peculiar, sterile, and thoroughly indeterminate novel? The only possible way to approach it is by way of an inquiry into not what it says, but how it says what it says; in other words, by way of an inquiry into its formal organization.

But perhaps the more pressing question is this. Why should one engage with *L'éducation sentimentale* in the first place?

There are many excellent reasons. Here's argument number one, articulated by Marcel Proust: Flaubert brings about a revolution in the history of French literature, and nowhere more dramatically than in *L'éducation sentimentale*.[7] And this upheaval radically changes the topography of the genre of the novel. I discussed Proust's argument at length in my chapter on *Madame Bovary,* stressing that it places questions of syntax at the center. It now remains to be seen how the syntactic revolution that started with *Madame Bovary* finds its culmination in

---

Why? Because it consisted of nothing but description. In comparing *Madame Bovary* and *L'éducation sentimentale,* Sarcey concluded that Monsieur Flaubert had only one novel "dans le ventre. " Jules Barbey d'Aurevilly was equally relentless. He, too, complained that there was too much description. The novel seemed to him like a magic lantern, projecting a never-ending sequence of tableaux—but ultimately unable to tell a story. Flaubert, indeed, was not only a "descripteur enragé" but also a "faiseur de bric-à-brac," indulging in atomistic descriptions that only blind the reader. See Jules Barbey d'Aurevilly, review of *L'éducation sentimentale, Le constitutionnel* (29 November 1869). On the overabundance of description and obsession with minute detail, see also Amédée de Cesena's review in *Le Figaro* (20 November 1869), and Edmond Duranty's review in *Paris-Journal* (14 December 1869).

[5] Henry James, introduction to *Madame Bovary,* in *French Writers,* vol. 2 of *Literary Criticism,* 326.

[6] Jonathan Culler, *Flaubert: The Uses of Uncertainty* (Ithaca, N.Y.: Cornell University Press, 1974), 147.

[7] Marcel Proust, "A propos du 'style' de Flaubert," in *Contre Sainte-Beuve précédé de Pastiches et mélanges et suivi de Essais et articles* (Paris: Gallimard, 1971), 586–600.

L'éducation sentimentale, how, in other words, impression is substituted for action.

Here's argument number two, articulated by Walter Benjamin: the appearance of *L'éducation sentimentale* marks the end of the narrative invention known as the novel. Benjamin even goes so far as to state that Flaubert's book signals the end of storytelling as such.[8] How can this be? The decline of storytelling starts as early as with the rise of the novel at the beginning of modern times, he suggests, for what sets the novel apart from the story is that the former is dependent on that invention known as the book—and with the book comes a whole new cultural situation: reading rather than listening, individual experience rather than collective counsel. To grapple with Flaubert's 1869 novel is therefore to grapple with the history of epic narration as such.

Here's argument number three, articulated by Michel Foucault: Flaubert is to the library what Manet is to the museum, for both are emblematic of a historically new culture in which citation has been substituted for emulation. Manet's *Déjeuner sur l'herbe* and *Olympia* are the first "museum" paintings, Foucault suggests. They would be unthinkable without the existence of art museums, that is, without the particular mode of being and interdependence that works of art acquire in such institutions. For the first time in the history of art, the archive is key. Flaubert and Manet thus "font venir au jour un fait essential à notre culture: chaque tableau appartient désormais à la grande surface quadrillée de la peinture; chaque oeuvre littéraire appartient au murmure indéfini de l'écrit [unearth an essential aspect of our culture: every painting now belongs within the squared and massive surface of painting and all literary works are confined to the indefinite murmur of writing]."[9]

Here's argument number four, articulated by Fredric Jameson: "*Sentimental Education* is one of the most fascinating and exasperating [novels] of world literature, at one and the same time the richest and the

---

[8] Walter Benjamin, "Der Erzähler. Betrachtungen zum Werk Nikolai Lesskows," in *Illuminationen* (Frankfurt am Main: Suhrkamp, 1977), 389, 400–1; translated by Harry Zohn as "The Storyteller: Reflections on the Works of Nikolai Leskov," in *Illuminations,* ed. Hannah Arendt (New York: Schocken, 1988), 87, 98–100. See also chapter 1, 52-4.

[9] Michel Foucault, "La bibliothèque fantastique," *Cahiers Renaud-Barrault,* no. 59 (March 1967); reprinted in *Travail de Flaubert,* ed. Gérard Genette and Tzvetan Todorov (Paris: Seuil, 1983), 107; "Fantasia of the Library," in *Language, Counter-memory, Practice: Selected Essays and Interviews,* trans. Donald. F. Bouchard and Sherry Simon (Oxford: Basil Blackwell, 1977), 92–3. Foucault's essay centers primarily on *La tentation,* but its perspectives apply equally well to Flaubert's 1869 novel. See also Foucault, *La peinture de Manet,* ed. Maryvonne Saison (Paris: Seuil, 2004), 21–47. For a substantial effort at establishing parallels between Manet and Flaubert, see Arden Reed, *Manet, Flaubert, and the Emergence of Modernism: Blurring Genre Boundaries* (Cambridge: Cambridge University Press, 2003).

emptiest of books, one immense failure and at one and the same time […] one of the rare novels to which one can return endlessly without exhausting it, a veritable summa of sentences, an encyclopedia of everything it is interesting to see narrative language do."[10]

That will have to do for now. For all their differences, these four critics have one thing in common: they hold that Flaubert's 1869 novel is a narrative construction that testifies to rhetorical, stylistic, and generic transformations of the highest historical interest. They also argue that Flaubert's novel is a product of the very literary archive it energetically seeks to negate. Pierre Bourdieu, in *Les règles de l'art* (1992), takes the argument a step further by suggesting that *L'éducation sentimentale* may usefully be read as a veritable objectification of the structure of the social world in which it was produced; in fact, it even offers an exact analysis of that world. More than anything else, *L'éducation sentimentale* is a formidable expression of the autonomization of the literary field.[11] This, indeed, is the murmur that can be heard between the lines in Flaubert.

What I shall be proposing in the following pages is that Flaubert's handling of the visible is a straightforward way of coming to terms with *L'éducation sentimentale* and its place in literary history. The visible is a rewarding site for the analysis of how Flaubert turns realism inside out, systematically reducing its ambitions to dust. Indeed, to trace the adventures of the seen through Flaubert's 1869 novel is to grasp, in precise and concrete detail, the utter strangeness at the heart of the tale about Frédéric Moreau, but also, and above all, the radical indeterminacy that has ensured it such a prominent position in the tradition of the novel.[12]

In short, along with *Madame Bovary* and *Trois contes*, *L'éducation sentimentale* occupies a crucial place in the literary history of the visible. What once began as an effort to reproduce the thereness of the real has now become a vehicle of derealization. Flaubert effects a thoroughgoing change that will reverberate far into the twentieth century, all the way through Proust and Joyce and beyond.

---

[10] Fredric Jameson, "The Ideology of the Text," in *The Ideologies of Theory: Essays, 1971–1986* (Minneapolis: University of Minnesota Press, 1988), 1:39.
[11] Pierre Bourdieu, *Les règles de l'art. Genèse et structure du champ littéraire* (Paris: Seuil, 1992); trans. by Susan Emanuel as *The Rules of Art: Genesis and Structure of the Literary Field* (Stanford: Stanford University Press, 1996).
[12] On Flaubertian indeterminacy, see Culler, *Flaubert*.

Like A Vision

The opening of *L'éducation sentimentale* is straightforward enough. The reader is immediately drawn into the specifics of a particular moment and of a particular location:

> Le 15 septembre 1840, vers six heures du matin, *la Ville-de-Montereau*, près de partir, fumait à gros tourbillons devant le quai Saint-Bernard.[13]

> On the 15th of September 1840, at six o'clock in the morning, the *Ville-de-Montereau* was lying alongside the Quai Saint-Bernard, ready to sail, with clouds of smoke pouring from its funnel.[14]

Following a time-honored pattern, Flaubert creates a typical realist illusion. Indeed, as Henri Mitterand suggests, Flaubert—like all nineteenth-century realists—wants to conjure up not a real world, but rather a possible world, a virtual world.[15] And this virtual world now comes before us in all its sensual immediacy, smoking and steaming, ringing and rustling.

> Des gens arrivaient hors d'haleine; des barriques, des câbles, des corbeilles de linge gênaient la circulation; les matelots ne répondaient à personne; on se heurtait; les colis montaient entre les deux tambours, et le tapage s'absorbait dans le bruissement de la vapeur, qui, s'échappant par des plaques de tôle, enveloppait tout d'une nuée blanchâtre, tandis que la cloche, à l'avant, tintait sans discontinuer.
>
> Enfin le navire partit; et les deux berges, peuplées de magasins, de chantiers et d'usines, filèrent comme deux large rubans que l'on déroule. (41)

> People came hurrying up, out of breath; barrels, ropes and baskets washing lay about in everybody's way; the sailors ignored all inquiries; people bumped into one another; the pile of baggage between the two paddle-wheels grew higher and higher; and the din merged into the hissing of the steam, which, escaping through some iron plates, wrapped the whole scene in a whitish mist, while the bell in the bows went on clanging incessantly.
>
> At last the boat moved off; and the two banks, lined with warehouses, yards, and factories, slipped past like two wide ribbons being unwound. (15)

---

[13] Gustave Flaubert, *L'éducation sentimentale*, ed. Pierre-Marc de Biasi (Paris: Livre de Poche, 2002), 41. Further page references are given in the main text.

[14] Flaubert, *Sentimental Education*, trans. Robert Baldick (London: Penguin, 1964), 15. Further page references are given in the main text.

[15] Henri Mitterand, "Flaubert: les jeux du regard," in *L'illusion réaliste. De Balzac à Aragon* (Paris: Presses Universitaires de France, 1994), 33.

Flaubert's narrative thus begins in the middle of things. But the immediacy of the moment is framed by a novelistic marker that suggests that something important will take place. In this way, Flaubert orchestrates the expectations of his reader. Why else would the narrator announce the year, the date, and the time of day?

This is realist precision in the manner of, say, Balzac. It is as though Flaubert, in offering us a seemingly significant date, sets the scene for a historical novel that will be filled with other significant dates; indeed, it is as though the initial sentence carried a promise of a certain generality lurking inside that stubborn particularity. However, this is Flaubert, not Balzac. The date turns out to be significant for one individual only: Frédéric Moreau.[16] He has just embarked on a boat that will take him to Nogent-sur-Seine, where his mother resides.

Just as the boat departs, so Flaubert's tale takes off. And just as the speed of the vessel makes the river banks appear as though they are sliding past the passengers, so this 1869 novel will present a seemingly endless series of moving tableaux that similarly slip past the reader.

What Flaubert here puts before us is a representation of something like a protocinematic experience. Numerous critics have noted this feature.[17] The tableau comes with an angle, and it is also presented in such a way that it presupposes the presence of an embodied spectator. But the implied eye is an anonymous one. We do not yet know who is looking, for the spectator in question remains to be introduced: that young man

---

[16] See Gisèle Séginger, *Flaubert. Une poétique de l'histoire* (Strasbourg: Presses Universitaires de Strasbourg, 2000), 86.

[17] See, for example, Victor Brombert, *The Novels of Flaubert: A Study of Themes and Techniques* (Princeton, N.J.: Princeton University Press, 1966), 141: "The image also suggests a film in slow motion." Mitterand, in a sentence-for-sentence analysis of the opening passages in *L'éducation sentimentale*, similarly underscores the cinematic character of the scene. The representation of the scenery that unfolds before Frédéric, he maintains, is not to be seen as description in the traditional sense; what Flaubert achieves here and elsewhere is rather a protocinematic representation: "N'employons pas le mot *description*, car ici le motif ne se fige pas, le temps ne s'immobilise pas, bien au contraire. Tout s'écoule et se transforme, récit et description se confondent. Ce sera la grande différence entre le cinéma et la photographie" ("Flaubert: les jeux du regard," 38). For an extensive analysis of the "cinematographic" in Flaubert, see Pierre Danger, *Sensations et objets dans le roman de Flaubert* (Paris: Armand Colin, 1973), ch. 4. "L'oeuvre de Flaubert est en effet exactement conçue comme une oeuvre cinématographique," writes Danger, "c'ést-à-dire que tout y est exprimé par l'image, le son et la perception du mouvement, sans qu'aucune analyse psychologique, aucun commentaire de l'auteur ne vienne jamais se superposer à la simple vision de la scène décrite" (186). Joseph Frank's discussion of the agricultural show in *Madame Bovary* remains a classic analysis of cinematic techniques in Flaubert; see Frank, "Spatial Form in Modern Literature," in *The Idea of Spatial Form* (New Brunswick: Rutgers University Press, 1991), esp. 16–21.

called Frédéric Moreau. There is, then, an object of observation that is being observed, but there is no observer. The action is in the animated landscape itself, and the banks have been endowed with syntactical agency: *les deux berges, peuplées de magasins, de chantiers et d'usines, filèrent...*[18]

This is what accords the tableau its proto-cinematic character. It is as though the vessel were at a standstill while the landscape is set in motion. The inanimate is animated, and vice versa. Flaubert, one might say, keeps the seen apart from the known. This is why Proust, in his article on Flaubert's style, devised the metaphor of the *trottoir roulant*; it captured the experience of reading *L'éducation sentimentale,* in particular the effect produced by Flaubert's syntactical idiosyncrasies. Things, settings, and humans all pass by at an even speed before that implied eye. Action has been substituted for impression.

In a few seconds, Frédéric will catch sight of a woman he does not know. At the same time, the plot will take off. For Frédéric's visual experience of the nameless woman will be decisive for the course of the next couple of decades of his life and, by implication, for the course of the novel also. In fact, all of the action of Flaubert's 1869 narrative flows from this luminous vision.

But first Flaubert makes sure to prepare the reader for what is to come. The singularity of the as yet unknown woman will be set off against the anonymous crowd of passengers. The individuals that make up the crowd may well stand out, to be sure, but they are anything but singular. Flaubert represents them as a group of immediately recognizable social types that, moreover, easily melt together.

> À part quelques bourgeois, aux Premières, c'étaient des ouvriers, des gens de boutique avec leurs femmes et leurs enfants. Comme on avait coutume alors de se vêtir sordidement en voyage, presque tous portaient de vieilles calottes grecques ou des chapeaux déteints, de maigres habits noirs, râpés par le frottement du bureau, ou des redingotes ouvrant la capsule de leurs boutons pour avoir trop servi au magasin; çà et là, quelque gilet à châle laissait voir une chemise de calicot, maculée de café; des épingles de chrysocale piquaient des cravates en lambeaux; des sous-pieds cousus retenaient des chaussons de lisière; deux ou trois gredins qui tenaient des bambous à ganse de cuir lançaient des regards obliques, et des pères de familles ouvraient de gros yeux, en faisant des questions. Ils causaient debout, ou bien accroupis sur leurs bagages; d'autres dormaient dans des

---

[18] This feature was noted—and attacked—by contemporary critics. Edmond Duranty, in his review of Flaubert's 1869 novel, remarked that "les vrais personnages du roman sont des bateaux à vapeur, des chambres, des rues, des escaliers et des paysages." In Duranty's view, it made for an utterly dry, heavy, and monotonous book.

coins; plusieurs mangeaient. Le pont était sali par des écales de noix, des bouts de cigares, des pelures de poires, des détritus de charcuterie apportée dans du papier; trois ébénistes, en blouse, stationnaient devant la cantine; un joueur de harpe en haillons se reposait, accoudé sur son instrument; on entendait par intervalles le bruit du charbon de terre dans le fourneau, un éclat de voix, un rire; – et le capitaine, sur la passerelle, marchait d'un tambour à l'autre, sans s'arrêter. Frédéric, pour rejoindre sa place, poussa la grille des Premières, dérangea deux chasseurs avec leurs chiens. (45–6)

[The passengers], apart from a few well-to-do people in the first class, were workmen and shopkeepers with their wives and children. As it was the custom in those days to put on one's oldest clothes for travelling, nearly all of them were wearing old skull-caps or faded hats, thread-bare black jackets worn thin by desk-work, or frock-coats with buttons which had burst their covers from too much service in the shop. Here and there a coffee-stained calico shirt showed under a knitted waistcoat, gilt tie-pins pierced tattered cravats, and trouser-straps were fastened to list slippers. Two or three louts, carrying bamboo canes with leather thongs, glanced shiftily from side to side, while the family men opened their eyes wide as they asked questions. Some stood about, chatting, or squatted on their luggage; others slept in corners; several had something to eat. The deck was littered with nutshells, cigar stubs, pear skins, and the remains of sausage-meat which had been brought along wrapped in paper. Three cabinet-makers in overalls stood in front of the bar; a harpist dressed in rags was resting with his elbow on his instrument; now and then one could hear the sound of the coal in the furnace, a burst of voices, or a roar of laughter. On the bridge the captain kept striding from one paddle-wheel to the other, without ever stopping. To get back to his seat, Frédéric pushed open the gate leading to the first-class section of the boat, disturbing a couple of sportsmen with their dogs. (17–8)

In terms of plot, these sentences are inconsequential. The passage is a mere preliminary: it serves as a counterpoint to the decisive moment that will follow immediately upon it. It could easily be removed; the story would suffer little damage. And yet it is a highly intricate piece of writing that reveals a great deal about the syntactic texture of Flauberts's works.

What animates the paragraph is not the people in it, nor the human action reported, nor the peculiar details on which the narrator lavishes such close attention. The passage acquires its force from the panoramic gaze that sweeps over the objects in the field of vision, moving from humans to worn buttons to fruit peel. Flaubert's narrator is not content merely to state that the workers' clothes are worn, that the floor is littered with waste, or that the scene is noisy. He wants us to really see before us the shabby jackets and the soiled shirts and the pear skin and the nut shells and the cigar butts; by the same token, he wants us to really hear that disembodied laughter and that busy furnace.

At first, it may seem as though the narrator merely describes what meets Frédéric's senses, in particular, his eyes, as he walks about on the boat. But there is more to these sentences, for the perceptual apparatus implied is a transformative one. Pear peel and cabinet-makers, cigar butts and family fathers, human voices and machine sounds: all are clustered together and placed on the same level. Flaubert wants to convey a sense of sensory presence, to be sure, but above all of messiness, that is, of a scene teeming with activities of many different kinds. To produce an effect of messiness, Flaubert needs order, an order that is provided by the logic of the catalogue. Here as so often in Flaubert, the use of the semicolon enacts the logic of the catalogue. The passage contains no fewer than ten such punctuation marks.

Flaubert has thus set the stage for the crucial encounter that awaits Frédéric. Now the narrative shifts gear. We leave the realm of the semicolon and enter that of the colon. In opening that inconspicuous door in the final sentence of the paragraph, Frédéric crosses a symbolic threshold—as does the reader. We move from the working classes to the bourgeoisie, from faded black attire to pink hat ribbons, from smelly sausage remains to the beauty of a straight nose. What is more, we move from the many to the one. In the meantime, and almost unnoticeably, we enter a radically different representational space:

> Frédéric, pour rejoindre sa place, poussa la grille des Premières, dérangea deux chasseurs avec leurs chiens.
> Ce fut comme une apparition:
> Elle était assise, au milieu du banc, toute seule; ou du moins il ne distingua personne, dans l'éblouissement que lui envoyèrent ses yeux. En même temps qu'il passait, elle leva la tête; il fléchit involontairement les épaules; et, quand il se fut mis plus loin, du même côté, il la regarda.
> Elle avait un large chapeau de paille, avec des rubans roses qui palpitaient au vent, derrière elle. Ses bandeaux noirs, contournant la pointe de ses grands sourcils, descendaient très bas et semblaient presser amoureusement l'ovale de sa figure. Sa robe de mousseline claire, tachetée de petits pois, se répandait à plis nombreux. Elle était en train de broder quelque chose; et son nez droit, son menton, toute sa personne se découpait sur le fond de l'air bleu. (46–7)

> Frédéric pushed open the gate leading to the first-class section of the boat, disturbing a couple of sportsmen with their dogs.
> It was like a vision:
> She was sitting in the middle of the bench, all alone; or at least he could not see anybody else in the dazzling light which her eyes cast upon him.

> Just as he passed her, she raised her head; he bowed automatically; and stopping a little way off, on the same side of the boat, he looked at her.
>   She was wearing a broad-brimmed straw hat, with pink ribbons which fluttered behind her in the wind. Her black hair, parted in the middle, hung in two long tresses which brushed the ends of her thick eyebrows and seemed to caress the oval of her face. Her dress of pale spotted muslin billowed out in countless folds. She was busy with a piece of embroidery; and her straight nose, her chin, her whole figure was silhouetted clearly against the background of the blue sky. (18)

What Frédéric catches sight of is not any passenger; it is *she*. The mature Flaubert—the author of *Madame Bovary, L'éducation sentimentale,* and *Trois contes*—would probably have been utterly incapable of writing a banal sentence like the following: "Frédéric noticed a ravishingly beautiful woman sitting on a bench all alone." Instead, he simply writes, "Elle était assise..."

This speedy introduction of the unknown woman, this simple yet willful *she*, is remarkably effective. The reader is made to understand, at one stroke, that the very moment the male protagonist casts his eyes on the creature on the bench, *she* has become an object of desire. We realize also that *she*, whoever she is, is likely to be a major presence in the novel.[19] A single word, and the story takes a leap.

The woman on the bench is presented as though in a full-length portrait. Devouring her being from head to toe, Frédéric's gaze moves from her straw hat down to the lining of her dress. The description of her external appearance is exclusively visual and meticulously detailed: the narrator reports that her eyebrows are thick, that her hat ribbons are pink and moving in the wind, and so on. Her beauty is everywhere implied, but Flaubert's narrator never once states that she is beautiful.

Flaubert's aestheticized representation of the unknown woman quickly turns into an independent entity. It is an island floating around in the narrative that surrounds it, self-contained and self-sufficient. What unfolds before the reader is not so much a description of a woman as rather an image—an autonomous image that has been carefully inserted into the

---

[19] This scene is a locus classicus in Flaubert criticism, and countless scholars have dwelt on the pictorial representation of Madame Arnoux. Jean Rousset, in his study of the first visual encounter, shows that Flaubert's scene partakes of a long narratological tradition: the action starts when the eyes of the protagonists first meet. See Rousset, *Leurs yeux se rencontrèrent. La scène de première vue dans le roman* (Paris: Corti, 1981), esp. 24–7. Rousset's title, incidentally, derives from Flaubert's episode. On the genesis of the scene, see Yoko Kudo's article on Flaubert's sketches, "Lecture d'un manuscrit. Etude de la scène d'apparition dans *L'Education sentimentale*," *Proceedings of the Department of Foreign Languages and Literatures* (Tokyo) 39, no. 2 (1991): 135–58.

diegesis.[20] We have seen a similar pictorial logic at work in numerous places in *Madame Bovary*. What is going on here is not description but rather perception: vision, looking, gazing. Indeed, the elaborate image is a record, not of the woman as such but of the woman being looked at. In fact, Frédéric is not merely looking at her; he already perceives her as image.[21] And the reader, as we shall see, is supposed to perceive things the same way.

Flaubert has already suggested as much. "*Ce fut comme une apparition*," he writes. He then adds a colon as well as a blank, two crucial typographic devices that serve a single purpose: to create a caesura. They highlight what is to come, lifting out the image of the narrative flow. The paragraph that renders Frédéric's vision thus literally stands out in relief against the letters on the page, attracting notice, sticking out, shining forth.[22] This typographic measure may seem like an insignificant detail, but it is fundamental to the episode. It is an attempt on Flaubert's part at reproducing a specifically pictorial logic within the realm of print—I am thinking especially of the frame, for it is the frame that turns the seen into a picture.

A glance at the early versions of the scene makes clear that although the episode went through numerous changes, one thing persists: Flaubert always makes sure to set off Frédéric's visual experience by introducing a blank and starting a new paragraph.[23] He clearly wants the representation of the nameless woman on the bench to strike the reader's eye; and

---

[20] See Diana Knight, *Flaubert's Characters* (Oxford: Oxford University Press, 1985), 86: "Mme Arnoux is real but Frédéric perceives her as if she were an image."

[21] Julianna Starr, in an article on male spectatorship, usefully suggests that Frédéric's gaze is a fetishistic one. "The sighting on the boat demonstrates Frédéric's fetishistic gaze; his look flattens and iconizes [Madame Arnoux's] image, as he describes her as a sort of cut-out figure or paper doll framed by her accoutrements against the blue background of the sky" (17). Stressing that this tendency persists throughout the novel, Starr observes that most women in the novel are subject to fragmentation and metonymization before Frédéric's eyes. See Julianna Starr, "Men Looking at Women Through Art: Male Gaze and Spectatorship in Three Nineteenth-Century French Novels," *Revue Frontenac*, 10–11 (1993–4): 8–34.

[22] The description of Madame Arnoux is divived into two paragraphs: the first one serves to render Frédéric's impression, that is, how the sight of the unknown woman imprints itself on him; the second paragraph details his willful study of her external appearance. To put it a little differently, Frédéric is at first the passive recipient of the visual impression, and then the active producer of it.

[23] For an incisive analysis of how Flaubert uses blanks and paragraph divisions, see Michel Sandras, "Le blanc, l'alinéa," *Communications* 19 (1972): 105–14. Sandras goes so far as to argue that Flaubert, along with Mallarmé, represents an entirely new mode of using blanks, one that ultimately creates a new kind of text, or *écriture*. He also notes that the blank represents a scission, a cut in the text that separates the seer/describer from the seen/described, as can be seen especially whenever Madame Arnoux appears in the narrative. I am grateful to Philippe Dufour for bringing this article to my attention.

the graphic design of the page is a crucial means to this end. Words, for Flaubert, are not enough: in order to be seen, things must acquire a visual tactility. Things must not only be told; they must also be shown. This is why he mobilizes punctuation marks and the graphic arrangement of the verbal material on the page.

The phrase, "Ce fut comme un apparition," is also there from the start. In the brouillons, Flaubert invariably closes the phrase with a period. The same occurs in the final version of the manuscript, as in the copyist's version: terminal punctuation. But as Flaubert read the page proofs, he apparently saw fit to change the period to a colon.[24] It is a change that reveals a great deal about the Flaubertian image, and especially this one. In fact, this is the only time in *L'éducation sentimentale* that Flaubert makes use of a colon in such an aesthetically elaborate way.[25] It foregrounds the utter narratological importance of the image of the anonymous woman. At the same time, it confirms the importance of the Flaubertian image at large.

Together with the blank, the colon serves as a syntactic traffic signal: it urges the reader to be attentive, to focus the mind as it flutters over the interpretive material, and then to move forward, with a heightened sense of awareness. The typographical break also signifies that the narrative is at a thematic crossroads.[26] *Ce fut comme une apparition*: the colon

---

[24] The corrected page proofs have been lost, but it is most likely that it is Flaubert who effected this typographic change. The first edition of *L'éducation sentimentale* contains a colon. Pierre-Marc de Biasi, who specializes in Flaubert's manuscripts, confirms the visual importance of the colon; he believes, moreover, that it was Flaubert who changed the punctuation. The typographic design practiced here is so idiosyncratic—from a conventional point of view, it is plain wrong—that only Flaubert could be behind it. In French, Biasi stresses, the material introduced by a colon typically begins with a lower-case letter, not a capital letter. And the blank following the colon is as idiosyncratic as is the capital letter; it really only occurs in drama where it serves to introduce speech. One might say, then, that the Flaubertian image is spatialized in the same way as dramatic dialogue. I thank Pierre-Marc de Biasi for discussing this and related matters with me. See "*L'éducation sentimentale*," Flaubert Papers, Institut des textes et des manuscrits modernes (CNRS-ENS), Paris, NAFR 17599, fols. 25v, 36v, 52, 55.

[25] It is matched by one thing only: the famous blank toward the end of the novel where the narrative unexpectedly changes gear and covers nineteen years in a single breath. For Proust this blank was the most beautiful element in Flaubert's novel; it demonstrated that Flaubert had managed to extract a musical rhythm from changes of narrative speed. In Proust's view, Flaubert's way of handling such temporal change demonstrated that Flaubert was the first to set temporal change to music. See Proust, "A propos du 'style' de Flaubert," 595.

[26] On the poetics of punctuation marks, see Adorno, "Satzzeichen," in *Noten zur Literatur* (Frankfurt am Main: Suhrkamp, 1981), 106–113; on the colon as traffic signal, 106; "Punctuation Marks," in *Notes to Literature,* trans. Shierry Weber Nicholsen (New York: Columbia University Press, 1991), 1:91–7. On the narrative function of the colon, particularly as framing device, see Italo Calvino, "Levels of Reality in Literature," in

both connects and separates. It connects by relating the extraordinary sight to Frédéric as perceptual agent; it separates by setting off the seen, ultimately insisting on the independence of the perceived, as though it were surrounded by an invisible frame.

The final sentence—"toute sa personne se découpait sur le fond de l'air bleu"—closes the vision, completes the framing, and turns the seen into a self-contained whole.[27] It also effects a flatness of the seen, transforming it into an image. Indeed, in stressing how the luminous woman on the bench is thrown into relief against the sky, the narrator strips the seen of depth, resolutely turning the representation into a two-dimensional one. As Reinhard Baumgart observes in his criticism of the famous episode: "Alles Menschengewimmel, die ganze Umwelt aus Rufen, Abfall, Hunden, Maschinenlärm, die seitenlang zusammenerzählt worden ist, alles versinkt, erlischt, die Zeit steht still, der Raum verliert seine Dreidimensionalität, wird zum gerahmten Bild, einem Madonnenbild vor Himmelsblau. So jedenfalls, als Ikone seiner Andakt, scheint Frédérics Blick diese Spätsommerdame zu erfassen."[28]

Indeed, it is as though the anonymous woman is stretched out on a flat backdrop; and behind this backdrop is yet another one: the sky. To the extent that there is depth in the seen, it is an effect produced by the implied relief.

Whoever she happens to be, the woman on the bench is always already perceived as image, by Frédéric as well as by the reader. In fact, the intricate way in which she is presented has certain affinities with the cinematic close-up. Or to put it in more accurate terms: theories of the close-up may help us understand what Flaubert seeks to achieve in these opening pages.[29] Generally speaking, the close-up pulls the image away from the diegesis, thus providing it with instant self-sufficiency. Indeed, no matter what the object filling the screen may be—a face, an eye, a tear, a door knob, a knife, a bug—the close-up strips the seen of

---

The Uses of Literature: Essays, trans. Patrick Creagh (New York: Harcourt Brace Jovanovich, 1986), 115–16. On the colon, see also Fredric Jameson, *Sartre: The Origins of a Style* (New York: Columbia University Press, 1984), 54–60, 160.

[27] That Flaubert has a penchant for framing his characters, especially his female characters, has been noted by numerous critics. See, for example, Knight, *Flaubert's Characters,* 86–7, 93–5. For Knight, this feature is intimately linked to what Sartre called derealization. See also Georges Jacques, "Cadrage, vernissage et encadrement. Pour une esthétique du figement," in *Flaubert et la théorie littéraire,* ed. Tanguy Logé and Marie-France Renard (Brussels: Facultés universitaires Saint-Louis, 2005), 207–21.

[28] Reinhard Baumgart, *Liebesspuren. Eine Lesereise durch die Weltliteratur* (Munich: Hanser, 2000), 14.

[29] For a critical survey of theories of the close-up, see Mary Ann Doane's excellent article, "The Close-Up: Scale and Detail in the Cinema," *differences* 14, no. 3 (2003): 89–111.

its narrative motivations by placing it within a tight frame. For a few seconds, off-screen space is suspended, even abolished; and the object of the shot, isolated as it is from its original context, becomes a visual entity of its own, independent and autonomous.

The close-up also effects a despatialization of the image. In extracting the visual object from its narrative mise-en-scène and turning it into an entity of its own, the close-up radically reduces the spectator's sense of depth. Three-dimensional space is flattened; the seen turns into surface. As a result, the close-up effectively upsets traditional rules of perspectival realism. "The image becomes, once more, an image rather than a threshold onto a world. Or rather, the world is reduced to this face, this object," Mary Ann Doane suggests.[30]

We can see a similar logic at work in Flaubert's passage: the description of Madame Arnoux is anything but a visual space into which the gaze may enter. It is anything but a threshold onto a world. Rather, what Flaubert seeks to render is how the world—Frédéric's as well as ours—is momentarily reduced to this appearance: this head, this face, these eyes.[31]

But there is more to the logic of the close-up. It always comes with a built-in "Here!" That is to say: the close-up is preeminently deictic. It points to the here and now, conjuring up the immediate: the presence of being. Christian Metz, in his attempt to elaborate a syntax of cinema, argues that cinema is organized by a semiotic order all its own. Cinema is always speech, practice, performance. It cannot be theorized on the order of language, because there is an essential ontological difference between the cinematic image and any verbal unit: cinema is at bottom indexical.

What is more, the smallest signifying unit of cinema—the image—is always already part of a sequence or, to use a linguistic metaphor, a sentence. Metz's example is a close-up of a revolver. It would be wrong to

---

[30] Doane, "The Close-Up," 91.

[31] I should stress that I am not suggesting that the image of Madame Arnoux is a close-up, only that theories of the close-up can help us articulate what Flauberts seeks to accomplish in this and many other similar passages: hereness, literality, indexicality. Calvino, in an essay on cinema and the novel, rightly maintains that the "close-up has no equivalent in a narrative fashioned of words." The reason is that in a written text, the distance between language and image is always the same. "Literature is totally lacking in any working method to enable it to isolate a single vastly enlarged detail in which one face comes forward to underline a state of mind or stress the importance of a single detail in comparison with the rest" ("Cinema and the Novel," in *The Uses of Literature,* trans. Patrick Creagh [New York: Harcourt Brace Jovanovich, 1986], 75). On the differences between literature and film, especially with regard to description, see David MacDougall, "Voice and Vision," in *The Corporeal Image: Film, Ethnography, and the Senses* (Princeton: Princeton University Press, 2006), 32–63.

approach the image of the shooting gun as a lexical unit, he maintains. The image does not mean "revolver." The close-up must be understood, he suggests, not as a word but rather as a sentence. As an absolute minimum, it says: "Here is a revolver!"[32] And that here, for Metz, is a pure index of actualization.

The revolver, in short, comes with that precious hereness. It is made present. It is actualized. The image of the revolver, then, is inseparable from a specifically photographic gesture, that of bringing forward. "The close-up, more than other types of shots, demonstrates the deictic nature of the cinematic image, its inevitable indexicality," Mary Ann Doane explains. "Mimicking the pointing finger, it requires no language and is not comparable to it."[33] The hereness of the cinematic image is at the core of Metz's semiotics of cinema.

Flaubert's description of the seated woman partakes—or, rather, wishes to partake—in such an indexical logic. This is why the colon is crucial. It is the narrator's pointing finger. It is a deictic gesture. It says: *Here!*

Flaubert wants indexicality, not semiotics. Indeed, he wants literality, not literature. By way of the colon, the passage seeks to effect a presentation rather than a representation. It wants to bring forward, to demonstrate, to show. In the end, these carefully crafted sentences seek less to signify than to actualize a presence, a singular because absolutely particular presence.

I am tempted to say that Flaubert's description wants to perform that which an image alone is capable of performing; put differently, it wants to enact a pragmatics of the pictorial image. It pursues the kind of indexicality that a verbal mode of representation can never achieve. The scene in effect does two things at once: first, it renders Frédéric's experience of the woman on the bench as an essential image experience; second, it seeks to make the reader also perceive that image. Hence the colon; and hence, indeed, the blank.

Yet Flaubert would not be Flaubert if the image of Madame Arnoux was readable only in this way. For all the particularity of the woman on the bench, and for all her breath-taking immediacy, she is also an emphatically generic figure. She is the one and only, to be sure, but she is many also. She is a stock figure, a romantic cliché, a standardized image—in Flaubert as well as in the history of Western literature, and Flau-

---

[32] Christian Metz, *Film Language: A Semiotics of the Cinema,* trans. Michael Taylor (New York: Oxford University Press, 1974), 67. I found the reference to Metz in Doane's article.
[33] Doane, "The Close-Up," 93.

bert obviously designed her that way. In an early version of the scene, he in fact writes: "Elle ressemblait aux héroïnes romantiques de Byron." [34]

That vague yet highly significant *she* appears in *Madame Bovary,* for instance, when Emma's second lover, Léon, ponders his passion for his extravagant mistress. In a rare moment of eloquence, and with a little help from Flaubert's cunning narrator, Léon muses apropos of Emma:

> Elle était l'amoureuse de tous les romans, l'héroïne de tous les drames, la vague *elle* de tous les volumes de vers. (397)

> She was the lover in every novel, the heroine in every play, the vague *she* in every volume of poetry. (215)

Flaubert's narrator surely knows what he is doing when he introduces the woman on the bench as a nameless presence, as that vague *she* in every romance. He implicitly underscores the fictitious nature of his female protagonist, and of Frédéric's hapless falling in love with her. *Here she is, the object of desire that comes with the territory and that is necessary to get the plot going.*

In stressing her novelistic character, and her imaginary nature as an object of desire, Flaubert's narrator seems at first merely to blink ironically at the reader, as though the story made no other claims than to being a story, as though it were little more than a narrative invention that readily admits its invented character.

But there is more to that *she*, for Flaubert has arranged a subtle reversal: by stressing the preeminently novelistic nature of the woman on the bench, the narrator is able to insist all the more on her "reality." In fact, it is as though Flaubert has placed not only her but the entire narrative within quotation marks—precisely so as to be able to craft the precious illusion of a real world: a possible world, a virtual world. Ultimately, one might say, those invisible quotation marks serve to authenticate the world of the novel. As Barthes would have suggested, they to put an end to meaning. They arrest signification. Those invisible quotation marks say: *This is the real.*

Soon enough, the woman on the bench will move out of Frédéric's field of vision, come to life, and acquire something like a reality of her own. She will be given a name, Madame Arnoux. She will also be given

---

[34] Flaubert then crosses out the section and begins anew, and after a few rounds of corrections, Madame Arnoux has turned into a romantic heroine at large: "Elle ressemblait aux femmes décrites alors dans les livres […]." See *"L'éducation sentimentale,"* Flaubert Papers, Institut des textes et des manuscrits modernes (CNRS-ENS), Paris, NAFR 17599, fol. 37v. Later on, Flaubert will delete the section in question; and all that remains in the final version of the scene is the simple yet mysterious *elle*.

a social status: she is the wife of the chatty man in red boots, monsieur Arnoux, art dealer and proprietor of the periodical *L'Art industriel*; in addition, she is the devoted mother of two well-behaved children. In this way, the luminous being on the bench is socially defined, for Flaubert and for us, but not for Frédéric. In his eyes, she will—and must—remain an otherworldly creature.[35]

Yet no matter how far we progress into Flaubert's narrative, the ways in which Madame Arnoux is described will retain that phantasmatic character. Indeed, when it comes to the representation of Frédéric's primary object of desire, we are always already located in the imaginary realm. Peter Brooks observes that Flaubert's reader is "never vouchsafed any 'objective' view of Mme Arnoux, any perspective that would allow us to step outside Frédéric's mystified vision of her."[36] The reason is simple. The ways in which Flaubert makes visible Madame Arnoux in the remainder of the narrative will almost always recall that first visual design, keeping alive that originary moment out of which the entire plot flows.

All this brings me little by little to the core of my argument. What I have been discussing so far is not description in the traditional sense. It is something else. Historically speaking, what Flaubert accomplishes by way of images such as the one of Madame Arnoux is the invention of a whole new representational space.

Where the Action Is

Throughout the novel, Madame Arnoux's appearance will strikingly often retain the almost formulaic flatness that characterizes the mode in which she was first represented, and her image will similarly be subjected to framing and reification. The following episode comes half way through the novel. Frédéric and Madame Arnoux now meet regularly, although the young man has yet to confess his passion. The representation of Madame Arnoux's appearance clearly refers us back to the very first impression of her, while at the same time reinforcing her reality as image.

> Le feu dans la cheminée ne brûlait pas, la pluie fouettait contre les vitres. Mme Arnoux, sans bouger, restait les deux mains sur les bras de son

---

[35] See also Baumgart, *Liebesspuren*, 15.
[36] Peter Brooks, "Retrospective Lust, or Flaubert's Perversities," in *Reading for the Plot* (Cambridge, Mass.: Harvard University Press, 1984), 186.

fauteuil; les pattes de son bonnet tombaient comme les bandelettes d'un sphinx; son profil pur se découpait en pâleur au milieu de l'ombre.
　　Il avait envie de se jeter à ses genoux. Un craquement se fit dans le couloir, il n'osa.
　　Il était empêché, d'ailleurs, par une sorte de crainte religieuse. Cette robe, se confondant avec les ténèbres, lui paraissait démesurée, infinie, insoulevable; et précisément à cause de cela son désir redoublait. Mais la peur de faire trop et de ne pas faire assez lui ôtait tout discernement. (308–9)

The fire in the hearth had gone out; the rain lashed against the windowpanes. Madame Arnoux sat motionless with her hands on the arms of her chair; the ribbons of her cap hung down like the head-bands of a sphinx; her clear-cut profile stood out in pale relief in the dusk.
　　He longed to throw himself on his knees. There was a creaking noise in the corridor; he did not dare.
　　Besides, he was restrained by a sort of religious awe. That dress of hers, merging into the shadows, struck him as enormous, infinite, impossible to lift; and precisely because of that his desire increased. But the fear of going too far, and that of not going far enough, robbed him all of power of judgement. (201–2)

　　The central image here is that of the sphinx. Everything in the passage congeals in this well-placed yet inconspicuous metaphor: the stillness of Madame Arnoux as she reclines in her armchair, her immutable immobility, her imposing silence, her utter impregnability. To be sure, the statuesque Madame Arnoux is the subject of an action, but that activity of hers is emphatically insignificant: *elle restait les deux mains sur les bras de son fauteuil*—that is all. What is more, her activity is leveled with that of her cap ribbons and her profile; both are grammatical subjects in their own right. Little by little, Madame Arnoux begins to resemble an impersonal sculpture, towering before Frédéric like a vast enigma made of stone. And no sooner has she been likened to a sphinx than her attire begins to acquire otherworldly features. In fact, Madame Arnoux and her dress are like communicating vessels: the more inanimate and petrified she herself appears, the more animated and lifelike is her dress.
　　Frédéric's visual impression is thus both lexically and syntactically coded. Indeed, Flaubert's lexical choice—the sphinx—oversees an entire syntactical drama, in which human agency is pushed into the background while things—a ribbon, a profile, a dress—move center stage and begin to act.
　　But the metaphor also has another crucial function: it serves to motivate Frédéric's exclusively visual experience of Madame Arnoux, and to urge on the reader a similar approach to the narrative content. And in

case the reader should have missed the metaphor and its manifold implications, Flaubert's narrator makes sure to stress that Madame Arnoux's pale profile stands out in relief against the darkness, just as it did in that paradigmatic scene in the opening pages. *Son profil pur se découpait en pâleur au milieu de l'ombre*: this verb—se découper—recurs remarkably often in Flaubert's descriptions of women and other things seen. Madame Arnoux again emerges as image, as a self-isolating visual entity hovering in the field of vision.

But there is even more to the image of the sphinx. A mental construct projected onto Madame Arnoux, it bespeaks Frédéric's propensity for failure, here and elsewhere. By way of this metaphor, Frédéric's utter impotence is at it were objectified in Madame Arnoux herself.

More than anything else, it is Frédéric's hopeless love for Madame Arnoux that gives coherence to *L'éducation sentimentale*, along with his feeble attempts at making his way in the world. But apart from this singular *amour fou*, Frédéric has other loves. To make his way in Paris society, he teams up with two strategically placed women, first Rosanette, also known as La Maréchale, or the Marshal, and then Madame Dambreuse. The former is a sought-after Parisian courtesan; the latter is the wealthy and powerful wife of an equally wealthy and powerful man, monsieur Dambreuse.

Attraction, immersion, framing: as a rule, whenever Frédéric is struck by desire for the female sex, the description of the woman in question tends to follow a remarkably homogeneous pattern. In such moments, as in the initial portrait of Madame Arnoux's silhouette, the plot slows down, the narrative flow comes to a halt, and little by little, a luminous vision takes shape.

In the following episode, Frédéric and Rosanette are on their way to the horse races. It is a sunny Sunday and the two are traveling through the empty shuttered streets of Paris. Frédéric has begun to actively pursue Rosanette. To increase his male prestige, and to satisfy her taste for luxury, he has done what he is expected to do: he has hired a carriage, a postilion, and two horses. Reclining in his seat as the carriage travels along the quiet streets, Frédéric watches Rosanette with an eager eye, taking pleasure in her delicious appearance.

> La voiture prit un train plus rapide [...]. Frédéric se laissait aller au bercement des soupentes. La Maréchale tournait la tête, à droite et à gauche, en souriant.
>
> Son chapeau de paille nacrée avait une garniture de dentelle noire. Le capuchon de son burnous flottait au vent; et elle s'abritait du soleil sous une ombrelle de satin lilas, pointue par le haut comme une pagode.

> – Quels amours de petits doigts! dit Frédéric, en lui prenant doucement l'autre main, la gauche, ornée d'un bracelet d'or, en forme de gourmette. (312–3)

> The carriage began to move faster [...]. Frédéric gave himself up to the rocking of the springs. The Marshal smilingly turned her head right and left.
>   Her hat of pearly straw was trimmed with black lace. The hood of her burnous fluttered in the breeze; and she sheltered from the sun under a parasol of lilac satin, rising to a point in the middle like a pagoda.
>   "What sweet little fingers!" said Frédéric, gently taking her free hand, the left hand, which wore a gold bracelet in the form of a curb-chain. (204–5)

The visual design of Madame Arnoux in the opening pages, and the ravishing beauty it seeks to convey, is echoed in the image of Rosanette, and not only on the syntactical level. Desire in Flaubert has a lexicon of its own, and a strangely limited one at that. Like Madame Arnoux before her, Rosanette sports a straw hat that elicits a detailed description of its shape, color, and structure; and by the time we learn that a textile object is fluttering in the wind, we intuit that the profane world of female fashion has been magically transformed into a very different realm: that of desire. In the opening pages, Madame Arnoux's profile could be seen against the sky while her pink hat ribbons palpitated in the breeze; here Rosanette's head is adorned by a hat whose hood flutters in the air. In the Flaubertian world of desire, there is almost always something that flutters, or flickers, or billows. It is as though Frédéric's inner agitation animates that ribbon, that hood, that skirt.

This much is in any case clear: in *Madame Bovary* and *L'éducation sentimentale,* the lived reality of the object of desire may seem eternally arrested in a flattened image, resolutely transmuted into a nature morte by the alienating power of the gaze of desire, but the still life is always provided with a dash of kinetic energy—this, besides, is why Flaubert's pictorial representations have so little in common with photography.[37] The figuration of desire, in Flaubert, always involves movement. So it

---

[37] But see Anne Green's interesting article on how contemporary photography—panoramic photographs, cartes de visite, pornographic images—may have influenced various aspects of *L'éducation sentimentale*. Green suggests that Flaubert's panoramic representations of Parisian sights, especially views of the Seine, owe much to contemporary photographic practices. She also discusses Gustave Le Gray's photographic studies of the trees in the Fontainebleu forest, suggesting that they may well have influenced the famous description of nature in the Fontainebleau episode. See Anne Green, "'Ce n'est jamais ça…' Ecriture et photographie chez Flaubert," in *Flaubert et la théorie littéraire*, 197–205.

is that desire, that transformative force otherwise invisible to the naked eye, is made visible by a pink hat ribbon fluttering in the breeze.

What does Rosanette herself see as she is being looked at by Frédéric? And what, if anything, does she think and feel? Flaubert does not say. Focalized through Frédéric, the passage concentrates on that which can be seen and that alone—until Frédéric catches sight of her delicious fingers, at which point visual fetishism gives way to tactility. But Rosanette herself is not focalized, and must not be. When looked at, she must be immersed in herself—as all female objects of desire in Flaubert must be immersed in themselves whenever they emerge into the field of visual desire. They must not look back, not return the gaze, not reciprocate, in much the same way as a film actor must never look into the camera.

Should the female object of desire be immersed in an activity, it must be an activity of an utterly insignificant kind. Accordingly, Rosanette is busy turning her head this way and that, meanwhile smiling. By the same token, Madame Arnoux is occupied with a piece of embroidery when Frédéric, in that paradigmatic first scene, makes her the object of his gaze; and in the sphinx scene, she rests her hands on the arms of the chair. And Emma, in *Madame Bovary,* is similarly immersed in various trivial activities when she is gazed at: she is holding her head to one side, or sewing a bandage, or sucking her fingers, or standing under an umbrella, or reclining in a chair. Not even when Charles looks Emma in the eyes that morning in the marital bed does she return the gaze.

This thematics of immersion persists throughout Flaubert's 1869 novel. What is more, it can also be traced in *Salammbô* (1862) and in *Trois contes* (1877). This puts Flaubert's mode of representing women squarely within the so-called antitheatrical paradigm that Michael Fried has mapped in his writings on French painting from the 1750s to the 1860s, tracing a critical current that stretches from David and Géricault to Courbet and Manet.[38]

But this also goes to show just how immersed Flaubert is in the pictorial as such. For while Fried describes the logic that served to regulate the relationship between the viewer and the object of perception (paint-

---

[38] Michael Fried's work on the so-called antitheatrical tradition in French premodernist painting forms a trilogy of books: *Absorption and Theatricality: Painting and Beholder in the Age of Diderot* (Chicago: University of Chicago Press, 1980); *Courbet's Realism* (Chicago: University of Chicago Press, 1990), and *Manet's Modernism; or, the Face of Painting in the 1860s* (Chicago: University of Chicago Press, 1990). For a critical discussion of Fried's theory of absorption, see Robert Pippin, "Authenticity in Painting: Remarks on Michael Fried's Art History," *Critical Inquiry 31* (2005): 575–98. Pippin foregrounds the essentially ontological framework of Fried's approach and its philosophical underpinnings, at the same time suggesting that the ideal of "absorption" might also be understood in historical, even historicizing, terms.

ings), we are concerned with the relation between the viewer and the object of perception (human subjects) as it is depicted within a cultural artifact. To put it another way, Fried is discussing a specific version of a relationship that is spectatorial already and that cannot be otherwise; we, however, are considering relationships between human subjects that, in Flaubert, are rendered as exclusively visual and one-sided ones. This confirms the pictorial thrust that everywhere makes itself felt in Flaubert. As an object of desire, woman is always already an image.

I shall have more to say about this thematics of immersion shortly, but first I want to gloss in more detail the syntactical logic that governs Flaubert's representation of female objects of desire.

After the horse races, Rosanette, Frédéric, and a few others are dining at a restaurant. Rosanette has had beef, shrimp, truffle, pineapple, vanilla sorbet, and bourgogne. Her appetite is as good as her lack of ceremony is striking. As she rounds off the meal with a piece of tropical fruit, Frédéric watches her with an irritated yet keen eye: this is the woman who has just had the nerve to humiliate his goddess, Madame Arnoux. What is more, she has done it in public. Yet Frédéric cannot help finding her irresistible. He looks at her. What does he see? Rosanette is absorbed by her munching; Frédéric, for his part, is absorbed by her image. And these two symmetrical appetites, distinct yet related, now merge into a single tantalizing vision overseen by so many candle flames and a pomegranate, that time-honored symbol of fertility.

> [Rosanette] mordait dans une grenade, le coude posé sur la table; les bougies du candélabre devant elle tremblaient au vent; cette lumière blanche pénétrait sa peau de tons nacrés, mettait du rose à ses paupières, faisait briller les globes de ses yeux; la rougeur du fruit se confondait avec le pourpre de ses lèvres, ses narines minces battaient; et toute sa personne avait quelque chose d'insolent, d'ivre et de noyé qui exaspérait Frédéric, et pourtant lui jetait au coeur des désirs fous. (327)

> [Rosanette] was biting into a pomegranate, with her elbow on the table; the flames of the candelabra in front of her flickered in the draught, and this white light steeped her skin with mother-of-pearl hues, tinged her eyelids with pink, and made her eyeballs glow; the redness of the fruit blended with the crimson of her lips; her slender nostrils quivered; and there was something insolent, intoxicated, and indefinable about her whole person which exasperated Frédéric, and yet filled his heart with mad desires. (214)

This feverish snapshot of Rosanette in the act of consuming a pomegranate speaks of her as a spectacle. It is a sparkling, dazzling, and utterly defamiliarizing description. In the first sentence, Rosanette appears as the grammatical subject, but the predicate attached to her—*mordait*—is perfectly inessential, as trivial as Madame Arnoux's resting her two hands on the arms of her chair. And then, in a characteristic move, Flaubert's narrator strips Rosanette of syntactical agency only to transpose it onto the candle flames, the light, and the red color: these now act on Rosanette's face, transforming it into a vast yet fragmented surface that may be consumed by the eye in much the same way as one consumes an exotic fruit. And all of it is delivered in one verbal flow, for the scene is held together in a single sentence.

The fantasmatic vision of Rosanette is topped off with a telling detail: those nostrils that set themselves free. To be sure, Rosanette possesses a certain agency and, therefore, intentionality; after all, she is said to bite into that fruit. But in language there is only so much agency to go around, and most of it has been deposited in the candlelight and the fruit. Indeed, from the first semi-colon onwards, intentionality is located in the realm of the inanimate. It is as though Rosanette's intentional consciousness had been temporarily evacuated. Left to themselves, her nostrils beat and tremble and shiver, as though they had a life of their own, as though they existed in a vacuum. This much is in any case clear: if the sphinx served to suggest impotence, the pomegranate carries sexual promise. Frédéric's love will soon be consummated.

To treat a given phenomenon—a human being, a setting, an object—as something to be looked at and little else may seem natural enough, especially in desire-driven representations such as the ones I have been discussing, but it still has to be motivated, and Flaubert goes to great lengths in order to naturalize an aestheticizing approach that is more or less exclusively visual.

For the sake of contrast, and to remind ourselves of the exceedingly visual thrust of Flaubert's tightly framed images, let us look briefly at a description of a woman as seen by a man in Jane Austen's *Pride and Prejudice* (1813). Elizabeth has become "an object of some interest" in the eyes of Mr. Darcy, and the all-seeing and all-knowing narrator sets out to explain the gentleman's grounds for finding her attractive.

> Mr. Darcy had at first scarcely allowed her to be pretty; he had looked at her without admiration at the ball; and when they next met, he looked at her only to criticize. But no sooner had he made it clear to himself and his friends that she had hardly a good feature in her face, than he began to find it was rendered uncommonly intelligent by the beautiful expression of her dark eyes. To this discovery succeeded some others equally mortifying. Though he had detected with a critical eye more than one failure of perfect symmetry in her form, he was forced to acknowledge her figure to be light and pleasing; and in spite of his asserting that her

> manners were not those of the fashionable world, he was caught by their easy playfulness.[39]

This passage is all about how Darcy's perception of Elizabeth has undergone a subtle yet palpable change. Two hundred and fifty pages later the two will be married. But although Austen dwells on Elizabeth's looks, there is nothing visually evocative about this passage. Indeed, nothing could be farther removed from Madame Arnoux's sphinx-like appearance or, for that matter, the description of how Emma Bovary's veins beat deliciously near her temples. In Austen, there is not a single metaphor, but also not a single concrete observation—except, perhaps, for the remark that the protagonist's eyes are dark. The passage contains impressions, judgments, and assessments, even conclusions and abstractions, but very little attention is paid to what actually founds them. We cannot really see Elizabeth before our eyes—to this end, the visual information is too scarce.

Remarkably enough, however, the passage still succeeds in delineating something like an appearance, and few readers would even notice the relative lack of external data and visible detail. Why? Because Austen makes no clear-cut distinction between the exterior and the interior. For her, the boundaries between character, behavior, and looks are always blurred. And these, moreover, form part of a coherent and intelligible system. Austen is a formidable analyst of those psychological mechanisms that are invisible to the naked eye. In her literary universe, human action and interaction are everything.

For Flaubert, the opposite is true. The visible reigns supreme, and the rest is silence. Flaubert makes repeated efforts at naturalizing an approach that insists on relating to the world as though it were an image. We have seen that the shape of Rosanette's umbrella was likened to a pagoda, and that Madame Arnoux's hair invited comparisons to the headbands of a sphinx. Let us now look at a description of Madame Dambreuse, with whom Frédéric will eventually have an affair. Frédéric has just entered her residence. It is a summer evening, and Madame Dambreuse is hosting a reception. Because Frédéric's railway shares have just increased in value, he enters the drawing-room with a certain sense of entitlement and looks eagerly for the hostess.

> La lumière était faible, malgré les lampes posées dans les coins; car les trois fenêtres, grandes ouvertes, dressaient parallèlement trois larges carrés d'ombre noire. Des jardinières, sous les tableaux, occupaient jusqu'à hauteur d'homme les intervalles de la muraille; et une théière d'argent

---
[39] Jane Austen, *Pride and Prejudice* (New York: Bantam, 1981), 16.

avec un samovar se mirait au fond, dans une glace. Un murmure de voix discrètes s'élevait. On entendait des escarpins craquer sur le tapis.

Il distingua des habits noirs, puis une table ronde éclairée par un grand abat-jour, sept ou huit femmes en toilettes d'été, et, un peu plus loin, Mme Dambreuse dans un fauteuil à bascule. Sa robe de taffetas lilas avait des manches à crevés, d'où s'échappaient des bouillons de mousseline, le ton doux de l'étoffe se mariant à la nuance de ses cheveux; et elle se tenait quelque peu renversée en arrière, avec le bout de son pied sur un coussin, — tranquille comme une oeuvre d'art pleine de délicatesse, une fleur de haute culture. (357–8)

In spite of the lamps standing in the corners, the light was dim; for the three windows were wide open, and formed three broad rectangles of darkness side by side. The spaces in between, under the pictures, were occupied by flower-stands five or six feet high; and a silver tea-pot with a samovar was reflected in a mirror in the distance. There was a discreet murmur of voices, and shoes could be heard squeaking on the carpet.

He made out a few tail-coats, then a round table lit by a big shaded lamp, seven or eight women in summer dresses, and, a little farther on, Madame Dambreuse in a rocking-chair. Her lilac taffeta dress had slashed sleeves with puffed muslin linings; the soft shade of the material harmonized with the colour of her hair; and she was leaning back a little, with the tip of her foot on a cushion, as calm as some delicate work of art or rare flower. (236–7)

We do not have to move very far into this passage to know that we have entered the domains of description and that Flaubert, once again, will be concerned with the intricacies of visual perception. The very first words make this clear: *la lumière était faible*. The piece of information given—that the room is poorly lit—justifies the central event in this artfully constructed passage: how Frédéric's gaze searches for and finally discovers Madame Dambreuse. For what Flaubert's narrator attempts to do here is to recreate the very temporality of Frédéric's perceptual activity as the latter crosses the threshold of the drawing-room and begins to scan the human content of the dim space. *Il distingua des habits noirs, puis une table ronde éclairée par un grand abat-jour, sept ou huit femmes en toilettes d'été, et, un peu plus loin, Mme Dambreuse dans un fauteuil à bascule.* Within the space of a single sentence, the narrator manages to cover considerable mental ground: he moves from perceptual difficulty to secure knowledge, from those metonymic black coats and that hasty estimate of the number of ladies present—seven? eight?—to the final identification of the object Frédéric has been looking for all along. Indeed, a few seconds ago Frédéric was able merely to distinguish a few part-objects and little more; now his gaze comes to a halt, fastens onto Madame Dambreuse, and absorbs her appearance in its entirety, poring over it, exploring it, assessing it, all the way from the color, shape, and material of her exquisite dress to the tip of her foot resting on a cushion. In rendering Frédéric's visual experience as it extends in time, the narrator thus seeks to represent its phenomenology to the reader.

It is only logical that the passage should end with a comparatio that underscores Frédéric's visual mode of approaching the hostess as she reclines gloriously in her chair. In fact, there are two such metaphors, the one piled on top of the other: *comme une oeuvre d'art pleine de délicatesse, une fleur de haute culture.* As so often in Flaubert, such images serve to justify the transformation of a phenomenal reality into an exclusively visual-perceptual one, while at the same time encouraging the reader to adopt a similar vantage point.

The female foot, in Flaubert, is a recurring fetishistic object, in *Madame Bovary* as well as in *L'éducation sentimentale.* Florence Emptaz, in a wonderfully eccentric study, has mapped the podological pathways that structure Flaubert's thematic universe.[40] But the foot also serves a very different purpose. The art of realist description has its rules. If a description of a character begins at the head, we can be sure that it will reach the foot in due course and then be terminated.[41] The foot is part of a textual machinery that works to orchestrate the reader's mode of processing the narrative content. The foot closes that Flaubertian space of representation that, time and again, insists on bursting into the narrative fabric. In other words, the foot makes desire flash into the present and then immediately plunges us back into the real.

With this episode, we have moved deep into the plot. Yet the singular vision of Madame Arnoux in the opening pages continues to have a shaping role in the unfolding of Flaubert's novel, particularly when it comes to the figuration of desire. One evening, Mademoiselle Vatnaz pays an unexpected visit to Frédéric. She looks around, inspects his belongings, and makes a joke about the women she assumes he receives in his elegantly decorated house. All of a sudden, she stands before Frédéric, so

---

[40] Florence Emptaz, *Aux pieds de Flaubert* (Paris: Grasset, 2002): "Tout lecteur averti s'avise bientôt que de toutes les parties du corps, le pied est celle qui est la plus souvent évoquée: rarement nu, chaussé presque toujours, parfois taré, bot, boiteux, difforme. Il y en a partout! Texte myriapode! Des pieds qui marchent, courent, valsent, battent le pavé, foulent les champs de bataille, éperonnent le flanc des chevaux, résonnent haut et fort! Les bruits de pas martèlent la page: claquements de sabots, craquements d'escarpins, désert sonore des trépignements des monstres malins. Un incessant ballet de chaussures nombreuses et variées, bottes, bottines, sabots, galoches, brodequins, souliers vernis, pantoufles, chaussons, sandales, cothurnes, hante le texte bruyamment" (18).
[41] See Philippe Hamon, "Qu'est-ce qu'une description?" *Poétique* 12 (1972): 465–85; "What Is a Description?" in *French Literary Theory Today,* ed. Tzvetan Todorov, trans. R. Carter (Cambridge: Cambridge University Press, 1982), 147–78.

close that he can perceive the scent of her hair. The narrative momentum is suspended.

> Et, amicalement, elle lui prit le menton. Il tressaillit au contact de ses longues mains, tout à la fois maigres et douces. Elle avait autour des poignets une bordure de dentelle et, sur le corsage de sa robe verte, des passementeries, comme un hussard. Son chapeau de tulle noir, à bords descendants, lui cachait un peu le front; ses yeux brillaient là-dessous; une odeur de patchouli s'échappait de ses bandeaux; la carcel posée sur un guéridon, en l'éclairant d'en bas comme une rampe de théâtre, faisait saillir sa mâchoire; — et tout à coup, devant cette femme laide qui avait dans la taille des ondulations de panthère, Frédéric sentit une convoitise énorme, un désir de volupté bestiale. (382–3)
>
> And she playfully took him by the chin. He shivered at the touch of her long hands, which were at once thin and soft. She had lace at her wrists, and the bodice of her green dress was trimmed with braid like a hussar's uniform. Her black tulle hat had a drooping brim, which partly concealed her forehead; beneath it, her eyes were glittering; and her hair gave off a scent of patchouli. The oil-lamp, which was standing on the table, lit up her face from below, like the footlights of a theatre, throwing her jaw into relief; and suddenly, in the presence of this ugly woman, with the lithe body of a panther, Frédéric felt an overwhelming lust, a longing for sensual pleasure. (255)

Mademoiselle Vatnaz is promptly transformed into spectacle; and Frédéric is as promptly pulled into the force-field of desire. Flaubert performs yet again a stylistic maneouvre whose mechanisms we now recognize: the passage opens with the straightforward reporting of an inessential action (*elle lui prit le menton*) and then offers a visual impression in which the subject of the initial action—Mademoiselle Vatnaz—is swiftly turned into a perceptual object, whose various attributes immediately take on a life of their own (*ses yeux brillaient*, and so on).

Who is Mademoiselle Vatnaz? She is everything that Madame Arnoux is not: unmarried, independent, self-assertive. She is also ugly. What is more, she is a feminist avant la lettre, with socialist leanings. But in this passage her image reenacts that of Madame Arnoux. Transformed by Frédéric's desire-laden gaze, her being turns into appearance and little more; she emerges as a bundle of insignificant and exclusively external features—fingers, lace, tulle, brim, eyes, hair. These features, in their turn, are carriers of qualities that stir Frédéric's senses, and the passage accordingly offers us a miniature inventory of smell, touch, and vision. But the faculty of vision prevails. It is the anaphorical oil-lamp—and the implied theatrical metaphor behind it—that presides over these lines, turning the sensory experience of the object of desire into pure image.

As happens so often in Flaubert, light is responsible for the action. Light solidifies, acting on the facial surface that simultaneously emerges into view. And no sooner has the lower part of Mademoiselle Vatnaz's face turned into a major scene of visual action, complete with those extravagant special effects produced by the light source below, than her jaw ceases to be an organic part of her face. In the sexual field of vision, female bodies are defamiliarized and dissolve into their component parts—and that jaw meanwhile becomes something like an aesthetic event, a spectacle within the spectacle.

Flaubert's novel contains innumerable such moments during which the female object of desire is first introduced and then artfully dissolved. An image is made and remade. In all these cases, the same sort of syntactical pattern can be observed: agency retreats from the human to the inanimate world, or else the former is leveled with the latter. We have already scrutinized the scene when Rosanette's lips merge with that exotic fruit while her nostrils begin to lead a life of their own, flapping and shivering. In another romantic restaurant scene, Rosanette similarly disintegrates into a catalogue of facial features and discrete body parts. The descriptive movement begins at the head and works its way down to her upper extremities, and these acquire syntactic agency:

> La table était près de la fenêtre, Rosanette en face de lui; et il contemplait son petit nez fin et blanc, ses lèvres retroussées, ses yeux clairs, ses bandeaux châtains qui bouffaient, sa jolie figure ovale. Sa robe de foulard écru collait à ses épaules un peu tombantes; et, sortant de leurs manchettes tout unies, ses deux mains découpaient, versaient à boire, s'avançaient sur la nappe. (485)

> The table was next to the window; and he sat opposite Rosanette, gazing at her delicate little white nose, her pouting lips, her bright eyes, her loosely combed chestnut hair, her pretty oval face. Her dress of raw silk clung to her slightly sloping shoulders, while her hands, emerging from their plain cuffs, cut up her food, poured out her wine, moved over the tablecloth. (324)

In this scene, Rosanette appears once again as an emblem of immersion, absorbed as she is by cutting her food into pieces, transporting wine from the bottle to the glass, and so on. Whether she is aware of it or not, she happily lets herself be looked at. In the first part of the passage, Frédéric is the subject of the syntactical action: he explicitly contemplates Rosanette's appearance. It is his gaze—and, by implication, his consciousness—that motivates the catalogue of that small white nose, those full lips, those dazzling eyes. In the second half of the passage, however, the syntactical order is turned upside down. The picture is remade. From a grammatical point of view, Frédéric's gaze retreats into the background, while Rosanette's two hands move center stage. The narrator amasses no fewer than three predicates that are attached to the improbable subject that we find presiding over the very last clause: *ses deux mains découpaient, versaient à boire, s'avançaient sur la nappe*. Acting by themselves, these hands turn into a spectacle before Frédéric's eyes. It is as though they were self-animating, as though they had been endowed with an uncanny intentionality all their own. Indeed, it is as though they were living creatures, capable of making perfectly meaningful decisions.

The result is something that we know and theorize under the rubric of "defamiliarization" or, alternatively, "estrangement." Half a century later James Joyce will pick up that aesthetic and push it to an extreme. In *Ulysses* (1922), eyes, hands, tongues, sausages, onions, tea spoons, umbrellas, and the like make up a vast sensory space crowded by animated objects that actively enter into dialogue with Leopold Bloom's sensory apparatus.

In cinematographic terms, one might say that Flaubert provides a close-up of Rosanette's independently moving hands. If the close-up produces instant autonomy by way of tight visual framing, Flaubert manages to create a similar effect by playing with rules of syntax, that is, by ascribing agency to a discrete body part. I do not mean to say that the rendering of Rosanette's hands are a close-up, nor that it is like a close-up. Cinematography, in any case, was invented only much later. But I would argue that theories of the close-up may help us understand the peculiarity of the Flaubertian image, especially its pragmatics.

Once an extremity has been reified and turned into a thing that acts on its own, it can be re-anthropomorphized, but in a whole new manner, as in the following episode. Madame Arnoux and Frédéric have begun to meet regularly and are on first-name basis. Their relationship, chaste but deliciously intimate, allows for rapturous moments of bliss. As Madame Arnoux is playing with the sunlight, she turns into an object of desire. In the meantime, her fingers acquire a life of their own.

> Quelquefois, les rayons du soleil, traversant la jalousie, tendaient depuis le plafond jusque sur les dalles comme les cordes d'une lyre, des brins de poussière tourbillonnaient dans ces barres lumineuses. Elle s'amusait à les fendre, avec sa main; – Frédéric la saisissait, doucement; et il contemplait l'entrelacs de ses veines, les grains de sa peau, la forme de ses doigts. Chacun de ses doigts était, pour lui, plus qu'une chose, presque une personne. (406)

> Sometimes the sunbeams, coming through the Venetian blind, would stretch what looked like the strings of a lyre from ceiling to floor, and specks of dust would whirl about in these luminous bars. [Madame Arnoux] amused herself by breaking them with her hand; Frédéric would gently seize it and gaze at the tracery of her veins, the grain of her skin, the shape of her fingers. For him, each of her fingers was something more than a thing, almost a person. (271)

What I have been trying to do so far is suggest just how central the pictorial mode is in Flaubert's 1869 novel and analyze in detail some of the syntactic mechanisms that organize the logic of the Flaubertian image. We have seen that Flaubert's descriptions of women are almost always exclusively visual. We have also seen that these descriptions tend to be presented as images. This must be understood in the strongest sense possible. As I have emphasized throughout my discussion of both *Madame Bovary* and *L'éducation sentimentale*, the point is not so much that these descriptions come across as literary images, which they no doubt do. They have all the plasticity, texture, and rhetorical power typically associated with the verbal image, all the way from the shield of Achilles to, say, Goethe's description of the lush landscape at the beginning of *Wahlverwandschaften*. The point I want to make is different: what accords the Flaubertian image a special place in the history of literary description and helps explain the radical novelty of his visual designs is that Flaubert's images are effectively *represented* as images. What is even more remarkable is that they are *perceived* as such. Indeed, the implied viewer approaches the seen—for example, a woman's appearance—as though it were an image and little else.

All this can be put a little differently. What Flaubert's images force us to realize is that when we talk about literary images, we necessarily do so in a manner of speaking. We mobilize a metaphor. In speaking of literary images in a narrative text, we usually have in mind such moments when the diegetic momentum slows down and we are made to visualize a phenomenon or other. We typically say that the text makes us see something before us: an object, a character, an action, a landscape, a view, or the like. It can be Odysseus's thigh, or Madame Vauquer's nose, or the muddy battlefields around Waterloo. That is to say, when our eyes travel along the lines of a page, fluttering over those clusters of black signs and interspersed blank spaces, we extract meaning. We see things. And what we see are mental constructs that we are prone to call "images."

But the Flaubertian image is a very different creature. To understand its specificity, we first need to ask a basic question. What is a picture?

Here is Léon Battista Alberti's famous definition of the picture, as summarized by Svetlana Alpers. "[A picture] is a framed surface or pane situated at a certain distance from a viewer who looks through it at a second or substitute world."[42] A vastly influential Renaissance architect and art theoretician, Alberti devised a theory of the picture that was to undergird academic painting for centuries, in particular, the mathematical rationalization of perspective. Alberti laid down precise rules for how to turn the surface into a window onto a perspectival world, so that the beholder's eye would approach the picture in much the same way as one looks through a window into a space.[43] In short, the picture was to be seen through, not to be looked at. This was key to Alberti's perspectival realism.

Whenever we come across what we typically call a literary image and proceed to visualize its contents, we similarly see through the black signs on the page. This is of course also true for Flaubert. But to see through the Flaubertian letter is to enter a peculiar visual order, because Flaubert's images almost always present themselves as images. They call attention to their very *Bildlichkeit*, that is, to the image-character of the image. Framed, flattened, autonomous, Flaubert's images tend to emerge as surfaces. We saw a similar logic at work in the cinematic close-up and how it overturns perspectival realism, reducing the world to this face, these eyes, these hands. All this brings me little by little to the point I want to make, which is that Flaubert's images appear not as windows into a space but rather as images. They are not transparent but rather opaque. They offer not substitute worlds but rather pictorial surfaces.

The features I have been describing here are a vital part of what I want to call Flaubert's pictorial aesthetic. And that aesthetic, in its turn, is crucial to the new representational space which is Flaubert's signal invention and which emerges on a grand scale in his later works, from 1857 onward.

My primary example so far has been the representation of women in *Madame Bovary* as well as in *L'éducation sentimentale*. In Flaubert, woman is image and little else, at least when she enters the sexual field of vision. The portrait of Madame Arnoux sitting alone on the bench is a particularly rich and striking example. Indeed, it is paradigmatic. And as we have seen on numerous occasions, these pictorial moments are

---
[42] Svetlana Alpers, *The Art of Describing: Dutch Art in the Seventeenth Century* (Chicago: University of Chicago Press, 1983), xix.
[43] See Léon Battista Alberti, *On Painting,* trans. Cecil Grayson (London: Penguin, 1991), esp. 37–59.

privileged ones in Flaubert. In *L'éducation sentimentale,* the entire plot derives from a single such visual experience: Frédéric Moreau, after all, falls in love not with Madame Arnoux but with an image. In Flaubert's 1869 novel, the image has thus acquired a central organizing importance that it did not quite have in *Madame Bovary,* although it was certainly prominent enough. It is an image—or, more specifically, an image-experience—that prompts the story about Frédéric's sentimental education, driving it forward through a connecting chain of similar visual experiences.

What I have been proposing is that Flaubert's pictorial aesthetic is intimately bound up with the idea of the feminine, that is, with woman as an object of desire. I have also sought to show that the visual division of labor that emerges in Flaubert's writings is a highly gendered affair. Consider the two protagonists I have been discussing. Whereas Emma is constantly made visible, subjected to excessive image-making even as she lies dying, Frédéric's external appearance remains an enigma. In short, Emma is a visual event; Frédéric is not.

And whereas Frédéric is constantly presented as an author of perception, focalizing a vast array of aestheticizing descriptions of women, Emma hardly ever emerges as a fastidious beholder of the male company she keeps. To be sure, Charles, Léon, and Rodolphe do occasionally flash into view, but their appearances fail to congeal into expansive images that release themselves from the narrative flow. Indeed, Flaubert's visual universe is a rigorously gendered one.

A parenthesis. We have seen that Madame Arnoux is something like a model, serving as a paradigm for the description of other female objects of desire in the novel. But the description of Madame Arnoux, too, has a model, a fact that adds a dimension to the gendered nature of Flaubert's visual universe. To be sure, the luminous woman on the bench can be traced back to the Madonna and other otherworldly creatures, as numerous critics and scholars have suggested, but there is also a quite different lineage: she recalls a courtesan whom Flaubert met on his trip to Egypt. Indeed, the celebrated passage about Madame Arnoux has a striking affinity with the way in which Flaubert, in his travel notes, describes the famous courtesan and dancer Koutchouck-Hânem. Flaubert dwells in detail on her looks and her dancing; he describes, too, his sexual activities with her. In writing *L'éducation sentimentale,* Flaubert recycled several phrases in modified form, for there are parallels between Madame Arnoux and Koutchouck-Hânem both on the syntactic level and the semantic one.

Flaubert's travel companion, Maxime Du Camp, also kept a diary; and he, too, described the courtesan's physical appearance. As Pierre-Marc de Biasi has emphasized, the phrase that Flaubert uses to open the description of Madame Arnoux—"Ce fut comme une apparition"—actually originates in Du Camp's account of how the courtesan flashes into view.[44] "Je poussai une porte fermée au loquet et j'entrai dans une petite cour sur laquelle descendait un étroit escalier extérieur," Du Camp writes in *Le Nil*. "Koutchouk-Hanem m'attendait. Je la vis en levant la tête; *ce fut comme une apparition*. Debout, sous les derniers rayons de soleil qui l'enveloppait de lumière, vêtue d'une simple petite chemise en gaze […] elle était superbe" (*L'éducation* 46n. 4).

Moreover, the sentence that closes the portrait of Madame Arnoux carries a distinct echo of the passage describing how Flaubert first catches sight of Koutchouck-Hânem: "Sur l'escalier, en face de nous, la lumière l'entourant et *se détachant sur le fond bleu du ciel,* une femme debout en pantalons roses, n'ayant autour du torse qu'une gaze d'un violet foncé," he writes (my italics). A little later, Flaubert adds: "Ses cheveux noirs, […] séparés en bandeaux par une raie fine sur le front […] allant se rattacher sur la nuque" (*L'éducation* 47n. 1). This last phrase clearly recalls the passage describing how Emma appears to Charles Bovary during their very first conversation; the courtesan's hair, like that of Emma, acquires syntactical agency and a life of its own. Interestingly, Flaubert worked on his Egyptian notes in the summer of 1851, just before embarking on *Madame Bovary*.[45]

Edward Said, in his discussion of Flaubert's orientalism, writes with great force about Koutchouck-Hânem and what she represented in the eyes of the French traveler: body, desire, sex. Said goes on to suggest that the Egyptian courtesan is "the prototype of several of his novels' female characters in her learned sensuality, delicacy, and (according to Flaubert) mindless coarseness." What Said has in mind are the characters of Salammbô and Salomé in *Salammbô*, "as well as all of the versions of carnal female temptation to which his Saint Anthony is subject."[46] Said's point is well taken. In fact, it can easily be shown that Koutchouck-Hânem's prototypicality extends even wider. Persisting throughout Flaubert's writings, the pattern is by no means limited to the female characters in *Salammbô* and *La tentation*. Whenever Flaubert represents a woman as an object of desire, be it Emma Bovary, or

---

[44] As Biasi stresses, it has long been known that Flaubert's celebrated phrase is in fact a loan from Du Camp's travel diary; see Flaubert, *Voyage en Egypte,* ed. by Pierre-Marc de Biasi (Paris: Grasset, 1991), 280.

[45] For the full description of Koutchouck-Hânem, see Flaubert, *Voyage en Egypte,* 280–9.

[46] Said, *Orientalism* (London: Peregrine, [1978] 1985), 186, 187.

Madame Arnoux, or Salammbô, the mode of representation is singularly unvaried. Almost all those syntactical, stylistic, and rhetorical features I have been analyzing in my discussion of Flaubert's mode of making women visible can be found in these Egyptian notes, for example, the predominance of the visual; the sovereignty of the male gaze; the objectification and reification of the female body; the autonomization of body parts; the levelling of human and non-human phenomena, and so on.

But what does it mean to say that Koutchouck-Hânem is prototypical? What made her so? The answer lies not in her personality traits, nor in her looks and behavior, but rather in the situation itself. Indeed, it was the carefully staged situation that motivated the precise nature of their exchange: he was the client, she was the purveyor; he was the spectator, she was the spectacle; he was all eyes, she was all body. The syntactical pattern that governed Flaubert's mode of describing the physical appearance of the Egyptian courtesan was thus determined by the situation. And this situation served to naturalize the gendered terms of the description and its utter prototypicality.

Narrate or Describe

My theme so far has been Flaubert's pictorial aesthetics, and I have sought to show that it is intimately bound up with female objects of desire. I said intimately, but not exclusively. For there is more to be said about this. What characterizes Flaubert's pictorial aesthetics is that it penetrates deeply into other domains as well, patterning them and re-patterning them. I have in mind two major thematic clusters: that of motion and that of the crowd. It is to these that I now turn, for it is only when we have considered how Flaubert treats these that we can begin to grasp more fully the scale and complexity of the new representational space that emerges in full-fledged form in the pages of *L'éducation sentimentale*. This, in turn, enables a more theoretically nuanced reading of Flaubert's mode of making things visible and, by extension, of late nineteenth-century realism. But we first need to retrace our steps and approach *L'éducation sentimentale* from a slightly different angle, for not all in Flaubert turns around appearance.

To explore the precise ways in which Flaubert treats the visible is to grasp an important part of the reason why his mode of writing is at once so exasperating and so influential. In Stendhal and Balzac, and especially in Zola, visual descriptions serve to make things known, to convey knowledge, and to authenticate. Philippe Hamon, in a semiotic analysis of the nature of description, argues that realist description tends to have a pedagogical function.[47] It is almost always a question of making things known, and perhaps nowhere so strongly as in Zola. As a novelist, Zola is above all out to describe, and to describe means to convey knowledge about a given society. Hamon demonstrates that Zola, for whom vraisemblance is a governing principle, goes to great lengths in order to motivate these descriptions—on the level of the construction of character, of setting, even of plot. Indeed, in Zola description is such a powerful presence and requires so much maneuvering that one might say that the narrative is reduced to the status of connecting tissue: it merely serves to motivate the descriptions. In *Les romanciers naturalistes,* Zola accordingly declared that the novelist's primary goal is no longer to tell a story but rather to describe.

Flaubert, too, rejected the idea that the task of the novelist is to craft a narrative. And in Flaubert, too, descriptions abound. But they serve a very different purpose. They seldom seek to transmit knowledge. Reading Flaubert, we will never learn how to print a wedding invitation, as in Balzac. We will also not learn how a locomotive works or how a department store is organized, as in Zola. We will also learn very little about the properties of objects. But we will learn all the more about how things and people and settings may appear in the field of vision.

This analysis, however, can also be turned around. For when it comes to Flaubert, description is in the end a strangely inadequate term. To approach the Flaubertian art of making things visible solely in descriptive terms is to neglect the peculiarity of his signal achievement, for what is at issue is not so much description as a new space of representation. And this designation must be understood in the strongest sense possible.

To inquire into the visible in Flaubert is to inquire into the heart of Flaubert's realism. That Flaubert's realism is an utterly complicated and perplexing affair is well known. It is not for nothing that Jean-Paul Sartre, in his three-volume study *L'idiot de la famille,* speaks of "derealization."[48] Such derealization, I want to suggest, is a direct consequence of Flaubert's mode of handling the visible.

---

[47] Philippe Hamon, "Qu'est-ce qu'une description?"; "What Is a Description?"
[48] Jean-Paul Sartre, *L'idiot de la famille,* rev. ed. (Paris: Gallimard, 1988). For a discussion of Sartre's notion of derealization, see Knight, *Flaubert's Characters,* 7–9, 89. For a general discussion of Sartre's work on Flaubert, see Hazel E. Barnes, *Sartre and Flaubert* (Chicago: University of Chicago Press, 1981). Sartre had plans for a fourth volume of *L'idiot de la famille,* one that would focus on *Madame Bovary* and provide a summa of the previous three volumes, but it was never finished. On the basis of Sartre's notes, Barnes offers an instructive reconstruction of the major arguments of this fourth and final volume; see *Sartre and Flaubert,* 340–87.

In Flaubert, the visible is configured in two major ways. The visible world that emerges in *Madame Bovary* and *L'éducation sentimentale* but also in *Trois contes* tends to come before us by way of observation, and such observation typically builds upon two different procedures. These procedures necessarily coexist: the new space of representation whose logic I have sought to outline in the preceding pages absolutely feeds on the tension between the one and the other. And as we shall see, this tension has its own dynamic.

On the one hand, Flaubert conjures up the visible world by what I would like to call an *ontological mode*, an *ontology of observation.* This means that a given description, or representation, is directed at what a phenomenon is. Things are simply named, or enumerated, or pointed at, and always in a more or less emphatic manner. The stress falls on what the phenomenon is, not on how it appears in the field of vision. The phenomenon—it may be an object, or a human being, or a landscape—is conjured up *per se,* as though language were a transparent medium. When things are subject to ontological observation, the act of observation does not involve problems of scale, or of perspective, or of angle. The implied space is an abstract one, just as the implied observer is a non-empirical and hence ideal entity.

On the other hand—and this is the second principle—the world is made visible by way of a *phenomenology of observation.* When I speak of "phenomenology," I do not mean phenomenology in a strictly philosophical sense. This is a heuristic definition. When I say "phenomenological," I mean to use it in contrast to "ontological," that is to say, as a representation of an act of observation that seeks to render how the phenomenon in question appears in the field of vision, in the eye of the beholder—not in some general sense, but here and now, in the immediacy of perception. The emphasis is now placed, not on being, but on appearance—on how a given phenomenon presents itself and emerges in a given field of vision.

Both of these procedures make themselves felt in all kinds of narration to a lesser or greater degree, but Flaubert puts them to systematic use. Indeed, as is so often the case in his work, it is the rigorous systematization of perfectly common stylistic features, not a high-minded philosophical system or, say, a grand rhetorical ambition, that allows for the radical novelty and utter strangeness of Flaubert's mode of writing. In other words, the features themselves are not new, but their usage is.

To make clear the difference between the ontological and the phenomenological, and to show how vital both are to the new representational space emerging in Flaubert, I have chosen from among numerous episodes a passage that is singularly illuminating. It has the further advantage of summing up many of the topics I have been discussing so far, while at the same time introducing yet another Flaubertian theme: that of motion.

The Universal Eye

The episode I have in mind takes place at the horse races. Seated in a luxurious carriage, Frédéric and Rosanette watch the horses shoot away. Meanwhile, they munch on *foie gras* and drink wine. All of a sudden Frédéric's secret love, Madame Arnoux, appears at the races and catches sight of the two. Frédéric is distressed. And as if that were not enough, the courtesan humiliates the married lady in public. Frédéric is even more troubled. To make things worse, Madame and Monsieur Dambreuse also appear at the races. Recognizing Frédéric, they are astonished to see him in the company of the courtesan. Frédéric longs to die. He tells the coachman to drive off immediately; and Frédéric and Rosanette travel along the streets in silence.

The passage that follows is a remarkable description of a traffic jam, written some three decades before the advent of the motor vehicle, at a time when the horse-driven carriage still reigned supreme. The passage is complex, from both a visual and a syntactic point of view, and deserves to be quoted at some length. Having just left the hippodrome in the Bois de Boulogne, Frédéric and Rosanette enter the streets of Paris. The drizzle soon turns into pouring rain.

> Et la berline se lança vers les Champs-Élysées au milieu des autres voitures, calèches, briskas, wurts, tandems, tilburys, dog-carts, tapissières à rideaux de cuir où chantaient des ouvriers en goguette, demi-fortune que dirigeaient avec prudence des pères de famille eux-mêmes. [...] L'averse cependant redoublait. On tirait les parapluies, les parasols, les mackintosh; on se criait de loin: "Bonjour! – Ça va bien? – Oui! – Non! – A tantôt!" et les figures se succédaient avec une vitesse d'ombres chinoises. Frédéric et Rosanette ne se parlaient pas, éprouvant une sorte d'hébétude à voir auprès d'eux, continuellement, toutes ces roues tourner.
>
> Par moments, les files de voitures, trop pressées, s'arrêtaient toutes à la fois sur plusieurs lignes. Alors, on restait les uns près des autres, et l'on s'examinait. Du bord des panneaux armoriés, des regards indifférents tombaient sur la foule; des yeux pleins d'envie brillaient au fond des fiacres; des sourires de dénigrement répondaient aux ports de tête orgueilleux; des bouches grandes ouvertes exprimaient des admirations imbéciles; et, çà et là, quelque flâneur, au milieu de la voie, se rejetait en arrière d'un bond, pour éviter un cavalier qui galopait entre les voi-

tures et parvenait à en sortir. Puis tout se remettait en mouvement; les cochers lâchaient les rênes, abaissaient leurs fouets; les chevaux, animés, secouant leur gourmette, jetaient de l'écume autour d'eux; et les croupes et les harnais humides fumaient dans la vapeur d'eau que le soleil couchant traversait. Passant sous l'Arc de Triomphe, il allongeait à hauteur d'homme une lumière roussâtre, qui faisait étinceler les moyeux des roues, les poignées des portières, le bout des timons, les anneaux des sellettes; et, sur les deux côtés de la grande avenue, – pareille à un fleuve où ondulaient des crinières, des vêtements, des têtes humaines, – les arbres tout reluisants de pluie se dressaient, comme deux murailles vertes. Le bleu du ciel, au-dessus, reparaissant à de certaines places, avait des douceurs de satin. (320–1)

And the berlin made off in the direction of the Champs-Élysées in the midst of the other carriages–barouches, britzkas, wurts, tandems, tilburies, dog-carts, covered waggonettes with leather curtains full of singing workmen out on the spree, and go-carts carefully driven by fathers of families. [...] In the meantime the downpour grew heavier. Umbrellas, parasols, and mackintoshes were brought out; shouts of "Good afternoon!"—"How are you keeping?"—"Fine!"—"Not so bad!"—"See you later"—were exchanged from a distance; and face followed face with the rapidity of Chinese shadows. Frédéric and Rosanette said nothing to each other, dazed as it were by the sight of all these carriage wheels continually revolving beside them.

Now and then the files of carriages, packed too closely together, would all stop at the same time in several lines. Forced to remain for a while side by side, everybody stared at his neighbour. From above emblazoned door-panels indifferent glances were cast at the crowd; eyes full of envy gleamed in the depths of cabs; sneering smiles replied to heads held arrogantly high; gaping mouths expressed stupid admiration; and here and there some pedestrian in the middle of the road would suddenly leap backwards to avoid a rider galloping between the carriages before succeeding in making his escape. Then everything moved off again; the coachmen slackened the reins and lowered their whips; the frisky horses, shaking their bits, scattered foam around them, while their damp cruppers and harness steamed in the watery mist. Piercing this haze, the setting sun cast through the Arc de Triomphe, a few feet above the ground, a ray of reddish light which sparkled on the wheel-hubs, the door-handles, the tips of the shafts, and the rings of the axle-trees; and on either side of the great avenue, which resembled a river carrying manes, clothes and human heads, the trees stood glistening with rain, like two green walls. The blue sky above, reappearing here and there, was as soft as satin. (209–10; translation amended)

This is vintage Flaubert. I am tempted to say that this is description pure and simple: dense, detailed, and visually evocative. But description of what? What is Flaubert trying to convey?

The material precision in the passage is excessive—from the initial catalogue of the various types of carriages that can be seen leaving the races to the reddish setting sun sparkling on the axle-trees in the last sentence. We can certainly see the street scene before us. But the more time Flaubert's narrator spends on the description of the slow-moving traffic and its intermittent speed, and the more detail he adds to the rainy tableau, the less real it becomes.

How can this be? Part of the reason is that Flaubert makes use of his poetic license and rewrites one reality in terms of another, so that the passage that started off with such excessive precision ends on a hallucinatory note. The busy avenue is likened to a river in which manes, clothing, and human heads are floating. This metaphor—this *comparatio*—makes possible the translation of the real into a phantasm. Add to this the details that immediately precede the uncanny image of the avenue—those glances, eyes, smiles, and gaping mouths, endowed with syntactic agency and acting on their own—and it becomes obvious that there is something nightmarish about Flaubert's tableau.

But there is another reason why this ultra-realistic scene ultimately has something utterly unreal about it, and the reason is that the narrator is speaking in two registers at once. For one thing is clear, and that is what Flaubert is not doing. He is not trying to tell us what it is like to travel in a horse-driven carriage along the streets of Paris as the rain is pouring down. He is trying to convey something very different, something that language can express only with great difficulty, and that something is silence.[49] The narrator wants us to experience the silence between the two in the carriage, the embarrassing, painful, deadening silence.

This is why the narrator describes in such painstaking detail what can be seen and heard and felt during the ride. Not any ride, but that particular ride, on that particular day, at that particular hour. Frédéric's attention is turned away from Rosanette, and vice versa. And in case the reader should have missed the point, the narrator makes plain that the two do not speak: *Frédéric et Rosanette ne se parlaient pas.* All the two can do, or want to do, is look out the window; and the intensity with which they engage in their respective visual activities is amplified by the frozen atmosphere in the carriage.

The tableau thus has a psychological correlate. By describing an exterior reality, including the ways in which it is processed, Flaubert man-

---

[49] Marcel Proust is, to my knowledge, the first to comment on the crucial role of silence in Flaubert; see Proust, "A propos du 'style' de Flaubert." See also Gérard Genette's essay, "Silences de Flaubert," in *Figures* (Paris: Seuil: 1976), 1:223–46; and Philippe Dufour, *Flaubert ou la prose du silence* (Paris: Nathan, 1997).

ages to convey an interior state, at least as experienced by the male protagonist. This is confirmed by the two sentences with which Flaubert's narrator rounds off the passage:

> Alors, Frédéric se rappela les jours déjà loin où il enviait l'inexprimable bonheur de se trouver dans une de ces voitures, à côté d'une de ces femmes. Il le possédait, ce bonheur-là, et n'en était pas plus joyeux. (322)

> Then Frédéric remembered those days, already distant, when he had longed for the ineffable joy of sitting in one of these carriages, next to one of these women. He now possessed that joy, and he was none the happier. (210)

This finale, in all its emotional suddenness, also makes the reader realize that the narratological perspective is focalized through Frédéric, at least partly.

Let us take a closer look at the passage. Flaubert's narrator begins by enumerating various types of carriages—he lists no less than twelve different kinds—and produces something like a taxonomy of these horse-driven vehicles.[50] Nothing is said about how the carriages look, nor about how they appear to Frédéric or, for that matter, Rosanette. These lines amount to an assertion of what can be seen and little else; they are not concerned with how things are seen. The carriages are conjured up per se, as though language were a transparent veil. They are simply named. Their reality is not insisted upon, merely brought forward. The vehicles carry no looked-at-ness. What Flaubert offers here is an ontology of observation.

By way of this mixed catalogue of carriages, the passage seeks to convey the uneasy atmosphere that emerges when the rich mix with the poor, when those who have are confronted with those who have little or nothing. In a word, the episode turns around the question of class;

---

[50] Interestingly enough, a similar catalogue of carriages is to be found in *Madame Bovary,* at the beginning of chapter four in part one (85–92). Emma and Charles are about to be married, and the forty-three wedding guests are making their way to the village. Flaubert opens the chapter with a list of the various vehicles arriving at the farm, at least five different kinds, an enumeration that serves to suggest the social stratification of the crowd. This enumeration is then matched of by another catalogue: of the various coats the male guests are wearing. This description, too, serves to give the reader a sense of the precise nature of the social hierarchy; Flaubert even underscores as much: "Suivant leur position sociale différente, ils avaient des habits, des redingotes, des vestes, des habits-vestes" and so on (86). The author of *L'éducation sentimentale,* however, is much less prone to signal to the reader that such catalogues are there for a reason, as witness the passage I have just quoted. Less is now more: the facts are made to speak for themselves. That is to say, Flaubert apparently counted on the contemporary reader to decode the implicit semiotics of class.

and this should come as no surprise in a nineteenth-century novel such as *L'éducation sentimentale,* in which the unfolding of extraordinary political events—in particular the 1848 revolution—is carefully, almost invisibly, calibrated with the events that take place on the psychological level.

Immediately after Flaubert's catalogue of carriages follow a few more assertions of what can be seen and heard: we see before us the umbrellas and the parasols and the mackintoshes, and we can hear those greetings swirling around in the air. Both of these actions—bringing out umbrellas and shouting "hello"—belong to syntactical subjects that are human; and Flaubert also represents these actions as such, using the impersonal "on": "On tirait les parapluies," he writes, and "on se criait de loin."

So far so good. But now Flaubert's narrator shifts gears. We find ourselves in a different rhetorical register altogether, and a new space of representation opens up. Flaubert writes: *et les figures se succédaient avec une vitesse d'ombres chinoises.* We have moved beyond notions of human agency, and all of a sudden a body part—the face—has achieved autonomy. This body part, moreover, is treated as a grammatical subject. Stendhal, say, might perhaps have written something like: "The rain was pouring down. Frédéric looked out the window and tried to catch a glimpse of the Parisians hiding in the carriages darting by, but he could hardly see anything."

Stendhal certainly would have produced a more captivating sentence, but the difference in narrative treatment should be clear. In Stendhal, body parts do not exist on their own, not even metaphorically speaking. The only possible exception that I can think of is Madame de Rênal's hand in *Le rouge et le noir.* But there is an important difference, for although that extremity of hers appears to Julien Sorel as an independent thing, that fantastic appearance is not reflected on the syntactic level, only on the semantic one. Her hand, in short, is not a grammatical subject.

In Flaubert, by contrast, hands and feet and faces readily act, leading a syntactic life of their own. Indeed, in the passage I have just quoted, what is typically believed to humanize a human character the most—the face—has been dehumanized and turned into a thing. And this facething, moreover, is accompanied by other face-things that have acquired agency.

A similar stylistic boldness makes itself felt a few lines further down. Glances act on their own, as do eyes and sneering smiles and gaping mouths: *des regards indifférents tombaient sur la foule; des yeux pleins d'envie brillaient au fond des fiacres; des sourires de dénigrement répondaient aux ports de tête orgueilleux; des bouches grandes ouvertes exprimaient des admirations imbéciles.* The force of these lines stems from the implied differentiation of the human body, whose various parts have been autonomized and endowed with an agency all their own. For there is plenty of action in these lines, but no human agency. Again, this is reflected on the syntactic level. Had Flaubert been a garden-variety realist writer, he might have written something like this: "Looking out the window, Frédéric saw how the wealthy count laughed condescendingly at the pedestrians in the street."

But in lieu of passing up such a conventional because anthropomorphic turn of phrase, Flaubert's narrator manipulates the syntax: he strips the sentence of human agency. And so body parts and facial expressions—eyes, mouths, smiles—rush in to fill the syntactical vacuum. As a result, the Parisian avenue is subject to defamiliarization avant la lettre. What is more, it is as though Flaubert's narrator made a distinction between seeing and knowing, as though he keeps to what he perceives, not to what he knows is there. We are now far removed from the ontological mode: appearance, not being, has moved center stage.

But who is the perceptual agent? To whom belongs that extraordinarily discriminating eye capable of looking at the avenue as though it were a river, in which manes, clothes, and human heads are floating? From the catalogue of those twelve carriage types to the river-like Parisian avenue, Flaubert has moved from the assertion of what can be seen to how things are seen. To put it differently, he has moved from an ontology of observation to a phenomenology of observation.

As we have seen on numerous occasions, such passages are common enough in Flaubert's writings, also when no psychological correlation can be discerned.[51] To whom, then, belongs that eye? To Frédéric? To Rosanette? To the implicit narrator? To be sure, the narratological perspective is partly focalized through Frédéric, but we have little reason to believe that Flaubert's protagonist is capable of looking at the phenomenal world, much less representing it, in such a sophisticated and thoroughly aestheticized way.

If a writer like, say, Proust had authored a passage like the one I have just quoted, we would probably assume that the aestheticized scene was a product of the narrator's will to style, that Proustian narrator who so passionately wants to become a writer and readily appropriates Ruskin's idea that the artist should keep to what he sees, not to what he knows.

---

[51] See, for example, Genette's analysis of the famous carriage ride in Emma Bovary in "Les silences de Flaubert."

169

But this is Flaubert, and all his anti-hero can lay claim to is that he is a *failed* artist, if anything. True, the scene is partly focalized through Frédéric, but the key word here is partly. Sitting as he does inside a covered carriage, Frédéric is unable to assume the point of view that the representation of the traffic jam presupposes. Clearly, an anonymous observer-narrator must also be present at the scene, one who is able to look at the traffic jam from above, from below, and from the side.

Is this observer-narrator an omniscient narrator? Again, this is Flaubert, and his weightless narrator is a very different creature from the one we find in, say, Stendhal's *Le rouge et le noir*, where the narrator happily chitchats with his readers, even his publisher, and makes sure his mighty personal presence animates long stretches of the novel. In Flaubert, we know, the omniscient narrator has moved off the scene, and the vacuum left behind is an essentially impersonal and indeterminate space of narration. Yet this does not prevent the perspective of the implied narrator from being aligned with that of a character. The one bleeds into the other, and this happens so frequently that it is close to impossible to pinpoint who is speaking, perceiving, thinking, or feeling in Flaubert.

I suggested earlier in discussing point of view in *Madame Bovary* that narratological indeterminacy readily translates into perceptual indeterminacy. And this feature is key to the historically original space of representation that emerges in Flaubert's mature works. If Flaubert is able to extract a whole new and complex order from the domain of the visible, this is because he has made sure to systematize narratological indeterminacy. We are now in a better position to grasp the precise patterning of that new space of representation. Thus: who sees? To whom belongs that attentive, fastidious, discriminating eye? Who is the author of perception?

In the end, these are misleading questions, for as I hope to have shown in my analysis of the traffic jam episode, the point is that this representational space is ultimately an impersonal one. And what is even more important, it is also an autonomous one. True, the visual representations I have been discussing in this book are always partly focalized through a given character, but that does not make them any less impersonal, nor less autonomous. For what I now would like to suggest is that in the final analysis such perceptual focalization is an enabling fiction. Flaubert's characters—Frédéric, Emma, Charles, Léon, Rodolphe, and others—do not really author images. Rather, they serve to motivate their coming into being. The traffic jam episode is a case in point. On the semantic level, the episode says: things are observed in such a way that a physiological perceiver must be present. Appearance, after all, is always appearance for someone. On the syntactical level, however, the action is located in the seen itself, not in some observer, for the perceived is not related to a perceiver. This is what affords the characteristic suspension between objectivity and subjectivity that we have traced in so many passages. And it is precisely this ambiguity, this fundamental and irreducible ambiguity, that produces that new space of representation that emerges with great force in the interstices of Flaubert's narrative text.

If there is a proto-cinematic impulse in Flaubert, it has everything to do with this ambiguity. The French film theorist André Bazin once remarked that if there is framing, there is perspective. And since the cinematographic mode of representing the visible world necessarily involves framing—the film camera, after all, is a visual framing device on wheels—the world represented always comes before us with an angle. Things are seen in all their empirical immediacy, but the seeing itself derives from an anonymous eye: the camera. Hence the affinity between Flaubert and cinema.

I mentioned above that three thematic clusters in particular are pulled into this new representational space: first, female objects of desire; second, things in motion or, alternatively, things as seen from vehicles or vessels in motion; and third, the crowd. In all three cases, the emphasis is placed on how they appear—to an anonymous eye, to an ever-present but never identified eye.

Before I move on to my concluding remarks, I would like to comment briefly on two passages. The first is drawn from the horse racing episode and renders a perfectly trivial non-event: a race. The second, meanwhile, is drawn from the representation of the 1848 revolution and renders a socially symbolic action of the highest interest, an event if there ever was one. Syntactically speaking, however, there is precious little that separates them. Horses or revolutionaries: in the end, it makes little difference, for Flaubert is above all concerned with the intricacies of visual perception.

In the following passage, Flaubert's narrator carefully motivates the extraordinary description of what will soon take place before Frédéric and Rosanette. Some of the spectators are said to climb on to the benches, the narrator makes clear, and some remain in their cabs and follow the race through field-glasses. We—the readers—can expect a spectacle of the first rank:

> Les spectateurs des tribunes avaient grimpé sur les bancs. Les autres, debout dans les voitures, suivaient avec des lorgnettes à la main l'évolution des jockeys; on les voyait filer comme des taches rouges, jaunes, blanches et bleues sur toute la longueur de la foule, qui bordait

le tour de l'Hippodrome. De loin, leur vitesse n'avait pas l'air excessif; à l'autre bout du Champ de Mars, ils semblaient même se ralentir, et ne plus avancer que par une sorte de glissement, où les ventres des chevaux touchaient la terre sans que leurs jambes étendues pliassent. Mais, revenant bien vite, ils grandissaient; leur passage coupait le vent, le sol tremblait, les cailloux volaient; l'air, s'engouffrant dans les casaques des jockeys, les faisait palpiter comme des voiles; à grands coups de cravache, ils fouaillaient leurs bêtes pour atteindre le poteau, c'était le but. (317–8)

The spectators in the stands had climbed on to the benches. The others, standing in their carriages, followed the jockeys' manoeuvres through field-glasses; they could be seen as red, yellow, blue, and white dots moving past the crowd which lined the whole circuit of the Hippodrome. At a distance their speed did not appear to be exceptional; at the far end of the Champ de Mars, they even seemed to slow down, so that they advanced only by a sort of gliding motion in which the horses touched the ground with their bellies without bending their outstretched legs. However, coming back quickly, they increased in size; they cut the air as they passed; the earth shook; pebbles flew; the wind, blowing into the jockeys' jackets, puffed them out like sails; and they lashed their horses with their whips as they strained towards the winning-post. The numbers were taken down; another were taken up; and, to the sound of applause, the winning horse dragged itself to the paddock, covered in sweat, with its knees rigid and its head down, while its rider held his sides as if he were dying in his saddle. (207–8)

This is a brilliant description of the visual experience of racing horses. For what Flaubert's narrator fastens onto is not the reality of the animals, nor the reality of the jockeys. What is represented here is the reality of the spectators. Indeed, this is a realism of visual perception. Flaubert's utterly matter-of-fact-like passage seeks to convey an optical illusion: at first the seeming slowness when the horses are at a large distance from the spectator, and then the tremendous power that transports itself into the body of the spectator and that makes the ground tremble as the horses come closer and eventually pass by.

In terms of plot, this passage is unimportant. What Flaubert offers us here is not a narrative event but rather a linguistic one. He turns a non-significant narrative event into a significant linguistic event. As we have seen on numerous occasions, this is a recurrent tendency in Flaubert.

What does Flaubert do? In the second sentence of this speed-infused paragraph, the jockeys are represented as so many color patches. Color, by the way, is not a primary property, but a secondary one. Flaubert's narrator seeks to reproduce a perceptual act, stressing scale and perspective, in particular. The narrator then moves over to the horses, stating that "ils grandissaient"; literally speaking, "they grew larger." Of course the horses are not growing, but it looks as though they do—in the eyes of the implicit spectator. Flaubert here insists on the difference between what you know is there and what you actually see. Meanwhile, this perfectly mundane scene transforms itself into an autonomous image that acquires a life of its own, independent of the narrative context that served to motivate it in the first place.

My final passage is drawn from an episode that comes two thirds into the novel. King Louis-Philippe has just left Paris, and a provisional government is about to be appointed. Frédéric and Hussonnet have entered the deserted royal palace. Walking about on the first floor, they inspect the paintings of important men lining the walls. All of a sudden a large group of people enters the building; and here's how Flaubert renders the historical agent behind the revolution:

> Tout à coup *la Marseillaise* retentit. Hussonnet et Frédéric se penchèrent sur la rampe. C'était le peuple. Il se précipita dans l'escalier, en secouant à flots vertigineux des têtes nues, des casques, des bonnets rouges, des baïonnettes et des épaules, si impétueusement que des gens disparaissaient dans cette masse grouillante qui montait toujours, comme un fleuve refoulé par une marée d'équinoxe, avec un long mugissement, sous une impulsion irrésistible. En haut, elle se répandit, et le chant tomba.
>
> On n'entendait plus que les piétinements de tous les souliers, avec le clapotement des voix. La foule inoffensive se contentait de regarder. Mais, de temps à autre, un coude trop à l'étroit enfonçait une vitre [...]. (429)

> Suddenly the *Marsellaise* rang out. Hussonnet and Frédéric leaned over the banisters. It was the mob. It swept up the staircase in a bewildering flood of bare heads, helmets, red caps, bayonets, and shoulders, surging forward so violently that people disappeared in the swarming mass as it went up and up, like a spring-tide pushing back a river, driven by an irresistible impulse and giving a continuous roar. At the top of the stairs it broke up and the singing stopped.
>
> Nothing more could be heard but the shuffling of shoes and the babble of voices. The mob was content to stare inoffensively. But now and then an elbow, cramped for room, smashed a window-pane [...]. (288)

The central character in this passage—the people—is first identified and then artfully dissolved. For one thing is clear, and that is what this crowd is *not*: it is not represented as a collective of human beings or individuals. The passage builds on the distinction between knowing and perceiving, between what you know is there and what you actually perceive.

On the one hand, Flaubert's narrator rewrites the people as a single vast and unruly body, as a natural phenomenon that sweeps through the

173

building.[52] As a consequence, the crowd is stripped of human agency. On the other hand, Flaubert rewrites the people as a cluster of metonymies: as parts that stand for the whole, as so many hats and helmets and shoulders. What Flaubert seeks to intimate is a view from above.

In both cases, the people are turned into an image, into something to be looked at, to be aestheticized. In *L'éducation sentimentale*, we learn little about the 1848 revolution but all the more about its visible manifestations. "He felt as if he were watching a play," Frédéric confesses in the midst of the gun smoke.

Realism and Derealization

Once we reach Flaubert in the history of the novel, perception moves into the foreground and becomes part of the narrative content. And with the increasing stress on subjective perception comes the increasing autonomy of the image. What happens with Flaubert is that the art of making things and persons visible has been replaced by the production of images, that is, autonomous images. As I have stressed throughout my discussion, such image production has little to do with embellishment or with illustration. Instead, Flaubert manages to invent a new representational space, one in which perception is exercised for perception's sake.

That realism is a tricky category has often been pointed out. The brief account I have given here goes some way toward explaining why this is so. It also shows that realism incorporates incompatible tendencies within itself. Or to put it a little different: that the realist enterprise contains the seeds of its own undermining. As practiced by Balzac, realist writing attempts to know, to penetrate, to conquer an increasingly abstract world by means of making each concrete appearance of the world visible. It is an epistemological project, if you wish, and as the intellectual historian Wolf Lepenies among others has shown, it is intimately related to a sociological imperative.[53] The privileged experience in *L'éducation sentimentale* has little to do with modes of knowing or modes of acting but has everything to do with modes of perceiving, so much so that perception turns into an almost self-sufficient activity. It is an aesthetic project that is radically incompatible with the epistemological thrust of, say, Balzac's writing.

---

[52] See Gisèle Séginger, Flaubert. *Une poétique de l'histoire* (Strasbourg: Presses Universitaires de Strasbourg, 2000), 86.
[53] Wolf Lepenies, *Die drei Kulturen* (Munich: Hanser, 1985).

What does it mean to make things visible? And what are the effects produced by the realist visibility? To look at the world, Adorno stressed, is not necessarily the same as to see through it. In other words, a piece of writing that renders the world visible is not necessarily the same as a piece of writing that renders the world intelligible. It is precisely this distinction that becomes apparent in that part of the history of the novel that I have discussed in the preceding pages. From the integration of the visual fact in Stendhal to the autonomy of the image in Flaubert: it is a remarkable historical irony—and an interesting intellectual problem—that the very movement that promoted the literal, the immanent, and the true-to-life should in fact pave the way for the separation of image and meaning, perception and knowledge, sensation and deduction.

Epilogue
The Scandal of Realism

Once you have reduced the glorious triumphs of nineteenth-century realism to rubble, what do you do next? Indeed, what do you do when you have turned the history of the novel into a smoldering ruin? When you have managed to write not just one but several books about nothing? When you have engineered a narrative machinery in which action is substituted for impression? When a gap has begun to yawn between linguistic events and narrative events?

In the years he had left before his death in 1880, Flaubert went on writing, but he published no more novels. Flaubert wrote the final version of the play *La Tentation de Saint Antoine* (1874), a book that was a giant failure; *Trois contes* (1877), three loosely connected tales set in the past; and *Bouvard et Pécuchet*, a good-humored satirical story about two copy-clerks that was published posthumously. To even think of a novel following in the wake of *L'éducation sentimentale* is almost as maddening as imagining Proust producing yet another encyclopedic work after *A la recherche du temps perdu* or, for that matter, Joyce crafting yet another meaty, massive, monumental book after *Ulysses*. Proust passed away upon the completion of his great novel; and as for Joyce, what could possibly follow upon that "little story of a day," as he once called his 1922 epic? Nothing, it seems, except *Finnegans Wake*. And what is *Finnegans Wake* if not maddening?

Indeed, Flaubert's last novel was *L'éducation sentimentale*. To be sure, *Bouvard et Pécuchet* is a narrative work in prose and might very well be called a novel, but it surely lacks the scope of Flaubert's previous works. Also, it was never brought to completion. What is more, *Bouvard et Pécuchet* utterly lacks the seriousness that characterizes *Madame Bovary* and *L'éducation sentimentale* and that, according to Erich Auerbach, defines modern realism from Stendhal and Balzac onward. The book is an odd literary creature; more than anything else, it is a comedy. It is about two copy clerks who, typically enough, are also bachelors. They devote their lives to copying books, mountains of books, in an attempt to collect all that can be known. It is an encyclopedic enterprise. And it is, of course, fruitless. As Hugh Kenner once said, the author of *Bouvard et Pécuchet* is a comedian of the enlightenment.[1]

The last book that Flaubert was to publish, *Trois contes* (1877), is what the title suggests: three tales. Not stories but tales, for Flaubert now explores the stuff of legends, and nowhere more so than in the centerpiece, "La légende de St. Julien." The book is everything that *Bouvard et Pécuchet* is not: it is deeply serious, even lofty and serene. It is concerned not with stupidity but with naiveté. It revels in unheard-of and marvelous events that recall Greek tragedy or folk tales—consider Julien and how he unwittingly comes to slay his parents.

Each tale features a story that tells the life of a person from beginning to end, and each can be likened to a medieval emblem. "La légende de St. Julien" is inspired by a stained-glass window in the Rouen cathedral; "Hérodias" owes a great deal to a tympanum on the front at the same cathedral; and the extraordinary opening tale, "Un coeur simple," which tells the story of a simple-minded and illiterate servant called Félicité, also seems to spring out of stained-glass windows—windows that figure in the tale itself and that Félicité studies during a church service. One shows the Holy Ghost looking down on Virgin Mary, another how the Virgin is kneeling before the infant Jesus.

Flaubert thus sets three iconic objects into motion. As Raymonde Debray Genette has suggested, this means that these tales are all second-degree narratives. They rely on narratives that have already been realized in another language, sculptural or pictorial.[2] And yet the tales emerge as a condensed version of all of Flaubert's works, a fact that underscores the great extent to which his achievement is truly a question of style.

What is remarkable about both *Bouvard et Pécuchet* and *Trois contes* is that there are virtually no images of the kind I have been discussing in this book. There is not much in the way of aestheticization and also no emphasis on acts of perception, on how things appear in the field of vision. Things are seen, and there is an abundance of things that are seen, but precious little attention is paid to *how* things are seen. What happened to that new space of representation?

Consider an episode in *Bouvard et Pécuchet*. Monsieur Bouvard has begun to court madame Bordin, the widowed wife of a real estate agent, and they share a sumptuous meal at her house. They have several courses

---

[1] Hugh Kenner, *Flaubert, Joyce, and Beckett: The Stoic Comedians* (London: Dalkey Archive Press, [1962] 2005).
[2] Raymonde Debray Genette, "Les figures du récit dans *Un coeur simple*," in *Métamorphoses du récit. Autour de Flaubert* (Paris: Seuil, 1988), 274.

and a great deal of wine, and Flaubert sums up this part of the evening in a single sentence. He then inserts a speed bump. The plot slows down, the magnifying glass comes out, for now we are made to see, in exquisitely minute and revelatory detail, how Bouvard's newfound object of desire approaches the end of the meal, her cup of coffee:

> Et Mme Bordin, en dilatant les narines, trempait dans la soucoupe sa lèvre charnue, ombrée légèrement d'un duvet noir.[3]

> They lingered over coffee—and Mme. Bordin, widening her nostrils, dipped her fleshy lip, lightly shaded by black down, into the cup.[4]

This is high comedy bordering on farce, but it is not an image. Certainly, the details dropped are all visual ones, and we can see the nose, the lips, and the downy mustache before us. But the seen refuses to congeal into an image. Although the sentence reports a number of visible particulars, it does not state how these things are seen. Indeed, for all the acute powers of observation on display here, this instant portrait is far removed from the kind of image that would emerge when Charles was looking at Emma as she was standing beneath her parasol, or when Frédéric was watching Rosanette as she was munching eagerly on that pomegranate.

Why is this so? Is it because *Bouvard et Pécuchet*, unlike *Madame Bovary* and *L'éducation sentimentale*, is ultimately not a tale about desire? Perhaps. But Flaubert has plenty of opportunities to indulge in image-making, for example, that evening when Bouvard finds his widow sitting by the fireplace in her living room. On a previous evening, he discovered the beauty of her shoulders, and caressed her arms and fantasized about her glorious curves. Now he pays a new visit to madame Bordin:

> Un soir, que la cuisine de Mélie l'avait dégoûté, il eut une joie en entrant dans le salon de Mme Bordin. C'est là qu'il aurait fallu vivre.
> Le globe de la lampe, couvert d'un papier rose, épandait une lumière tranquille. Elle était assise auprès du feu; et son pied passait le bord de sa robe. Dès les premiers mots, l'entretien tomba.
> Cependant elle le regardait, les cils à demi fermés, d'une manière langoureuse, avec obstination.
> Bouvard n'y tint plus! et s'agenouillant sur le parquet, il bredouilla:
> "Je vous aime! Marions-nous!"[5]

---

[3] Flaubert, *Bouvard et Pécuchet,* in *Oeuvres,* ed. Albert Thibaudet and René Dumesnil (Paris: Gallimard, 1952), 2:875.
[4] Flaubert, *Bouvard and Pécuchet,* trans. Mark Polizzotti (Normal, Ill.: Dalkey Archive Press, 2005), 165.
[5] Flaubert, *Bouvard et Pécuchet,* 2:876.

> One evening, when Mélie's cooking had nauseated him, he felt a great joy upon entering Mme. Bordin's parlor. This was where he wanted to live!
> The globe of the lamp, covered in pink paper, gave off a peaceful glow. She was sitting by the fire, and her foot peeked out from the hem of her skirt. After a few words, their conversation fell silent.
> Still, she was looking at him, her eyes half closed, in a languorous pose, insistently.
> Bouvard could stand it no longer! And kneeling on the wooden floor, he stammered, "I love you! Marry me!"[6]

This scene is vintage Flaubert, complete with a light source and a lone foot. Recall, there is plenty of foot fetishism in Flaubert. Whenever there is a woman, there is a foot—think of madame Bovary before the fireplace at the Yonville inn, or madame Dambreuse reclining in a chair with the tip of her foot on a cushion. We have also seen that a foot may serve to put an end to visual descriptions of women, closing off that libidinally charged space of looking and taking us back to the boring facts of everyday life.

All this is present in the passage about madame Bordin as well. Yet the scene is strangely thin. No image unfolds. Indeed, all the usual motivations are there—desire, woman, immersion, clothing, a lamp—but between the glowing light and that deliciously enticing foot, nothing happens. No picture of madame Bordin, no canvas, no tableau. And above all: no aestheticization. To put matters a little differently, Flaubert refrains from opening up that new space of representation. Is it because monsieur Bouvard is possibly more interested in madame Bordin's cooking than in her body? Is it because of her mustache? Or is it because this mature woman, unlike her sisters in Flaubert's other novels, is actually returning Bouvard's gaze?

All this applies equally well to the parallel episode, the one that revolves around Pécuchet's infatuation with Mélie. Pécuchet is mad with desire and takes pleasure in looking at the maid; he even goes so far as to kiss the nape of her neck. But this episode, too, refuses to yield thinglike images in which the female object of desire stands out in relief against a flat background. Why? Ultimately, I think, the explanation for this absence of images has to be sought elsewhere, not on the levels of the episode or plot. Unlike *Madame Bovary* and *L'éducation sentimentale, Bouvard et Pécuchet* is not preoccupied with aesthetics. It does not seek to redeem the material world by way of its aestheticization. It is content merely to expose the world—in all its massive and mind-boggling stupidity.

---

[6] Flaubert, *Bouvard and Pécuchet,* 165.

So what happens to that specifically Flaubertian space of representation in his last books? The discrepancy that I have discussed in these pages—the growing polarization between narrative event and linguistic event, or between action and impression, that emerges in *Madame Bovary* and even more so in *L'éducation sentimentale*—can in fact be traced in Flaubert's last works. But it now looks very different. It has reached its last stage: disconnection. It does not make itself felt within these works but rather *between* them. The polarization is now complete and has bifurcated into an absolute contrast. To push things as far as possible, we might say that two new and distinct paths emerge in the wake of *L'éducation sentimentale*. From now on narrative events and linguistic events go separate ways. The one path is embodied by *Bouvard et Pécuchet*, the other by *Trois contes*. Schematically speaking, we might say that the former book represents a narrative purged of linguistic events, that is, of images. Conversely, the latter represents images, or linguistic events, purged of narrative.

At the same time, however, a peculiar transformation has taken place. If *Bouvard et Pécuchet* is a narrative, it is a narrative without events. Things happen, but no events take place. Indeed, if Flaubert ever succeeded in his odd ambition to write a novel about nothing, then this book fits the bill—beautifully so. And just as *Bouvard et Pécuchet* is a narrative without narrative events, so *Trois contes* are images without image events. For although *Trois contes* springs out of three emblematic images that have been expanded and set in motion, the tales themselves do not offer much in the way of literary images proper, at least not of the aestheticized kind I have been discussing. Why? Because we are already inside the domain of the image. With *Trois contes,* we are inside the pictorial as such.

Indeed, images are redundant in this book because each tale is a complete and expansive image in itself. We are not asked to look at those three emblematic panes as though we were looking through windows onto a world; we are also not encouraged to approach them as pictorial surfaces. Rather, we are now to plunge into those animated images as though they were worlds unto themselves. In a strange reversal, the visible finally reigns supreme. And ultimately, the visible is able to reign supreme because it has been refracted through the image form. This is why *Trois contes* is Flaubert's great triumph. In this final work, he achieves the transparency of language to which so much of his writing aspires.

I opened this book by explicating Italo Calvino's reflection on the realist novel and the metaphor of the closed shutters, and I have attempted to throw light on some of the things that happen when, in the nineteenth century, those shutters are thrust open. I have sought to show that the nineteenth-century quest for the visible as a trace that connects the book to the world involves a history of realism that ends in an unlikely place: either in a pile of stupid, useless, ridiculous books, as in *Bouvard et Pécuchet,* or in a majestic cathedral, in the wondrous opacity of a stained-glass window, as in *Trois contes*. Between the open shutters and the opaque stained-glass window, the realist project unfolds. Flaubert manages precisely this: the book is finally connected to the world by way of the visible, but only because the world is already an image.

*

Now that I have reached the end of this book, it occurs to me that I have placed more emphasis on the image than on the visible as such. What happened to the visible? What happened to that blue soap?

I also realize that a number of questions have been left unanswered. What is the historical meaning of the advent of visibility in the novel? Why, indeed, does the art of making things visible gain a new urgency in the nineteenth century, beginning with Stendhal and Balzac? And how are we to contextualize the passionate impulse to make things visible that everywhere comes to the fore in Flaubert?

These are all questions that turn around the issue of *why*. In this book, I have concentrated more on *how* than on why. To understand *why*, these questions need to be articulated and answered in a significantly larger context, that of history.

What about French impressionism? Flaubert's life coincided with one of the most innovative periods in the history of French painting, from Ingres, Corot, and Courbet to impressionists such as Manet, Monet, Renoir, and Degas. He died in 1880, a decade and a half before the advent of commercial cinematography. Does not painting, especially impressionism, present a striking parallel? Is not impressionist painting ideally suited to highlight the peculiarity of the Flaubertian image, especially its insistent flatness, its two-dimensional pictorial plane, and the intricate ways in which it upsets perspectival realism? And what about the other great nineteenth-century pictorial revolution, that mechanical means of visual representation we know as photography?

Surely, impressionistic painting from Manet onward—at least from the late 1860s onward—is similarly preoccupied with flatness and with the visual datum as such. This is why Michael Fried speaks of Manet's "ocular realism."[7] Manet rigorously pursued the actually seen as op-

---

[7] See Michael Fried, *Manet's Modernism, or, The Face of Painting in the 1860s* (Chi-

posed to the known. Tracing the origins of Manet's ocular realism in a general shift that took place around 1860, Fried stresses that painters such as Manet, Degas, Whistler, and Fantin-Latour now began to execute a new kind of self-portrait, one that set out to render exactly what the artist-viewer saw and that alone. This meant that the artists kept true to the reversed mirror image rather than trying to correct the picture so that it corresponded to how his face and body were in fact seen by others. In other words, they pursued the exact nature of what the observer sees as distinct from what he or she knows is there. Consider, for example, *The Races at Longchamp* (1865), a speed-infused black and white lithograph. In this picture, Manet equips the horses galloping toward the viewer with two legs, not four; and yet the movement described has all the powerful plasticity one could wish for.[8] This is Manet's optical realism in a nutshell. He depicts not the reality of the horses but the reality of the viewer. We know that horses have four legs, but that is not necessarily what we see when the animals dart toward us.

In the chapter on *L'éducation sentimentale* (1869), I foregrounded a similar feature in the horse-racing episode. Flaubert's narrator, too, seizes on the reality of the implicit spectator. At first, the galloping horses hardly seem to move at all. Indeed, when seen from afar, moving along the far end of the Hippodrome, they appear to merely glide forward on their bellies with outstretched legs. Then, as the horses come closer, they seem to grow larger; and Flaubert now depicts their massive speed by emphasizing how the ground begins to tremble and how the jockey's jackets look like stiffened sails.

Why does Flaubert incorporate this study of the intricacies of visual perception into an episode that renders the beginnings of Frédéric's love affair with Rosanette? Hard to say. But this much is clear: the lengthy description of the races is a purely linguistic event. Perfectly detachable and transportable, it could easily be removed. It does nothing to advance the plot, nor does it add anything to the reader's understanding of the two characters. It is an event that takes place in language, and in language alone.

That Flaubert is to the novel what Manet is to painting is something of a commonplace, which of course does not mean that the parallels are not worth stressing; on the contrary, they are both intriguing and instruc-

---

cago: University of Chicago Press, 1996).

[8] See E. H. Gombrich, *The Story of Art,* rev. ed. (London: Phaidon, 1995), 516-7. See also the oil painting with the same title (1866), where the ocular aspect is less conspicuous, as Manet has dust stir up behind the front legs of the galloping horses—the dust connotes speed, but it also serves to create the illusion that the back legs are really there, only concealed by the dirt blowing about.

tive.[9] Think of the flattened perspective in Manet's *The Balcony* (1868-9), and especially of how the three figures in the painting appear like well-dressed paper dolls whose silhouettes seem pinned onto a backdrop of darkness—the male behind the two women is even reduced to a head, a shirt breast, and two hands as his dark-clad body melts into the black background. There can be no doubt that Flaubert, like Manet and other painters at the time, is intent on exploring a realism of visual perception and representing its phenomenology to the reader.

What is more, impressionistic painters paid close attention to matters of light, so much so that light became a character in its own right—consider the shifting, flickering, tremulous light in Renoir's *La Grenouillère* (1869) or, for an even more luminous example, the famous canvas *Dance at the Moulin de la Galette* (1876). In Flaubert, too, light solidifies. It turns into a syntactical agent that sculpts faces, heads, and bodies, even space itself. As for framing in Flaubert, we need only consider photography and the new modes of pictorial framing that it enabled, especially of human faces, body parts, and inanimate objects. It is hard to think of a more beautiful appropriation of photographic means of representing human bodies in action than Degas's tightly framed paintings of ballets dancers from the late 1870s.

All these parallels deserve to be articulated and explored. There is a certain degree of comparability between Flaubert and impressionist painting. Both are indefatigable in their pursuit of a realism of embodied perception. Ultimately, however, I think that these parallels are of limited value. They say very little about Flaubert. And if we want a historical explanation of Flaubert's will to pictorial style, they say even less.

First, if Fried is right, then the origins of impressionism can be traced back to circa 1860. This means that *L'éducation sentimentale* may usefully be juxtaposed with French impressionistic painting, but also that *Madame Bovary* (1857) is left out of the picture. How are we then to account for that flickering light playing on Emma's cheeks, not to mention the striking flatness that often characterizes her image?

Second, the Flaubertian image moves. Hat ribbons flutter, sumptuous skirts billow, hoods move in the wind—and, yes, light flickers. The Flaubertian image thus extends in time and comes with a temporality, meaning that the thing seen enjoys a certain duration in the perceptual field. For this reason, Flaubert's images can only partially be understood on the order of painting, impressionistic or otherwise. And this is also

---

[9] See Arden Reed, *Manet, Flaubert, and the Emergence of Modernism: Blurring Genre Boundaries* (Cambridge: Cambridge University Press, 2003).

why I have sometimes chosen to use the language of cinema, although it is something of an anachronistic maneuver. All this is to say that there exists no critical vocabulary that can adequately account for the specificity of the new representational space that emerges in Flaubert's pathbreaking novels.

To track down parallels is one thing, historical explanation quite another. The larger question still remains. How are we to contextualize the powerful inclination to make things visible that makes itself felt in Flaubert? It is a question of methodology. Carlo Ginzburg gets to the heart of the matter in his work on the art historians associated with the Warburg school. "The art historian appeals to literature, the literary scholar has recourse to art, and both invoke philosophy when they cannot explain certain problems within their fields."[10] Such interdisciplinary connections may be productive, Ginzburg points out, but the methodological problem still remains open. It is not historical explanation.[11] Tracing a lineage that stretches from Aby Warburg to E. H. Gombrich, Ginzburg explores the ways in which they conceived of how art relates to history. To put things simply: if, as Wölfflin once said, all paintings owe more to other paintings than they owe to direct observation, then how does the art historian explain stylistic change?

The problem becomes especially pressing if he or she holds that paintings can be understood neither by psychology, nor by communications theory, nor by drawing on an art history that is content merely to trace how painters borrow from other painters, or how art schools borrow from other art schools.[12] From Warburg to Gombrich, this problem was a standing preoccupation. They all sought to combine formal analysis with history, and went further than most art-historical scholars in the attempt at doing so.

I bring up this issue merely to emphasize the methodological difficulties inherent in any attempt at contextualizing questions of style and stylistic change. First, although the comparisons between Flaubert and impressionist painting are worth making, the overlap is limited. There are indeed features in Flaubert that can be called impressionistic ones, but his enterprise cannot.

---

[10] Carlo Ginzburg, "From Aby Warburg to E. H. Gombrich: A Problem of Method," in *Clues, Myths, and the Historical Method*, trans. John and Anne Tedeschi (Baltimore: Johns Hopkins University Press, 1989), 56.
[11] For a discussion of historical explanation in art history, see also Michael Baxandall, *Patterns of Intention: On the Historical Explanation of Pictures* (New Haven: Yale University Press, 1985), esp.1-11, 74-104.
[12] Ginzburg, "From Aby Warburg to E. H. Gombrich," 58.

Second, even if we were able to demonstrate that the concerns of Flaubert—especially those that are made manifest in and through the Flaubertian image—coincide to a surprisingly large degree with those of the impressionists, what would we actually have managed to show? And even more important, why—for Flaubert as well as for the impressionists—would it seem desirable, perhaps even necessary, to manage the world by way of its aestheticization? The question of history reasserts itself.

All this brings me to the point I wish to make. To grasp what had a bearing on Flaubert's writings and why they are crafted the way they are, I would suggest looking elsewhere. What is essential to an understanding of Flaubert's preoccupation with visibility is not the world of images but rather that of words. And in Flaubert's time, this means: the world of print. Flaubert's will to make things visible should be seen as a response, as a historically mediated response to a situation determined by—let's call it constant murmur. We know that the nineteenth century sees an explosion of printed matter. We also know that this historical period sees an unprecedented proliferation of discourse and the full-fledged emergence of that new space called public opinion. These historical facts take us straight to the core of Flaubert's enterprise.

And this is why, in the chapter on *Madame Bovary,* I dwelt at length on Flaubert versus Homais, on how the novel interfoliates Homais's journalistic versions of the very events that the narrator himself has just rendered, but in a very different register. *Madame Bovary* is more than just a book about other books. It is a book about all kinds of printed matter—and about what happens to language, meaning, and signification in a world crowded by ever more printed matter. Like no other novel before it, *Madame Bovary* thematizes the expansion and standardization of semiotic noise. It navigates a verbal universe cluttered by words that engender other words, endlessly, compulsively, hysterically. This is the context in which Flaubert's quest for *le mot juste* is best understood. To find the right word is to find the trace that connects the book to the world.

Style, for Flaubert, was a question of exactitude; and so words were a trouble. They were generic, blunt, diluted, vague. They were mere approximations. Flaubert wanted the literal, not the literary. This is why precision was imperative, and also why observation was essential. Language traffics in the general; meanwhile, through language, Flaubert tried to tease out the particular.

This is where the visible enters the picture. In this book, I have sought to show that the visible penetrates Flaubert's writings in two major ways. On the one hand, there is the order of the blue soap, an order based in what I have called an ontology of observation. Things are simply seen, noted, listed; perhaps they acquire an adjective, but that is all. (This is the place to disclose where that famous blue soap occurs: in "Un coeur simple," in a short passage describing the interior of Félicité's bedroom. On the table next to her bed, Flaubert informs his reader, are a few combs, a water-jug, and a bar of blue soap. No more, no less.)

On the other hand, there is the order of the image—of, say, Emma Bovary smiling beneath that parasol as the waterdrops are falling down onto the taut fabric, or madame Arnoux sitting alone on that boat, her head standing out in relief against the blue sky. This is an order based in a phenomenology of observation. The emphasis is now placed on how things appear in the field of vision—to an ever-present and distinguished yet anonymous eye. Ultimately, however, both orders are governed by one and the same impulse: to capture the presence of being.

What is represented in the new representational space that emerges in Flaubert? A new experience of the world, where the world offers itself as the occasion for perception for perception's sake. All the senses are called upon, to be sure, but in Flaubert the sense of vision reigns supreme. Nothing is pursued more aggressively than things seen. And very often the world of things seen is engaged with as though it were an image. The world, indeed, is frequently recreated in its own image. On a splendid number of occasions, Emma is reduced to her image and experienced as such. Flaubert takes great care to motivate this way of approaching Emma, so much so that the idea that Emma is an image, or even a work of art, begins to inflect his metaphors. Now Emma's body is likened to a *statue de cire,* an image made of wax; now her face is likened to marble. Or else Flaubert may choose to place Emma in an armchair before her lover, stressing that the yellow wallpaper behind her head emerges like a golden backdrop, as though to imply that the entire sight represents an icon; to top things off, Flaubert makes sure that the impression of her head is reflected in the glass (357-8/189).

But nowhere does this impulse—this will to turn things seen into image—make itself felt as strongly as in *L'éducation sentimentale,* because in this book, the inclination to recreate the world as image is effectively also thematized. Indeed, the tendency to impart an image form to the visible is not only implicit in descriptions of things seen—women, crowds, landscape. It is also thematized on the level of plot. When Frédéric bears witness to the revolution as it unfolds before his eyes in February 1848, he observes that wounded and dead people litter the streets. But nothing seems real. To be sure, he hears the drums and the cries, and he sees the damaged bodies on the ground, but as the narrator emphasizes, to Frédéric it all seems rather like a play: "Il lui semblait assister à un spectacle (318/286).

Among the things I have sought to do in the preceding pages is to expose the emergence of a new literary object, the Flaubertian image. And in doing so, I have also sought to expose a new kind of experience. To ask about the historical meaning of the advent of visibility is to ask about the historical conditions of this experience. Such an inquiry is a formidable task, of course, and it falls outside the scope of this study, but I hope to return to the issue in another book.

My theme in these pages has been the career of the visible in the nineteenth century. To trace the art of making things visible through the history of the realist novel is to bear witness to an evolution as remarkable as it is bewildering. What began as an attempt to invite the solidity of the quotidian real into the novel necessarily triggers a palpable separation between impression and action, between narrative event and linguistic event, between perception and knowledge. Flaubert takes the realist art of making things visible to extremes. In so doing, he turns realism inside out. This means that realism, that vastly ambitious project to conjure up the visible world, contains the seeds of its own undoing. Indeed, for all his stubborn interest in the visible surface of the world, Flaubert offers not so much *vraisemblance*, or verisimilitude, as *derealization.* What is more, Flaubert offers us derealization in the name of precision, specificity, and concreteness. This, indeed, is the scandal of the visible. And in the end, this is the scandal of realism itself.

Bibliography

Works by Gustave Flaubert

Oeuvres. 2 vols. Edited by Albert Thibaudet and René Dumesnil. Bibliothèque de la Pléiade. Paris: Gallimard, 1952.
Correspondance. 4 vols. Edited by Jean Bruneau. Bibliothèque de la Pléiade. Paris: Gallimard, 1973–98.
L'éducation sentimentale. Historie d'un jeune homme. 1869. 2 vols. Paris: Michel Lévy Frères, 1870.
L'éducation sentimentale. Edited, introduced, and annotated by Pierre-Marc de Biasi. Paris: Livre de Poche, 2002.
Madame Bovary. Edited, introduced, and annotated by Philippe Neefs. Paris: Livre de Poche, 1999.
Voyage en Egypte. Edited, introduced, and annotated by Pierre-Marc de Biasi. Paris: Grasset, 1991.

Works by Flaubert in English Translation

Bouvard and Pécuchet. Translated with an introduction by Mark Polizzotti. Normal, Ill.: Dalkey Archive Press, 2005.
Flaubert in Egypt: A Sensibility on Tour. Translated and edited with an introduction by Francis Steegmuller. New York: Penguin, 1996.
The Letters of Gustave Flaubert. Selected, edited, and translated by Francis Steegmuller. London: Picador, 2001.
Madame Bovary. Translated by Lowell Bair. New York: Bantam, 1981.
Madame Bovary: Provincial Manners. Translated by Margaret Mauldon. Oxford: Oxford University Press, 2004.
Madame Bovary: Provincial Lives. Translated with an introduction by Geoffrey Wall. London: Penguin, 1992.
Sentimental Education. Translated with an introduction by Robert Baldick. London: Penguin, 1964.
Three Tales. Translated by Roger Whitehouse. Edited by Geoffrey Wall. London: Penguin, 2005.

Other Works Cited

Adorno, Theodor W. *Noten zur Literatur.* Edited by Rolf Tiedemann. Frankfurt am Main: Suhrkamp, 1981. Translated by Shierry Weber Nicholsen as *Notes to Literature.* 2 vols. New York: Columbia University Press, 1991.

Ahlström, Anna. *Etude sur la langue de Flaubert.* Macon: Protat Frères, 1899.

Alberti, Leon Battista. *On Painting.* Edited, introduced, and annotated by Martin Kemp. Translated by Cecil Grayson. London: Penguin, 1991.

Alpers, Svetlana. *The Art of Describing: Dutch Art in the Seventeenth Century.* Chicago: University of Chicago Press, 1983.

Angenot, Marc. *1889. Un état du discours social.* Québec: Préambule, 1989.

Aristotle. *Poetics.* Translated by Stephen Halliwell. Loeb Library. Cambridge, Mass.: Harvard University Press, 1995.

Armstrong, Nancy. *Fiction in the Age of Photography: The Legacy of British Realism.* Cambridge, Mass.: Harvard University Press, 1999.

Auerbach, Erich. *Mimesis. Dargestellte Wirklichkeit in der abendländischen Literatur.* Tübingen: Francke, 1946. Translated by Willard R. Trask as *Mimesis: The Representation of Reality in Western Literature.* Princeton: Princeton University Press, 1968.

Austen, Jane. *Pride and Prejudice.* New York: Bantam, 1981.

Bal, Mieke. *Narratology: Introduction to the Theory of Narrative.* 2d ed. Toronto: University of Toronto Press, 1997.

Bally, Charles. "Le style indirect libre en français moderne I." *Germanisch-Romanische Monatsschrift* 4, no. 10 (1912): 549–56.

———. "Le style indirect libre en français moderne II." *Germanisch-Romanische Monatsschrift* 4, no. 11 (1912): 597–606.

Balzac, Honoré de. *Illusions perdues.* Edited, introduced, and annotated by Philippe Berthier. Paris: Flammarion, 1990. Translated by Herbert J. Hunt as *Lost Illusions.* London: Penguin, 1971.

Barbey d'Aurevilly, Jules. Review of *L'éducation sentimentale. Le constitutionnel.* November 29, 1869.

Barnes, Hazel E. *Sartre and Flaubert.* Chicago: University of Chicago Press, 1981.

Barnes, Julian. *Flaubert's Parrot.* London: Picador, 1984.

Barthes, Roland. *Oeuvres complètes.* Edited by Eric Marty. 3 vols. Paris: Seuil, 1993–95.

———. *Writing Degree Zero.* Translated by Annette Lavers and Colin Smith. New York: Noonday Press, 1968.

———. "The Reality Effect." In *French Literary Theory Today.* Edited by Tzvetan Todorov. Translated by R. Carter. Cambridge: Cambridge University Press, 1982.

Baumgart, Reinhard. *Addio. Abschied von der Literatur.* Munich: Hanser, 1995.

———. *Liebesspuren. Eine Lesereise durch die Weltliteratur.* Munich: Hanser, 2000.

Baxandall, Michael. *Painting and Experience in Fifteenth Century Italy: A Primer in the Social History of Pictorial Style.* 2nd ed. New York: Oxford University Press, 1972.

Becker, George J., ed. *Documents of Modern Literary Realism.* Princeton: Princeton University Press, 1963.

Benjamin, Walter. "Der Erzähler. Betrachtungen zum Werk Nikolai Lesskows." In *Illuminationen,* edited by Siegfried Unseld, 385–410. Frankfurt am Main: Suhrkamp, 1977. Translated by Harry Zohn as "The Storyteller: Reflections on the Works of Nikolai Leskov," in *Illuminations,* edited by Hannah Arendt, 83–109. New York: Schocken, 1988.

Bernhard, Thomas. *Auslöschung. Ein Zerfall.* Frankfurt am Main: Suhrkamp, 1986.

Bernheimer, Charles. "The Psychogenesis of Flaubert's Style." In *Emma Bovary,* edited by Harold Bloom, 81–90. New York: Chelsea House Publishers, 1994.

Bersani, Leo. Introduction to *Madame Bovary.* Translated by Lowell Bair. New York: Bantam, 1981.

Bosquet, Amélie. Review of *L'éducation sentimentale. Le droit des femmes.* December 11, 1869.

Bouillaguet, Annick. *Proust lecteur de Balzac et de Flaubert. L'imitation cryptée.* Paris: Honoré Champion, 2000.

Bourdieu, Pierre. *Les règles de l'art. Genèse et structure du champ littéraire.* 2d ed., rev. Paris: Seuil, 1998. First edition translated by Susan Emanuel as *The Rules of Art: Genesis and Structure of the Literary Field.* Stanford: Stanford University Press, 1996.

Bowie, Malcolm. *Proust Among the Stars.* London: Harper Collins, 1998.

Brombert, Victor. *The Novels of Flaubert: A Study of Themes and Techniques.* Princeton: Princeton University Press, 1966.

———. "Flaubert and the Status of the Subject." In *Flaubert and Postmodernism,* edited. by Naomi Schor and Henry F. Majewski, 100–115. Lincoln: University of Nebraska Press, 1984.

Brooks, Peter. *Body Work: Objects of Desire in Modern Narrative.* Cambridge, Mass.: Harvard University Press, 1993.

———. *Reading for the Plot: Design and Intention in Narrative.* 1984. Cambridge, Mass.: Harvard University Press, 1992.

———. *Realist Vision.* New Haven: Yale University Press, 2005.

Brown, Bill. *A Sense of Things: The Object Matter of American Literature.* Chicago: University of Chicago Press, 2003.

———. ed. Special issue on "Things." *Critical Inquiry* 28, no. 1 (fall 2001).

Buck-Morss, Susan. *The Dialectics of Seeing: Walter Benjamin and the Arcades Project.* Cambridge, Mass.: MIT Press, 1989.

Calvino, Italo. *Lezioni americane. Sei proposte per il prossimo millennio.* Milano: Mondadori, 1993. Translated by Patrick Creagh as *Six Memos for the Next Millennium.* Cambridge, Mass.: Harvard University Press, 1988.

———. "Cinema and the Novel: Problems of Narrative." In *The Uses of Literature.* Translated by Patrick Creagh. New York: Harcourt Brace Jovanovich, 1986.

———. "Gustave Flaubert, *Trois contes.*" In *Perché leggere i classici,* 167–169. Milano: Mondadori, 1995. Translated by Martin McLaughlin as "Gustave Flaubert, *Trois contes.*" In *Why Read the Classics?,* 151–153. New York: Pantheon, 1999.

Cavell, Stanley. *The World Viewed: Reflections on the Ontology of Film.* Enl. ed. Cambridge, Mass.: Harvard University Press, 1979.

Cesena, Amédée de. Review of *L'éducation sentimentale. Le Figaro.* November 20, 1869.

Clark, T. J. *The Painting of Modern Life: Paris in the Art of Manet and His Followers.* Princeton: Princeton University Press, 1984.

Cohen, Margaret. *The Sentimental Education of the Novel.* Princeton: Princeton University Press, 1999.

Cohen, Margaret, and Christopher Prendergast, eds. *Spectacles of Realism: Body, Gender, Genre.* Minneapolis: University of Minnesota Press, 1995.

Colwell, D. J., "Bibliography: Flaubert Studies, 1989–97." In *New Approaches in Flaubert Studies,* edited by Tony Williams and Mary Orr, 207–34. Lewiston, N.Y.: Edwin Mellen Press, 1999.

Compagnon, Antoine. *Le démon de la théorie. Littérature et sens commun.* Paris: Seuil, 1998. Translated by Carol Cosman as *Literature, Theory, and Common Sense.* Princeton: Princeton University Press, 2004.

Crary, Jonathan. *Techniques of the Observer: On Vision and Modernity in the Nineteenth Century.* Cambridge, Mass.: MIT Press, 1990.

Culler, Jonathan. *Flaubert: The Uses of Uncertainty.* Ithaca, N.Y.: Cornell University Press, 1974.

Danger, Pierre. *Sensation et objets dans le roman de Flaubert.* Paris: Armand Colin, 1973.

Daunais, Isabelle. *Frontière du roman. Le personnage réaliste et ses fictions.* Montréal: Les Presses de l'Université de Montreal, 2002.

———. *Flaubert et la scénographie romanesque.* Paris: Nizet, 1993.

Debray-Genette, Raymonde. "Flaubert: Science et écriture." *Littérature* (October 1974): 41–51.

———. "Du mode narrative dans les 'Trois contes.'" *Littérature* 2 (May 1971): 39–70.

Doane, Mary Ann. "The Close-Up: Scale and Detail in the Cinema." *differences* 14, no. 3 (2003): 89–111.

Dubois, Jacques. *Romanciers français de l'instantané au XIXe siècle.* Brussels: Palais des Académies, 1963.

Duchet, Claude. "Roman et objets." In *Travail de Flaubert,* edited by Gérard Genette and Tzvetan Todorov, 11–43. Paris: Seuil, 1983.

———. "Signifiance et in-signifiance. Le discours italique dans *Madame Bovary.*" In *La production du sens chez Flaubert,* edited by Claudine Gothot-Mersch, 358–78. Paris: UGE, 1975.

Dufour, Philippe. *Flaubert ou la prose du silence.* Paris: Nathan, 1997.

———. *Flaubert et le pignouf.* Saint-Denis: Presses universitaires de Vincennes, 1993.

———. *La pensée romanesque du langage.* Paris: Seuil, 2004.

———. *Le réalisme.* Paris: Presses universitaires de France, 1998.

Duranty, Edmond. Review of *L'éducation sentimentale. Paris-Journal.* December 14, 1869.

Eco, Umberto. *Six Walks in the Fictional Woods.* Cambridge, Mass.: Harvard University Press, 1994.

———. *On Literature.* Translated by Martin McLaughlin. London: Secker & Warburg, 2005.

Emptaz, Florence. *Aux pieds de Flaubert.* Paris: Bernard Grasset, 2002.

Ezrahi, Yaron. *The Descent of Icarus: Science and the Tranformation of Contemporary Democracy.* Cambridge, Mass.: Harvard University Press, 1990.

Foster, Hal. Preface to *Vision and Visuality,* ix–xiv. Seattle: Bay Press, 1988.

Foucault, Michel. *La peinture de Manet.* Edited by Maryvonne Saison. Paris: Seuil, 2004.

———. "La bibliothèque fantastique." *Cahiers Renaud-Barrault,* no. 59 (March 1967). Reprinted in *Travail de Flaubert,* edited by Gérard Genette and Tzvetan Todorov, 103–22. Paris: Seuil, 1983. Translated by Donald F. Bouchard and Sherry Simon as "Fantasia of the Library." In *Language, Counter-memory, Practice: Selected Essays and Interviews,* edited by Donald F. Bouchard, 87–109. Oxford: Basil Blackwell, 1977.

France, Anatole. "Le trottoir roulant." *Le Figaro,* 1. April 18, 1900.

Frank, Joseph. *The Idea of Spatial Form.* New Brunswick: Rutgers University Press, 1991.

Fried, Michael. *Absorption and Theatricality: Painting and Beholder in the Age of Diderot.* 1980. Chicago: University of Chicago Press, 1988.

———. *Courbet's Realism.* Chicago: University of Chicago Press, 1990.

———. *Manet's Modernism; or, the Face of Painting in the 1860s.* Chicago: University of Chicago Press, 1996.

Friedrich, Hugo. *Drei Klassiker des französischen Romans. Stendhal, Balzac, Flaubert.* 6th ed. Frankfurt am Main: Vittorio Klostermann, 1970.

Frølich, Juliette. *Des hommes, des femmes et des choses. Langages de l'objet dans le roman de Balzac à Proust.* Saint-Denis: Presses universitaires de Vincennes, 1997.

———. *Au parloir du roman de Balzac à Flaubert.* Oslo: Solum, 1991.

Frye, Northrop. *Anatomy of Criticism.* Princeton: Princeton University Press, 1957.

Gans, Eric. *Madame Bovary: The End of Romance.* Boston: Twayne, 1989.

Genette, Gérard. "Flaubert par Proust." *L'Arc* 79 (1980): 3–17.

———. "Silences de Flaubert." In *Figures,* 1:223–246. Paris: Seuil, 1976. Translated by Alan Sheridan as "Flaubert's Silences." In *Figures of Literary Discourse,* 183–202. Oxford: Basil Blackwell, 1982.

Genette, Gérard and Tzvetan Todorov, eds. *Littérature et réalité.* Paris: Seuil, 1982.

———. eds. *Travail de Flaubert.* Paris: Seuil, 1983.

Ginsburg, Michal Peled. *Flaubert Writing: A Study in Narrative Strategies.* Stanford: Stanford University Press, 1986.

———. "Free Indirect Discourse: A Reconsideration." *Language and Style* 15 (1982): 133–49.

———. "Vision and Language: Teaching *Madame Bovary* in a Course on the Novel." In *Approaches to Teaching Madame Bovary,* edited by Lawrence M. Porter and Eugene F. Gray, 61–8. New York: The Modern Language Association of America, 1995.

Ginzburg, Carlo. "Making Things Strange: The Prehistory of a Literary Device." *Representations* 56 (fall 1996): 8–28.

———. "Reflections on a Blank." In *History, Rhetoric, and Proof*, 92–110. Hanover: University Press of New England, 1999.

Girard, René. *Mensonge romantique et verité romanesque.* Paris: Grasset, 1961. Translated by Yvonne Freccero as *Deceit, Desire, and the Novel: Self and Other in Literary Structure.* Baltimore: Johns Hopkins University Press, 1965.

Gothot-Mersch, Claudine. *La genèse de "Madame Bovary."* Paris: José Corti, 1966.

———. "La description des visages dans *Madame Bovary.*" *Littérature* 15 (1974): 17–26.

———. "La parole des personnages." In *Travail de Flaubert,* edited by Gérard Genette and Tzvetan Todorov, 199–221. Paris: Seuil, 1983.

Green, Anne. "'Ce n'est jamais ça. . .' Ecriture et photographie chez Flaubert." In *Flaubert et la théorie littéraire,* edited by Tanguy Logé and Marie-France Renard, 197–205. Brussels: Facultés universitares Saint-Louis, 2005.

Halliwell, Stephen. *The Aesthetics of Mimesis: Ancient Texts and Modern Problems.* Princeton: Princeton University Press, 2002.

Hamon, Philippe. *Du descriptif.* Paris: Hachette, 1993.

———. *Imageries. Littérature et image au XIXe siècle.* Paris: José Corti, 2001.

———. "Qu'est-ce qu'une description?" *Poétique* 12 (1972): 465–85. Translated by R. Carter as "What Is a Description?" In *French Literary Theory Today,* edited by Tzvetan Todorov, 147–78. Cambridge: Cambridge University Press, 1982.

Harvey, David. *Paris, Capital of Modernity.* New York: Routledge, 2003.

Hassan, Ihab. "Realism, Truth, and Trust in Postmodern Perspective." *Third Text* 17, no. 1 (2003): 1–13.

Heffernan, James A. W. *Museum of Words: The Poetics of Ekphrasis from Homer to Ashbery.* Chicago: University of Chicago Press, 1993.

Israel-Pelletier, Aimée. "Flaubert and the Visual." In *The Cambridge Companion to Flaubert,* edited by Timothy Unwin, 180–95. Cambridge: Cambridge University Press, 2004.

Jacques, Georges. "Cadrage, vernissage et encadrement. Pour une esthétique du figement." In *Flaubert et la théorie littéraire. En homage à Claudine Gothot-Mersch,* edited by Tanguy Logé and Marie-France Renard, 207–21. Brussels: Facultés universitaires Saint-Louis, 2005.

Jakobson, Roman. "On Realism in Art." In *Readings in Russian Poetics: Formalist and Structuralist Views,* edited by Ladislav Matejka and Krystna Pomorska. Cambridge: MIT, 1971.

———. "Two Aspects of Language and Two Types of Aphasic Disturbances." In R. Jakobson and Morris Halle, *Fundamentals of Language,* 69–96. 2d, rev. ed. The Hague: Mouton, 1971.

James, Henry. *Literary Criticism: French Writers, Other European Writers.* New York: The Library of America, 1984.

Jameson, Fredric. *Fables of Aggression: Wyndham Lewis, the Modernist as Fascist.* Berkeley and Los Angeles: University of California Press, 1979.

———. *The Ideologies of Theory: Essays, 1971–1986.* 2 vols. With a foreword by Neil Larsen. Minneapolis: University of Minnesota Press, 1988.

———. *The Political Unconscious: Narrative as a Socially Symbolic Act.* Ithaca, N.Y.: Cornell University Press, 1981.

———. *Sartre: The Origins of A Style.* New Haven: Yale University Press, 1961.

———. *Signatures of the Visible.* New York: Routledge, 1990.

———. *A Singular Modernity: Essay on the Ontology of the Present.* London: Verso, 2002.

———. "Marc Angenot, Literary History, and the Study of Culture in the Nineteenth Century." *Yale Journal of Criticism* 17, no. 2 (2004): 233–53.

———. "Reflections in Conclusion." In *Aesthetics and Politics,* edited by Perry Anderson, 196–213. London: Verso, 1980.

Janouch, Gustav. *Gespräche mit Kafka.* Enl. ed. Frankfurt am Main: Fischer, 1968.

Jay, Martin. *Downcast Eyes: The Denigration of Vision in Twentieth-Century Thought.* Berkeley and Los Angeles: University of California Press, 1993.

———. *Songs of Experience: Modern American and European Variations on a Universal Theme.* Berkeley and Los Angeles: University of California Press, 2005.

Kleist, Heinrich von. "Die Marquise von O..." In *Erzählungen,* 117–60. Frankfurt am Main: Insel, 1997. Translated by David Luke and Nigel Reeves as "The Marquise of O—," in *The Marquise of O— and Other Stories,* 68–113. London: Penguin, 1978.

Knight, Diana. *Flaubert's Characters: The Language of Illusion.* Oxford: Oxford University Press, 1985.

Krieger, Murray. "The Ekphrastic Principle and the Still Moment of Poetry; or *Laokoön* Revisited." In *The Play and Place of Criticism,* 105–28. Baltimore: Johns Hopkins University Press, 1967.

Kudo, Yoko. "Lecture d'un manuscrit. Etude de la scène d'apparition dans *L'Education sentimentale.*" *Proceedings of the Department of Foreign Languages and Literatures* (Tokyo) 39, no. 2 (1991): 135–58.

Landgren, Bengt. "Salammbô – en roman om februarirevolutionen? Några perspektiv, problem och tolkningar i nyare Flaubertforskning." *Samlaren* (1983): 61–8.

Lanson, Gustave. *L'art de la prose.* Paris: Fayard, 1908.

Lepenies, Wolf. *Die drei Kulturen.* Munich: Hanser, 1985.

Lessing, G. E. *Laokoon oder über die Grenzen der Malerei und Poesie.* Stuttgart: Reclam, 2001.

Levin, David Michael, ed. *Modernity and the Hegemony of Vision.* Berkeley and Los Angeles: University of California Press, 1993.

Levin, Harry. *The Gates of Horn: A Study of Five French Realists.* New York: Oxford University Press, 1963.

Lukács, Georg. *Die Theorie des Romans. Ein geschichtsphilosophischer Versuch über die Formen der grossen Epik.* 1920. Munich: Deutscher Taschenbuch Verlag, 1994. Translated by Anna Bostock as *The Theory of the Novel: A Historico-Philosophical Essay in the Forms of Great Epic Literature.* London: Merlin, 1971.

———. "Erzählen oder Beschreiben? Zur Diskussion über Naturalismus und Formalismus." In *Probleme des Realismus,* 103–45. Berlin: Aufbau, 1955.

Lynch, Michael P., ed. *The Nature of Truth: Classic and Contemporary Perspectives.* Cambridge, Mass.: The MIT Press, 2001.

MacDougall, David. *The Corporeal Image: Film, Ethnography, and the Senses.* Princeton: Princeton University Press, 2006.

Maraini, Dacia. *Searching for Emma: Gustave Flaubert and Madame Bovary.* Translated by Vincent J. Bertolini. Chicago: University of Chicago Press, 1998.

Masson, Bernard. "Le corps d'Emma." In *Flaubert, la femme, la ville,* 13–22. Paris: Presses universitaires de France, 1983.

Mayr, Monika. *Ut pictura descriptio? Poetik und Praxis kuenstlerischer Beschreibung bei Flaubert, Proust, Belyi, Simon.* Tuebingen: Gunter Narr Verlag, 2001.

Metz, Christian. *Film Language: A Semiotics of the Cinema.* Translated by Michael Taylor. New York: Oxford University Press, 1974.

Mitchell, W. J. T. "Ekphrasis and the Other." In *Picture Theory,* 151–81. Chicago: University of Chicago Press, 1994.

Mitterand, Henri. *Le regard et le signe.* Paris: Presses universitaires de France, 1987.

———. *L'illusion réaliste. De Balzac à Aragon.* Paris: Presses universitaires de France, 1994.

Moretti, Franco. *The Way of the World: The "Bildungsroman" in European Culture.* London: Verso, 1987.

Morris, Pam. *Realism.* London: Routledge, 2003.

Mulvey, Laura. "Visual Pleasure and Narrative Cinema." In *Visual and Other Pleasures,* 14–26. London: Macmillan, 1989.

Nelson, Robert S., ed. *Visuality Before and Beyond the Renaissance: Seeing as Others Saw.* Cambridge: Cambridge University Press, 2000.

Nochlin, Linda. *Realism.* Harmondsworth: Penguin, 1971.

Orr, Mary. *Flaubert: Writing the Masculine.* Oxford: Oxford University Press, 2000.

Ortel, Philippe. *La littérature à l'ère de la photographie. Enquête sur une révolution invisible.* Nîmes: Jacqueline Chambon, 2002.

Pavel, Thomas. *La pensée du roman.* Paris: Gallimard, 2003.

Perruchot, Claude. "Le style indirect libre et la question du sujet dans *Madame Bovary.*" In *La production du sens chez Flaubert. Actes du Colloque de Cérisy,* edited by Claudine Gothot-Mersch, 253–86. Paris: UGE, 1975.

Pettersson, Torsten. "Den gemensamma världen. Realismen som litteraturform." I *Dolda principer. Kultur- och litteraturteoretiska studier,* 149–71. Lund: Studentlitteratur, 2002.

Philippe, Gilles. *Sujet, verbe, complément. Le moment grammatical de la littérature française 1890–1940.* Paris: Gallimard, 2002.

———. ed. *Flaubert savait-il écrire? Une querelle grammaticale (1919–1921).* Grenoble: Ellug, 2002.

Pippin, Robert. "Authenticity in Painting: Remarks on Michael Fried's Art History." *Critical Inquiry* 31 (2005): 575–98.

Prendergast, Christopher. *The Order of Mimesis: Balzac, Stendhal, Nerval, Flaubert.* Cambridge: Cambridge University Press, 1986.

Proust, Marcel. *Contre Sainte-Beuve précédé de Pastiches et mélanges et suivi de Essais et articles*. Edited by Pierre Clarac and Yves Sandre. Bibliothèque de la Pléiade. Paris: Gallimard, 1971.

———. "A propos du 'style' de Flaubert." *La Nouvelle Revue Française* 76 (January 1920): 72–90.

Quintilian. *The Orator's Education*. Translated by Donald A. Russell. Loeb Library. Cambridge, Mass.: Harvard University Press, 2001.

Rabatel, Alain. *La construction textuelle du point de vue*. Lausanne: Delachaux et Niestlé, 1998.

Reed, Arden. *Manet, Flaubert, and the Emergence of Modernism: Blurring Genre Boundaries*. Cambridge: Cambridge University Press, 2003.

Richard, Jean-Pierre. *Stendhal Flaubert*. Paris: Seuil, 1970.

Robert, Marthe. *Roman des origines et origines du roman*. Paris: Gallimard, 1972.

Roberts, John. *The Art of Interruption: Realism, Photography, and the Everyday*. Manchester: Manchester University Press, 1998.

Ronell, Avital. *On Stupidity*. Urbana, Ill.: University of Illinois Press, 2002.

Rosanvallon, Pierre. *Le peuple introuvable. Histoire de la représentation démocratique en France*. Paris: Gallimard, 1998.

Rousset, Jean. *Leurs yeux se rencontrèrent. La scène de première vue dans le roman*. Paris: José Corti, 1981.

———. "*Madame Bovary* ou le livre sur rien." In *Forme et signification*, 109–33. Paris: José Corti, 1962.

Said, Edward. *Orientalism*. 1978. London: Peregrine, 1985.

Sandras, Michel. "Le blanc, l'alinéa." *Communications* 19 (1972): 105–14.

Sarcey, Françisque. Review of *L'éducation sentimentale*. *Le Gaulois,* December 3–4, 1869.

Sarraute, Nathalie. "Flaubert le précurseur." *Preuves* (February 1965): 3–11.

Sartre, Jean-Paul. *L'idiot de la famille*. Rev. ed. 3 vols. Paris: Gallimard, 1988.

———. "La conscience de classe chez Flaubert, II." *Les temps modernes* 21, no. 241 (June 1966): 2113–53.

Schehr, Lawrence R. *Figures of Alterity: French Realism and Its Others*. Stanford: Stanford University Press, 2003.

Schlossman, Beryl. "Flaubert's Moving Sidewalk." In *Approaches to Teaching Flaubert's "Madame Bovary,"* edited by Lawrence M. Porter and Eugene F. Gray, 69–76. New York: The Modern Language Association of America, 1995.

Schor, Naomi. *Breaking the Chain: Women, Theory, and French Realist Fiction*. New York: Columbia University Press, 1985.

———. *George Sand and Idealism*. New York: Columbia University Press, 1993.

———. *Reading in Detail: Aesthetics and the Feminine*. New York: Routledge, 1987.

Schor, Naomi and Henry F. Majewski, eds. *Flaubert and Postmodernism*. Lincoln: University of Nebraska Press, 1984.

Segeberg, Harro, ed. *Die Mobilisierung des Sehens. Zur Vor- und Frühgeschichte des Films in Literatur und Kunst*. Munich: Fink, 1996.

Séginger, Gisèle. *Flaubert. Une poétique de l'histoire.* Strasbourg: Presses universitaires de Strasbourg, 2000.

Shapiro, Gary. *Archaeologies of Vision: Foucault and Nietzsche on Seeing and Saying.* Chicago: University of Chicago Press, 2003.

Shaw, Harry E. *Narrating Reality: Austen, Scott, Eliot.* Ithaca, N.Y.: Cornell University Press, 1999.

Spitzer, Leo. "Zur Entstehung der sog. erlebten Rede." *Germanisch-Romanische Monatsschrift* 16, no. 7–8 (1928): 327–32.

Starobinski, Jean. *La relation critique.* Paris: Gallimard, 1970.

Starr, Juliana. "Men Looking at Women Through Art: Male Gaze and Spectatorship in Three Nineteenth-Century French Novels." *Revue Frontenac* 10–11 (1993–1994): 8–34.

Stendhal [Henri Beyle]. *Racine et Shakespeare.* Paris: Jean-Jacques Pauvert, 1965.

———. *Le rouge et le noir.* Edited by Michel Crouzet. Paris: Livre de Poche, 1997.

Stiegler, Bernd. *Philologie des Auges. Die photographische Entdeckung der Welt im 19. Jahrhundert.* Munich: Fink, 2001.

Svenbro, Jesper. "Om fönsterluckor." In *Ljuset och rummet. Rom 1949 fotograferat av Lennart af Petersens,* 29–40. Stockholm: Wahlström & Widstrand, 2004.

Thibaudet, Albert. *Gustave Flaubert.* Rev. ed. Paris: Gallimard, 1935.

———. "Lettre à M. Marcel Proust." *La Nouvelle Revue Française* 78 (March 1920): 426–41.

———. "Le style de Flaubert." *La Nouvelle Revue Française* 74 (November 1919): 942–53.

Tooke, Adrianne. *Flaubert and the Pictorial Arts: From Image to Text.* Oxford: Oxford University Press, 2000.

Tygstryp, Frederik. *På sporet af virkeligheten. Essays.* Copenhagen: Gyldendal, 2000.

Ullman, Annika. *Stiftarinnegenerationen. Sofi Almquist, Anna Sandström, Anna Ahlström.* Stockholm: Stockholmia, 2004.

Swahn, Sigbrit. "Omkring Anna Ahlströms avhandling om Flaubert 1899." In *Anna Ahlström. Vår första kvinnliga doktor i romanska språk år 1899.* Edited by Kerstin Jonasson and Gunilla Ransbo, 41–5. Uppsala: Acta Universitatis Upsaliensis, 2000.

Wall, Geoffrey. *Flaubert: A Life.* London: Faber and Faber, 2001.

———. Introduction to *Madame Bovary.* Translated by Geoffrey Wall. London: Penguin, 1992.

Watson, Janell. *Literature and Material Culture from Balzac to Proust: The Collection and Consumption of Curiosities.* Cambridge: Cambridge University Press, 1999.

Watt, Ian. *The Rise of the Novel: Studies in Defoe, Richardson, and Fielding.* 1957. Harmondsworth: Penguin, 1983.

Weinberg, Henry H. "The Function of Italics in *Madame Bovary.*" *Nineteenth-Century French Studies* 3, no. 1–2 (fall-winter 1974–75): 97–111.

White, Hayden. *Figural Realism: Studies in the Mimesis Effect.* Baltimore: Johns Hopkins University Press, 1999.

———. "The Problem of Style in Realistic Representation: Marx and Flaubert." In *The Concept of Style,* edited by Berel Lang, 213–29. Philadelphia: University of Pennsylvania Press, 1979.

Williams, Tony, and Mary Orr, eds. *New Approaches in Flaubert Studies.* Lewiston: Edwin Mellen Press, 1999.

Wing, Nathaniel. "Emma's Stories: Narrative, Repetition, and Desire in *Madame Bovary.*" In *Emma Bovary,* edited by Harold Bloom, 133–64. New York: Chelsea House Publishers, 1994.

Zola, Emile. *Les romanciers naturalistes.* Paris: Charpentier, 1890.

Index

Adorno, Theodor, W., 45-58, 108, 139n.
Ahlström, Anna, 106
Alberti, Léon Battista, 158
Alpers, Svetlana, 158
Angenot, Marc, 123
Aristotle, 22n., 68n.
Armstrong, Nancy, 34
Auerbach, Erich, 23n., 25, 77n., 177
Austen, Jane, 22, 150-1

Bally, Charles, 65n.
Balzac, Honoré de, 11-12, 16, 29, 33, 35-58, 73, 74, 124-5, 127, 133, 157, 174, 177
Barbey d'Aurevilly, Jules, 70n., 129n.
Barnes, Hazel E., 162n.
Barthes, Roland, 20-1, 34n., 54n., 55, 120, 143, 161
Baudelaire, Charles, 103
Baumgart, Reinhard, 49n., 140, 144n.
Baxandall, Michael, 8n.
Benjamin, Walter, 35, 51-4, 130
Bernhard, Thomas, 108
Bernheimer, Charles, 104n.
Bersani, Leo, 93
Berthier, Philippe, 47
Biasi, Pierre-Marc de, 139n., 160
Bouilhet, Louis, 115n., 116
Bouillaguet, Annick, 72n.
Bonnard, Pierre, 24-5
Botticelli, 24-5
Bourdieu, Pierre, 62, 131
Bowie, Malcolm, 49n.
Brecht, Bertolt, 52
Brombert, Victor, 65n., 77, 133n.

Brooks, Peter, 14n., 73n., 144
Brown, Bill, 27n.
Buck-Morss, Susan, 51n.
Burckhardt, Sigurd, 28

Calvino, Italo, 9-16, 36n., 139n., 141n., 181-2
Canaletto, 92
Cervantes, Miguel de, 12
Cesena, Amédée de, 129n.
Clark, T. J., 35n.
Colet, Louise, 76-7, 113-5,
Compagnon, Antoine, 22n.
Conrad, Joseph, 17, 74-5
Constant, Benjamin, 12
Courbet, Gustave, 27
Crary, Jonathan, 15n.
Culler, Jonathan, 73n., 129, 131n.

Danger, Pierre, 63n., 133
Daunais, Isabelle, 33-4, 59n.
Degas, Edgar, 34
Doane, Mary Ann, 140n., 141-2
Du Camp, Maxime, 61n., 160
Duchet, Claude, 109
Dufour, Philippe, 104, 166n.
Duranty, Edmond, 129n., 134

Eco, Umberto, 22n., 29n., 112n.
Emptaz, Florence, 153

Flaubert, Gustave, *Bouvard et Pécuchet,* 177-81; "Un coeur simple," 21, 178; correspondence, 76-8, 113-16; *Dictionnaire des idées reçues,* 124; *L'éducation sentimentale,* 16-17, 67, 69, 72, 78,

127-75, 177, 179-81 "Hérodias," 178; "La légende de St. Julien," 178; manuscripts, 89n., 96n., 139, 143n., *Madame Bovary*, 9, 16, 32-4, 59-126, 129, 137, 147-8, 151, 153, 15-60, 163, 170, 177, 179-81; *La Tentation de Saint Antoine,* 177; *Trois contes,* 9-10, 69, 137, 148, 163, 177, 178, 181; *Salammbô,* 148

Foucault, Michel, 130
Foster, Hal, 14n.
France, Anatole, 72
Frank, Joseph, 133n.
Freud, Sigmund, 103
Fried, Michael, 148-9, 182-4
Friedrich, Hugo, 63n.
Frye, Northrop, 26
Frølich, Juliette, 27n.
Fumaroli, Marc, 33n.

Gans, Eric, 61n.
Genette, Gérard, 67n., 166n., 169n.
Genette, Raymonde Debray, 178
Ginsburg, Michal Peled, 65n., 66
Ginzburg, Carlo, 61n., 185
Girard, René, 35n.
Goethe, Johann Wolfgang von, 22, 128, 157
Gothot-Mersch, Claudine, 36n., 83n., 85n., 90n., 110n., 115n., 116n., 119, 124n.
Green, Anne, 147

Habermas, Jürgen, 53n.
Halliwell, Stephen, 54
Hamon, Philippe, 27n., 30-3, 59n., 70n., 161-2
Harvey, David, 35n.
Heffernan, James, 28
Homer, 12, 28, 157
Hugo, Victor, 127

Israel-Pelletier, Aimée, 59n.

Jacques, Georges, 140n.
Jakobson, Roman, 31
James, Henry, 41, 129

Jameson, Fredric, 55n., 57n., 74-5, 123n., 130-1, 140n.
Jay, Martin, 15n., 35n., 53n.
Jonasson, Kerstin, 106n.
Joyce, James, 12, 17, 75, 102, 131, 156, 177

Kafka, Franz, 13n., 17
Kenner, Hugh, 178
Kleist, Heinrich von, 19-20, 22
Knight, Diana, 138n., 140n., 162
Krieger, Murray, 28n.
Kudo, Yoko, 137n.

Lepenies, Wolf, 174
Leskov, Nikolai, 52
Lessing, Gotthold Ephraim, 20
Levin, David Michael, 15n.

MacDougall, David, 141n.
Manet, Edouard, 34, 182-4
Maraini, Dacia, 104
Masson, Bernard, 78n.
Maupassant, Guy de, 33
Metz, Christian, 141-2
Mitchell, W. J. T., 28
Mitterand, Henri, 59n., 132
Monet, Claude, 34
Moretti, Franco, 61-2, 127
Mulvey, Laura, 15n.

Nabokov, Vladimir, 17, 75
Neefs, Philippe, 32n.

Lafayette, Madame de, 12
Landgren, Bengt, 69n.
Lukács, Georg, 25, 26n.,

Ortel, Philippe, 34n.

Pavel, Thomas, 77
Perruchot, Claude, 65n.
Pettersson, Torsten, 25
Philippe, Gilles, 65n., 68n., 106n.
Plato, 22n., 112-3
Pippin, Robert, 148n.
Prendergast, Christopher, 109
Proust, Marcel, 11, 17, 33, 67-73, 84n., 129, 131, 139n., 166n., 177

Quintilian, 29, 112n., 118

Rabatel, Alain, 65n.
Reed, Arden, 130n.
Ricoeur, Paul, 22n.
Ronell, Avital, 124
Rousset, Jean, 66n., 79n., 87, 137n.

Said, Edward, 160
Sand, George, 22, 127
Sandras, Michel, 138n.
Sarcey, Françisque, 128
Sarraute, Nathalie, 75-6
Sartre, Jean-Paul, 72n., 102n., 124n., 162
Schlossman, Beryl, 69n.
Schor, Naomi, 22n., 27n., 99-104
Schehr, Lawrence, 61n.
Séginger, Gisèle, 133n., 174n.
Shaw, Harry E., 27n.
Starr, Julianna, 138n.
Stein, Gertrude, 17
Stendhal [Henri Beyle], 11-12, 16, 22-3, 26, 44, 62, 73-4, 157, 161, 168-9

Stiegler, Bernd, 34n.
Svenbro, Jesper, 13n.
Swahn, Sigbrit, 106n.

Thibaudet, Albert, 65n., 67-8, 72n., 103n., 106n.
Tooke, Adrianne, 59n., 81n.
Tygstrup, Frederik, 85n.

Ullman, Annika, 106

Valéry, Paul, 26-7
Virgil, 112

Wall, Geoffrey, 60n., 76n., 100, 112n.
Watson, Janelle, 27n., 63n
Watt, Ian, 25n.
Weber, Max, 50, 51
Weinberg, Henry H., 109n.
Wey, Francis, 27
White, Hayden, 24, 49n
Wing, Nathaniel, 65n.
Woolf, Virginia, 12

Zola, Emile, 16, 22, 27, 29, 161-2

ACTA UNIVERSITATIS UPSALIENSIS
Historia litterarum
Editores: Bengt Landgren et Torsten Pettersson

1. *Östen Södergård,* Essais sur la création littéraire de George Sand d'après un roman remanié: Lélia. 1962.
2. *Lars Gustafsson,* Le poète masqué et démasqué. Étude sur la mise en valeur du poète sincère dans la poétique du classicisme et du préromantisme. 1968.
3. *Egil Törnqvist,* A Drama of Souls. Studies in O'Neill's Supernaturalistic Technique. 1968.
4. *Staffan Bergsten,* Jaget och världen. Kosmiska analogier i svensk 1900-talslyrik. 1971. (The Self and the World. Cosmic Analogies in Twentieth Century Swedish Poetry.)
5. *Göran Stockenström,* Ismael i öknen. Strindberg som mystiker. 1972. (Ishmael in the Desert, Strindberg as Mystic.)
6. *Bengt Landgren,* Hjalmar Gullberg och beredskapslitteraturen. Studier i svensk dikt och politisk debatt 1933–1942. 1975. (Hjalmar Gullberg und die Literatur der Mobilisierungsjahre. Studien zur schwedischen Dichtung und politischen Debatte 1933–1942.)
7. *Tore Wretö,* Det förklarade ögonblicket. Studier i västerländsk idyll från Theokritos till Strindberg. 1977. (The Transfigured Moment. Studies in European Idyll from Theocritus to Strindberg.)
8. *Bengt Landgren,* Hermann Brochs Der Tod des Vergil. Studier i romanens källor, struktur och idéinnehåll. 1978. (Hermann Brochs Roman Der Tod des Vergil.)
9. *Bengt Landgren,* De fyra elementen. Studier i Johannes Edfelts diktning från Högmässa till Bråddjupt eko. 1979. (Die vier Elemente. Studien zur Dichtung Johannes Edfelts.)
10. *Marie-Christine Skuncke,* Sweden and European Drama 1772–1796. A study of translation and adaptations. 1981.
11. *Bengt Landgren,* Den poetiska världen. Strukturanalytiska studier i den unge Gunnar Ekelöfs lyrik. 1982. (Le Monde poétique. Analyse structurale de la poésie de Gunnar Ekelöf entre 1927 et 1934.)
12. *Lars Gustafsson,* Litteraturhistorikern Schück. Vetenskapssyn och historieuppfattning i Henrik Schücks tidigare produktion. 1983. (Der Literaturhistoriker Schück. Wissenschaftssicht und Geschichtsauffassung in Henrik Schücks früher Produktion.)
13. *Thure Stenström,* Existentialismen i Sverige. Mottagande och inflytande 1900–1950. 1984. (Réception et influence de l'existentialisme en Suède 1900–1950.)
14. *Tore Wretö,* Folkvisans upptäckare. Receptionsstudier från Montaigne och Schefferus till Herder. 1984. (Die Entdecker des Volkliedes. Rezeptionsstudien von Montaigne und Schefferus bis Herder.)

15. *Erik G. Thygesen,* Gunnar Ekelöf's Open-Form Poem A *Mölna Elegy*: Problems of Genesis, Structure and Influence. 1985.
16. *Lars Gustafsson,* Estetik i förvandling. Estetik och litteraturhistoria i Uppsala från P. D. A. Atterbom till B. E. Malmström. 1986. (Asthetik in Verwandlung. Asthetik und Literaturgeschichte in Uppsala von P. D. A. Atterbom bis B. E. Malmström.)
17. *Lars-Åke Skalin,* Karaktär och perspektiv: Att tolka litterära gestalter i det mimetiska språkspelet. 1991. (Character and Perspective: Reading Fictional Figures in the Mimetic Language Game.)
18. *Claes Ahlund,* Medusas huvud. Dekadensens tematik i svensk sekelskiftesprosa. 1994. (The Head of Medusa. The Theme of Decadence in Swedish Prose of the Turn of the Century.)
19. *Thure Stenström,* Gyllensten i hjärtats öken. Strövtåg i Lars Gyllenstens författarskap, särskilt *Grottan i öknen.* 1996. (Gyllensten in der Wüstenei des Herzens. Streifzüge im Werk von Lars Gyllensten mit besonderer Berücksichtigung der *Grotte in der Wüstenei.*)
20. *Bengt Landgren,* Polyederns gåta. En introduktion till Gunnar Ekelöfs Färjesång. 1998. (The Enigma of the Polygon: An Introduction to Gunnar Ekelöf's "Ferry-Boat Song".)
21. *Bengt Landgren,* Dödsteman. Läsningar av Rilke Edfelt Lindegren. 1999. (Themes of Death: Readings of Rilke Edfelt Lindgren.)
22. *Ulf Malm,* Dolssor Conina. Lust, the Bawdy, and Obscenity in Medieval Occitan and Galician-Portuguese Troubadour Poetry and Latin Secular Love Song. 2001.
23. *Lars Gustafsson,* Romanens väg till poesin. En linje i klassicistisk, romantisk och postromantisk romanteori. 2002. (Der Weg des Romans zur Poesie: Eine Entwicklungslinie klassizistischer, romantischer und postromantischer Romantheorie.)
24. *Claes Ahlund & Bengt Landgren,* Från etableringsfas till konsolidering. Svensk akademisk litteraturundervisning 1890–1946. 2003. (From Foundation to Consolidation: The Teaching of Literary History at Swedish Universities, 1890–1946.)
25. *Bengt Landgren* (red.), Universitetsämne i brytningstider. Studier i svensk akademisk litteraturundervisning 1947–1995. 2005. (A University Discipline in Transition: Studies in Swedish Academic Literature Instruction 1947–1995.)
26. *Sara Danius,* The Prose of the World. Flaubert and the Art of Making Things Visible. 2006.